D1259265

British science fiction television
A hitchhiker's guide

EDITED BY JOHN R. COOK AND PETER WRIGHT

I.B. TAURIS
LONDON · NEW YORK

Published in 2006 by
I.B.Tauris & Co. Ltd
6 Salem Rd, London w2 4bu
175 Fifth Avenue, New York ny 10010
www.ibtauris.com

In the United States and Canada distributed by Palgrave Macmillan,
a division of St. Martin's Press, 175 Fifth Avenue, New York, ny 10010

All photographs are courtesy of BFI Stills, Posters and Designs, to which
grateful acknowledgement is made.

isbn 1 84511 047 1 (Hb)
isbn 1 84511 048 x (Pb)
ean   978 1 84511 047 5 (Hb)
ean   978 1 84511 048 2 (Pb)

A full CIP record for this book is available from the British Library
A full CIP record for this book is available from the Library of Congress
Library of Congress catalog card: available

Typeset in Monotype Garamond by illuminati, Grosmont,
www.illuminatibooks.co.uk
Printed and bound in Great Britain by MPG Books Ltd, Bodmin, Cornwall

Contents

Acknowledgements

We would both like to thank Philippa Brewster, our editor at I.B. Tauris, for agreeing to take on this project and for sticking with it and supporting it through all the various stages of its development. Special thanks in this regard must also go to James Chapman, Series Editor as well as one of the sterling contributors to this collection, for seeing the merits of the project at the very outset and for encouraging us to submit it to Tauris as part of the 'Popular Television Genres' series. His support throughout has been invaluable.

Another contributor to this volume to whom we both owe a special debt of thanks is Professor Nicholas J. Cull for his very kind offer to us of publication of his 2003 interview with Gerry Anderson. As evidenced by his contributions to this volume, Nick has been a very enthusiastic supporter of this project throughout, even to the extent of inviting one of the editors (John R. Cook) to join him for lunch with Anderson during his 2003 'Visions of the Future' conference at the University of Leicester, at which Anderson was an invited guest. His kindness as well as enthusiasm both for the subject of TV science fiction and this book have been truly inspirational.

In addition to the above, John R. Cook would particularly like to thank all his friends, family and colleagues who have helped (knowingly or unknowingly) in the process of putting this collection together, including those colleagues and students at his current university, Glasgow Caledonian University, and those hitherto at De Montfort

University, Leicester, where he taught a module on 'Science Fiction Television' in the late 1990s whence the original spark for this volume came. Amongst all these, particular thanks to Ian (I.Q.) Hunter of De Montfort, who edited *British Science Fiction Cinema* (Routledge, 1999) through which he and Peter Wright first made contact and came to formulate this current project, as well as to Dr Catriona Miller of Glasgow Caledonian University, whose role as editorial assistant was invaluable to this volume during the final stages of its preparation.

Peter Wright would also like to thank Catriona Miller for her above role, in addition to Professor Alastair McCulloch at Edge Hill College of Higher Education for supporting his research for the book. Thanks are especially also due from him to Jenni Woodward, to whom he dedicates his work on the book.

Finally, photographic illustrations were provided by BFI Stills, Posters and Designs and the BBC Photographic Library. Our thanks to Simone Potter of BFI Stills and Tariq Hussain of the BBC Photographic Library for their help and research. Our acknowledgements to the copyright holders of the stills. While every reasonable effort has been made to obtain the necessary permissions, we invite the parties concerned to contact the publishers in the event of any oversight or incorrect attribution.

I

'Futures past':
an introduction to and brief survey
of British science fiction television

JOHN R. COOK AND PETER WRIGHT

As this volume hopes to illustrate in abundance, British science fiction (or sf) television is a fascinating, if under-researched, area of media and cultural criticism. Too often it has been dismissed as laughably cheap in comparison to bigger-budget American rivals such as the various series of the *Star Trek* franchise (NBC, 1966–69; 1987–2005), or severely wanting in terms of its quality of aspiration when regarded alongside sf cinema on the one hand and sf literature on the other. There is, however, a sizeable sf fan community around the world that cherishes British science fiction television and its distinctive contribution to envisioning and re-imagining the future in the many forms that may take. One can find evidence of this community's considerable energy and voracious appetite in the pages of science fiction and cult TV magazines, including *Starburst* (1977–), *TV Zone* (1989–) and *Cult Times* (1995–), not to mention the cornucopia of Internet websites devoted to particular British sf TV series that are still genuinely loved by their adherents, years after their original broadcasts have ended.[1]

Within the academy, whence most of the contributors to this volume originate, there has, in the past, been a certain sniffiness towards British science fiction television. The exponential growth of media and cultural studies in universities and colleges has legitimised the study of film and television as an academic discipline, and science fiction studies has also consolidated itself as part of literary or media-related academic programmes. But science fiction TV has perhaps too often been a neglected cousin, falling between the dense, ideas-laden creation of alternative worlds characteristic of literary sf and the big-budget, special-effects-laden 'sci-fi' cinema of spectacle that in many ways has now become the dominant template for commercial movie-making. Among dedicated scholars of science fiction, the differing attitudes are perhaps best encapsulated by differences in nomenclature: the term 'sf' being traditionally reserved for 'serious' forms such as the literary science fiction novel, in contrast to the popular generic label 'sci-fi', from which there has in the past been considerable distancing among science fiction critical circles on account of its ascribed connotations of pulp commercialised mass product, unworthy of serious cultural attention.

Happily, such attitudes are changing and one of the aims of this book is to build a constructive bridge between the academic and the fan communities in terms of helping to legitimise science fiction television as a worthy object of sustained critical study and to do so in a way that will hopefully be accessible and of interest to scholars and aficionados alike. In this regard, *British Science Fiction Television* sees itself as an informal companion to *British Science Fiction Cinema* (Routledge, 1999) – an earlier collection of academic essays that tried to rescue British sf cinema from the shadow of its dominant Hollywood counterpart and to which a number of writers in this current volume, including its two editors, made contributions.[2] There have, of course, been other scholarly, critical works which have considered science fiction television before, though these have tended to focus on particular iconic series rather than offering a general national survey, or, as in the case, for example, of John Tulloch and Henry Jenkins's *Science Fiction Television Audiences: Watching Star Trek and Doctor Who* (Routledge, 1995), they have engaged in a cross-cultural analysis concerned with the reception practices of particular sf TV fan communities.[3] By contrast, the preoccupation of this volume is less with the study of audiences and more with critical consideration of the texts themselves and how these might help illuminate wider social, political and cultural contexts exclusively in relation to Britain and notions of 'Britishness'.

This is the value, we hope, of such a volume to the wider media and cultural community in terms of both critics and historians, since it is our contention that analysis of past 'visions of the future' can very much help us to understand the preoccupations, hopes and fears of the society and culture which produced them at particular points in time; perhaps more potently than analysis of any other equivalent cultural form can do. Throughout its history, British science fiction television, being unable to afford the big-budget special effects of its cinema counterpart, was ideas-led, though on the level of plot, character and situation rather than having the luxury of detailed descriptive re-creations of alternative worlds axiomatic of literary sf. Its plots often functioned as metaphors or allegories, reflecting wider social and cultural preoccupations at the time of their production, particularly political tensions, or anxieties about the effects of new technology. Analysis of these 'futures past' thus offers us a fascinating window on to British society and culture as seen at different points in its recent history. Because of its displacement of social, political and technological concerns on to an outlandish, imaginative plane, British science fiction TV could often be more freely truthful about those concerns than any number of news broadcasts or current affairs analyses of the period could ever be, precisely because of the very indirectness of its metaphorical approach.

British science fiction creators were helped in this regard by the nature of the TV medium itself. Particularly in its early days, the crabbed conditions of viewing meant that in stark contrast to the public spectacle of the cinema screen, television was very much a private medium of domestic intimacy. Sf TV practitioners were able to reach right inside the home, communicating powerful messages and where necessary manipulating audiences' fears, because programmes were watched by viewers in their own private space with all their public defences down and so in that sense they became personal. This, in turn, may account for why numerous British science fiction television shows have become so iconic, remembered and celebrated years after they originally ended. Television is inextricably bound up with our own personal history and individual programmes can evoke a tremendous nostalgia. While the 'terrors' sparked by particular shows may rapidly fade, audiences still feel affection for them because they grew up with them, to such an extent that these 'visions of the future' paradoxically become a window not on to the future anymore but rather on to their own past, in a manner not entirely dissimilar to the way in which we have already suggested such texts can be used by cultural analysts.

At the same time, this does not explain why British science fiction television has proved so culturally exportable. While popular indigenous TV drama, such as crime series and soap opera, seldom has much impact overseas, particularly in the United States, British science fiction television is different. Partly this may be just a symptom of a global audience appetite for science fiction and fantasy of all kinds and the intense fan interest these genres especially attract. Shows like *Doctor Who* (BBC TV, 1963–89; 1996; 2005–) and *The Prisoner* (ITC, 1967–68), which have sold around the world and spawned international fan followings and conventions, also, however, seem to be offering something more, to which overseas audiences are responding. Comparison with *Star Trek* is instructive here: as Nicholas J. Cull argues in this volume in his essay examining *Doctor Who*'s complex relationship with the United States, the voyages of the Starship *Enterprise* in the 1960s were, in many ways, 'expansionist; integrating and co-ordinating newly discovered worlds into the inter-galactic federation' – in short, representing the forging of a kind of 'United States in space' in which 'Captain Kirk therefore seemed like an all-American hero' (see Nicholas J. Cull's chapter, 'Tardis at the OK Corral').

British sf TV was different. While America was assured of its leadership role in the emerging space race and could look with confidence to the stars as an extension of the utopian frontier possibilities of the American Dream, Britain was having to cope anxiously in the same period with the loss of empire and general decline as a world power. Thus the notion of the British in space was not only a depressing impossibility but an outright absurdity. Some of the basic differences in character between British and US science fiction TV may be traceable to this: where archetypal US series like *Star Trek* often confronted the future with a sense of gung-ho optimism, British equivalents were more prone to view it with pessimism, anxiety or, especially later with such shows as *The Hitchhiker's Guide to the Galaxy* (BBC TV, 1981) and *Red Dwarf* (BBC TV, 1988–99), an alternative response of absurdist humour; laughter rather than despair perhaps being the preferable long-term survival option in such circumstances. In US science fiction TV, space was frequently shown to be a conquest of noble courage and a feat of collective national enterprise; in

Britain, by stark contrast, it was more often the realm of whimsical individual eccentrics which, as with the Victorian frock-coated owner of the Tardis in *Doctor Who*, was less about boldly going into the future than using good old-fashioned British invention and ingenuity to step back in time.

Hence British TV exported to global audiences a more sceptical, perhaps even more 'realistic', view of the science fiction future than American equivalents could traditionally provide, and this manifested itself by way either of ironic humour and whimsical eccentricity, or frequently of something altogether more dark and despairing. Certainly, as we shall see evidenced in this volume, there is an underlying pessimism to much British TV sf – many of the fictions are about national catastrophe or future political nightmare, and in this they stand in a proud tradition of British anti-utopian writing that includes such iconic texts as Aldous Huxley's *Brave New World* (1932) and George Orwell's *Nineteen Eighty-Four* (1949). This darker, more 'political' vision can be seen reflected if we now trace, briefly, the history and development of science fiction on British television, concentrating in particular on some of the key texts that individual contributors discuss in their essays.

The foundations for British sf TV's political content were laid on 11 February 1938 when BBC TV broadcast a truncated adaptation of Czech writer Carel Kapek's stage play *RUR* (1920). This was the first ever piece of British science fiction television. The BBC had been running a regular scheduled television service from Alexandra Palace since 2 November 1936, and early TV drama output included adaptations from stage plays. Most significantly for the future development of British TV science fiction, *RUR* was a dark parable – it dealt with themes of dehumanisation, mass production and the abuse of power in its depiction of an android revolt which destroys humanity.

If *RUR* was the first example of British science fiction TV, another was not broadcast until January 1949, when producer Robert Barr staged a live studio version of H.G. Wells's famous 1895 novel, *The Time Machine*. This was a technically bold hour-long production, employing filmed inserts and back projection; it was the first occasion that British TV science fiction acknowledged the narrative potential of special effects.[4] More importantly, Barr's teleplay placed the figure of the scientist – the Time Traveller – in a central narrative position: a characteristic that would prove influential for the subsequent development of the genre on British television.

The Time Machine's technical experimentation signalled the need for 'updating' what drama producer Rudolph Cartier perceived in 1952 as the 'stagy' qualities of BBC drama.[5] Cartier's fervour for narrative and stylistic innovation led to the wellspring of much British TV sf: writer Nigel Kneale's technically ambitious *Quatermass* trilogy of the 1950s, which Cartier directed and produced. As James Chapman shows in his chapter in this volume, the *Quatermass* trilogy, in its reflection of contemporary British scientific endeavour, its post-war settings and general Cold War ambience, marks the true origins and indeed is arguably the epitome of adult British science fiction on television.

Kneale shared Cartier's impatience with theatre-like dramas that failed to exploit television's technical potential and with the suggestion that television should foster a reassuringly intimate relationship between producer and consumer. While, as Chapman shows, the commissioning of the first six-part *Quatermass* serial may have been the ad hoc result of the BBC discovering a gap in its summer schedules, Kneale's decision to reach for science fiction served his creative ambitions well. Unhampered by the restrictions of realism, sf could confront viewers with drama to challenge their perception of a changing medium and a changing world. Hence the title of Kneale's first serial in the eventual trilogy, *The Quatermass Experiment* (BBC TV, 1953), connotes both the subject matter and its creative approach to television drama.

As with Barr's earlier *The Time Machine*, in the *Quatermass* trilogy the scientist and the implications of developments in science and new technology are placed centre stage. Each *Quatermass* drama is a variant on the theme of an alien invasion uncovered by Professor Bernard Quatermass. Eschewing spectacle in favour of invasion by stealth, Kneale captures the fear and suspicion prevalent in the 1950s. In an interview in 1996, he reflected on how

> That decade has sometimes been called one of paranoia, which means abnormal, sick attitudes and irrational fears. I don't think it was irrational to be fearful at that time: there was a lot to be frightened of and stories like mine were a sort of controlled paranoia; inoculation against the real horrors.[6]

While challenging the expectations of television audiences, Kneale was also sublimating their fears of earthly conflict. In the final drama of the 1950s trilogy, *Quatermass and the Pit* (BBC TV, 1958–59), the scientist Quatermass discovers human aggression to be the consequence of evolutionary tampering by ancient, antagonistic Martians. 'If we cannot control the inheritance within us,' he warns at the conclusion, 'this will be their [the Martians'] second dead planet.'[7] With this polemical speech, delivered straight to camera, the sublimatory strategies of the earlier serials are stripped away so that the audience is directly engaged with the harsh political realities of the 1950s. The fact it is spoken by a scientist, albeit a fictional one, gives the warning extra weight.

By the end of the 1950s, the *Quatermass* trilogy had helped establish two of the key characteristics of British TV sf: the centrality of the scientist and the reflection of Cold War fears. In the 1960s, these remained fundamental but their dramatic presentation began to change, with much more of an explicitly anti-establishment stance adopted. In 1961, for example, the seven-part BBC TV serial *A for Andromeda* was bold in its condemnation of the political and military conscription of science and scientists. Where such criticism had been implicit or personalised in *Quatermass*, *A for Andromeda* showed a scientific community distrusted by and accountable to Whitehall. Written by astronomer Fred Hoyle and scripted by BBC producer John Elliot, it pitted an idealistic scientist, John Fleming (played by Peter Halliday), against a seemingly hostile alien supercomputer; a myopic British government; an unscrupulous multinational corporation; and a US general intent on selfishly safeguarding 'aircraft-carrier Britain'. In so doing, *A for Andromeda* re-emphasised the moral and intellectual superiority of scientists over politicians, first established in *Quatermass*.[8]

The notion of a salvatory scientist as a politically and socially critical figure became fundamental to the characterisation of perhaps the most famous renegade scientist in the history of British TV sf: Doctor Who. As Nicholas J. Cull comprehensively analyses in his chapter, 'Tardis at the OK Corral', *Doctor Who* was initiated by a Canadian, Sydney Newman, who had experience of working in US commercial television, and the drama's genesis was profoundly influenced by America. At the same time, however, it also reflected a very British liberal political and social agenda synonymous with the BBC's public service broadcasting ethos of the period. The Doctor was a humanist scientist who occupied the neutral ground of 'tolerance' and 'balance', from which the misdoings of the official and the powerful could be challenged and corrected, regardless of which side of the political and social spectrum these evils emanated from.

The serial was thus a classic BBC public service form of 'balanced', 'responsible' entertainment. It had originally been conceived partly to assist the teaching of science and history to children and with an avowed determination on BBC Head of TV Drama Sydney Newman's part to avoid what he dismissed as 'the Bug Eyed Monster (BEM) Syndrome' of pulp science fiction. As Cull makes clear, however, it soon became apparent to the show's producers that the closer the Doctor came to Bug-Eyed Monsters and outer space adventures, the better the ratings. Thus as Cull puts it: '*Doctor Who* had found his niche as a British character living American B-movie adventures.' As Cull then goes on to demonstrate, it was the influence and dominance of America that would increasingly pull at the show in the decades to come, until, by the 1980s and 1990s, *Doctor Who* ended up as something of 'a pawn in the transatlantic media game'.

This touches on a very important point in relation to some of the most successful British television science fiction: the need, often, for it to be internationally exportable, particularly to the lucrative United States market. Each of the next three contributions in this collection discusses filmed series of the 1960s that were made for commercial television and commissioned (all by famous TV mogul Lew Grade) with at least one eye on programme sales abroad. In 'Countering the Counterculture', Sue Short discusses perhaps the archetypal TV fantasy of the 1960s: *The Prisoner* (ITC, 1967–68). Created by and starring Patrick McGoohan, this famous series united the paranoid uncertainties of espionage narratives with sf's interest in psychology and altered states of consciousness in order to produce a provoca-tive political and philosophical discourse on the nature of freedom. McGoohan plays Number Six, an agent who resigns from the secret service but finds he cannot escape after he is abducted and taken to 'The Village': a bizarre amalgamation of holiday resort and detention centre for the politically inconvenient. Here, he enters a battle of wits with a series of administrators (called 'Number Two'), all of whom are determined to uncover why he resigned. The Prisoner's own quest, however, is to find Number One: the real manipulator of events and the mastermind behind 'The Village'.

As Short argues, the series stands in a problematical relationship to the 1960s' counterculture and the cultural ferment of its times. On one level, it seems to be the very epitome of that decade's anti-establishment, libertarian values, yet there is an underlying social and cultural conservatism which at times leads creator McGoohan to attack such values and their representatives, particularly in 'Fall Out', the surreal final episode (1st tx. ITV, 2 February 1968). Indeed the whole series seems steeped in an ambiguity of intention and motive and it is this which arguably continues to fuel its fascination for analysts and fans alike all around the world, since it leaves itself purposively open to all sorts of differing readings and interpretations. As such, it remains a uniquely challenging and ingenious series, dramatising the dilemmas involved in understanding and safeguarding one's individuality in a world of increasing technological surveillance, together with the corresponding dangers of political and social conformity this might bring.

If *The Prisoner* is therefore a classic example of the segueing of British telefantasy with science fiction TV,[9] it also seems to demonstrate how some of the most iconic texts we now associate as synonymous with the changes and challenges of the 1960s are actually, if one analyses them, deeply ambiguous about and conflicted by the enormous social and cultural upheavals wrought by that decade. This is a theme which John R. Cook takes up in his chapter, 'The Age of Aquarius: Utopia and Anti-Utopia in Late 1960s' and Early 1970s' British Science Fiction Television'. Following on from Short, Cook's focus is firmly on how the hopes and ideals of the late 1960s' 'Aquarian' counterculture were reflected and mediated across a number of key British sf TV texts of the period.

As we have seen, British science fiction television tends not to do optimism very well, but in the late 1960s and early 1970s as society started to liberalise and individuals began to experience a greater sense of freedom and 'permissiveness' in their own personal lives, this was one period when it could dare to dream with some sense of genuine hope. Sf TV thus became a natural vehicle for mediating some of the utopian dreams of the 1960s of a better future. It was, Cook argues, the young who were the principal locus of these hopes and who were seen as at the vanguard of social change. Hence it was perhaps not surprising that science fiction television aimed at children was often where the expression of utopian sentiments during this period were at their most pronounced.

Cook traces the spirit of utopianism across a number of diverse children's sf texts such as *Joe 90* (ITV, 1968–69) and Thames TV's *The Tomorrow People* (ITV, 1973–79). He also considers its more adult variation in what he labels 'the veritable sexual playground' of the technological utopian future presented by *UFO* (Century 21 for ITC, 1969–70): the first attempt by producer Gerry Anderson's company, Century 21, to break away from making science fiction puppet series for children and to move into live-action production for a more adult audience; an effort that met with only mixed results. Yet while commercial television, with eyes firmly fixed on international programme sales, was selling dreams of a bright, 'permissive' future of gadgets and girls to a mass audience, *Quatermass* writer Nigel Kneale was using the greater experimental freedoms of the single television play at the BBC to present a very different vision of the implications of the 'permissive society'. Like McGoohan with *The Prisoner*, his was much more of a sceptical attitude. His 1968 TV play *The Year of the Sex Olympics* was the worm in the bud of late 1960s' utopianism in the sense that he extrapolated the logic of a future Aquarian world of complete liberty, much vaunted by the counterculture at the time, and showed how the removal of all restrictions might create the very antithesis of the promised freedoms. Kneale's resulting drama is one which still has resonance for our own times, and perhaps it was most appropriate that it should be the creator of *Quatermass* who with this play moved British science fiction TV back to its more familiar dramatic territory: that of outright anti-utopianism.

Throughout its history, science fiction television has always had to contend with assumptions that its dreams of the future and of other worlds are fit only for children. As Cook suggests in his chapter, this was a common assumption among controllers and regulators of television during this period and it is certainly one which producer Gerry Anderson had to contend with throughout his distinguished career, as evidenced by his mixed fortunes with *UFO* and other live-action sf series aimed at adults. We are very pleased to be able to reproduce an interview with Gerry Anderson in this book – an on-stage interview that contributor Nicholas Cull conducted with Anderson as part of the 'Visions of the Future' cultural history conference, held at the University of Leicester in July 2003. Anderson, of course, is most famous and celebrated as the producer of the famous *Thunderbirds* 'supermarionation' series of the mid-1960s (Century 21 for ITC, 1965–66), as well as *Stingray* (Century 21 for ITC, 1964–65), *Captain Scarlet and the Mysterons* (Century 21 for ITC, 1967–68) and numerous others. But he has also worked in feature films and alongside *UFO*, has produced live action TV series such as *The Protectors* (ITC, 1972–74) and *Space: 1999* (ITC, 1975–76). He is still active within the industry and recently completed a new CGI (computer-generated imagery) version of *Captain Scarlet*, which premiered on ITV in spring 2005.

Relative to some of the key themes of British sf TV explored in this volume, Anderson's first-hand account is valuable in terms of illustrating the utopian values which as a practitioner he was keen to instil in those of his series aimed specifically at children. As he puts it: 'I had all sorts of fancy ideas about the future. You know, we had the United Nations and I imagined that the world would come together and there would be a world government...' His attitude was: 'I ... thought, well, hundreds of millions of children are watching these programmes and I don't want to contribute to a global conflict between two superpowers!' (see below, 'The Man Who Made *Thunderbirds*: An Interview with Gerry Anderson'). At the same time, more sadly, as his account of the demise of the original *Thunderbirds* demonstrates, his brand of expensive filmed series for commercial television was highly dependent on television sales to the United States networks such that when these dried up, series that were still tremendously popular and iconic in Britain nevertheless had to fold.[10]

As the utopian hedonism of the 1960s gave way to the more sobering realities of the 1970s, British sf TV similarly tended to turn inwards, away from international rescues and programme sales and more towards a growing concern with domestic political issues. Human influence on the environment became a principal preoccupation at this time. *Doomwatch* (BBC TV, 1970–72), for example, followed the efforts of a government department to safeguard environmental and public safety from scientific, military or corporate negligence. Created

SCIENTIST AS SAVIOUR   *Doomwatch* (BBC TV, 1970–72).

by *Doctor Who* script editor Gerry Davis and environmentalist Dr Kit Pedler, the series responded to growing scientific concerns over pollution, resource depletion and ecological mismanagement.

A comparable insularity is found in Terry Nation's *Survivors* (BBC TV, 1975–77), in which the remnants of British society struggle to rebuild civilization after a plague kills 95 per cent of the world's population. As Andy Sawyer argues in his chapter, the series explodes the myth of cosy, middle-class self-sufficiency popular in the 1970s (and typified by the exactly contemporaneous BBC TV sitcom *The Good Life*). Instead, it exposes the difficulties of returning to a less industrialised existence. Its focus on middle-class characters in crisis, together with its tone of cautious optimism and its combination of political modelling and social criticism, borrows from the traditions of British literary catastrophe fiction. Its politics, however, often appear to be avowedly nationalistic and isolationist (perhaps as a reaction against Britain's growing involvement with Europe and the

Common Market during the time of its production). The penultimate episode, 'Long Live the King' (1st tx. BBC 1, 1 June 1977),
seems to embrace conservatism over change, advocating the socially
uniting benefits of a constitutional monarchy. Meanwhile, the aptly
named final episode, 'Power' (1st tx. BBC 1, 8 June 1977), appears
to suggest real power will lie with a self-reliant feudal society ruled
over by warlords, where everybody will know their place. As Sawyer
comments: 'Either way, we seem not to be offered much hope for
the future of post-industrial society.'

The collapse of society in the wake of national catastrophe is also
central to David Seed's exploration of what he terms 'TV Docudrama
and the Nuclear Subject'. He examines two British documentary
drama-style representations from different historical periods, each
depicting what might happen to society if there were ever a nuclear
attack on British soil: director Peter Watkins's seminal *The War Game*
(BBC TV, 1965), which was controversially banned from television
for 20 years, despite going on to win an Oscar in 1967, and writer
Barry Hines and director Mick Jackson's *Threads* (BBC TV, 1984). Seed
also compares these with a US TV example from the same period
as *Threads*: *The Day After* (ABC 1983, dir. Nicholas Meyer).

In his discussion, Seed points out similarities between the three
'docudramas' but also highlights significant differences. *Threads* and
The Day After situate their nuclear nightmare within more conventional
dramatic narratives, following the effects of devastation on identity-
inviting families played by professional actors. Watkins, by contrast,
uses non-professionals, together with hand-held cinematography,
natural lighting and sound, in order to simulate the effects of a
nuclear attack on Kent, just as if the audience were witnessing it in
an actual documentary. In *Threads*, Hines and Jackson consider what
might happen if there were a nuclear strike on Sheffield. As Seed
suggests, they evoke the image of civil society as a web in the sense
of its interconnectedness but also its fragility, such that if one strand
is broken, many other threads may start to unravel too. By the end
of the drama, British society is shown to have reverted to a state
of medievalism only thirteen years after the Bomb has dropped, the
web having been almost completely shattered.

Threads formed part of a series of dramas and documentaries
made by BBC TV on 'the nuclear subject', and its screening in 1984

paved the way for the first television screening of *The War Game* in 1985. These programming decisions were very much a reaction to a renewed increase in tensions in the Cold War during the early 1980s. This was the period of Reaganite foreign policy with its determination to stoke up the Cold War against the Soviet Union, whilst at home Thatcherism was starting, in its own way, to unravel many of the threads of the British liberal post-war consensus. One key British science fiction television series coterminous with the early years of Thatcherism, and which seemed to reflect much of the pessimism of the period in terms of the hopelessness of the possibility of any kind of future social emancipation, was *Blake's 7* (BBC TV, 1978–81). As Una McCormack suggests in her chapter examining this iconic series, *Blake's 7* reclaimed the conventions of space opera for a British context at a time when the American *Star Wars* movies (US 1977; 1980; 1983; prod. George Lucas) were conquering the world's cinema screens. Created by Terry Nation, the series followed a rebellion by a group of criminals led by idealist Roj Blake (Gareth Thomas) and cynic Kerr Avon (Paul Darrow) against the despotic activities of Earth's Federation, commanded over by the ruthless, Thatcherite-style President Servalan (Jacqueline Pearce). Taking inspiration from the anti-utopian writings of Orwell and Huxley, *Blake's 7*, as McCormack shows, was the antithesis of *Star Trek* in the 1960s. The camaraderie of the crew in the latter series was replaced with hostility and distrust among the principal characters that made up Blake's band of renegades and outlaws; the seemingly benign United Federation of Planets was countered with the militaristic Federation in the British series, while heroic individuals were supplanted by ambivalent characters with ambiguous motives. Where *Star Trek* advocated triumphant expansionism, the dystopian space opera of *Blake's 7* chronicled a series of hollow victories and bitter defeats. By 1981 and the series' end, the climax of Blake's ineffective rebellion, which saw all but one of the rebels killed, reflected the sullen mood of a Britain beset by economic decline, mass unemployment and civil unrest, all presided over by the increasingly strident premiership of Margaret Thatcher.

As McCormack also points out, *Blake's 7* marked the BBC's last attempt at producing a mainstream, politically orientated science fiction TV series of discrete self-enclosed episodes for a primetime slot on BBC 1. In the more sober 1980s' world of greater Thatcherite 'realism', speculations about what the future might hold would henceforth tend to be consigned to minority slots or channels, or be considered suitable for treatment only within flagship serial drama form. The heyday of science fiction on British TV – which had peaked in the 1960s and 1970s – appeared to have passed. Over on ITV, however, one last gasp for serious use of the form in a primetime slot was *Sapphire and Steel* (ATV, 1979–82), a twice-weekly series of adventures created by crime drama writer P.J. Hammond. In his chapter on *Sapphire and Steel*, Peter Wright reads the series as a direct reflection on Thatcher's premiership: a political allegory of the triumph of Conservative order over social chaos in a drama that is as sombre as it is deeply symbolic. Wright demonstrates how the programme synthesises tropes from the Gothic and the English ghost story with the rational, investigative processes of science fiction and the golden age crime novel, in order to structure a conflict between the metaphorical representatives of perceived contemporary social malaise – militant groups, 'wet' or ineffective politicians, immigration, faceless bureaucracy – and the eponymous Thatcherite protagonists, Sapphire and Steel. Authoritarian and uncompromising, Sapphire (Joanna Lumley) and Steel (David McCallum) are guardians of the social and temporal order. Fittingly, for its Thatcherite times, the programme held them up as heroic figures, despite or perhaps rather because of their obdurate, misanthropic attitudes.

By 1981, however, as economic recession bit hard, riots erupted in the inner cities and old liberal certainties found themselves inexorably eroded by the emerging Thatcherite agenda, it was becoming increasingly hard to take science fiction on British TV seriously at all, as opposed to in the cinema where huge technical advances in special effects had made the physical representations of such visions of the future now highly believable. Faced with such circumstances, perhaps the only option left for British science fiction TV was to have a laugh at itself. This was something which ex-*Doctor Who* script editor Douglas Adams had already intrinsically recognised with his hit Radio 4 serial *The Hitchhiker's Guide to the Galaxy* (1978), and when it transferred to TV in 1981, the serial's absurdist humour continued with it. As a writer of science fiction, Adams was conscious not only of the meaninglessness of human existence but also the folly of searching for meaning, and he understood that humour is often the only defence against such a bleak realisation. *The Hitchhiker's Guide* employs comedy to recount a science fiction story that exposes the general absurdity of the cosmos and articulates a sobering and melancholy misanthropy. In its anarchic, encyclopaedic plotting, the importance of human existence is undermined, the pettiness of human officialdom mocked, and the scale of human achievement parodied.

As contributor M.J. Simpson points out in his chapter, however, the TV *The Hitchhiker's Guide* has been unfairly compared in retrospect as inferior to the radio serial which preceded it, when in fact its special effects were state-of-the-art for the period, and the serial also succeeded in bringing Adams's humour and rich ideas to a mass audience for the first time, so much so that for a great many people their memory of *The Hitchhiker's Guide to the Galaxy* is the TV version. Simpson is the author of a well-received commercial biography of Douglas Adams, as well as a popular critical guide to *The Hitchhiker's Guide to the Galaxy*, and as a non-academic contributor he is able to bring the perspective of a genuine fan, as well as expert, to his analysis of the serial, in keeping with the volume's wish to bridge the gap between the academic and the fan communities. Playfully borrowing his title from Adams's own dig at academic criticism in Episode 2 of *The Hitchhiker's Guide*, Simpson's chapter, 'Counterpointing the Surrealism of the Underlying Metaphor', also replicates some of the encyclopaedic breadth of Adams's own work in its analysis of biographical sources for many of the late writer's highly striking ideas.

As *Doctor Who* tottered towards cancellation in 1989, the lesson from Adams – that humour was going to be the key to future survival of British science fiction TV in a harsher cultural climate – was not lost on Rob Grant and Doug Naylor's *Red Dwarf* (BBC TV, 1988–99), which used the situation comedy format to revivify the various conventions and conceits of TV science fiction, much to the delight of British sf TV fans, starved of any more serious fodder on television for much of this period. Like *The Hitchhiker's Guide*, *Red Dwarf* resists denigrating generic conventions to mere devices in order to enliven standard comedy situations. However, where *The Hitchhiker's Guide* parodied bureaucracy, human hubris and the notion of ultimate knowledge in order to offer a wry account of humanity's shortcomings, *Red Dwarf*'s humour is more intimate, deriving from personal, class and masculine conflict between its characters. As Elyce Rae Helford argues in her chapter on *Red Dwarf*, the programme's futuristic setting opens up a potentially 'post-patriarchal space' in which the politics of gender, representation, masculine anxiety and male desire can take centre stage, even though, as she also comprehensively demonstrates, its male characters choose in the series to cling tenaciously to traditional patriarchal norms.

By the 1990s, however, *Red Dwarf* appeared to be just about the only successful example of British television science fiction still in production, precisely because it *was* a comedy, the genre as a whole seemingly no longer taken seriously by British television commissioners and producers. Instead, particularly at the BBC, there seemed to be more and more of a reliance on filling the vacuum left by the demise of the iconic *Doctor Who* through importing and repeating increasing numbers of US TV series with their bigger budgets and more elaborate special effects, including the various series of the *Star Trek* franchise; *The X-Files* (Fox Television, 1993–2002); *Quantum Leap* (Universal Television, 1989–93); *Sliders* (Fox Television, 1995–2000) and genre fantasies such as *Buffy the Vampire Slayer* (Warners/UPN, 1997–2003), all of which supplanted indigenous TV sf. When *Doctor Who* returned as a one-off television movie in 1996 (a pilot for a putative series that never was), it exemplified the loss, in an increasingly globalised entertainment market, of the form's quintessential Britishness. Co-produced by the BBC's Worldwide division, Universal and Fox Television, *Doctor Who* the TV movie avoided the original serial's public service politics of humane scientific liberalism in favour of a more 'globalised' Doctor, reinvented by writer Matthew Jacobs and producer Philip Segal as a kind of Byronic romantic hero (played by Paul McGann), who even at one point shares a chaste kiss with his new American assistant, Grace (Daphne Ashbrook). Revisionist intertexts, transformations of character and generic shifts had thus brought the hitherto itinerant time traveller bang into line with the homogenised requirements of international television production for a new global market.

As Catriona Miller goes on to examine in the final chapter in this volume, in the late 1990s, however, a renewed interest among

British television executives in commissioning sf drama resulted in a number of new home-grown serials being produced. In her chapter, she relates this to the phenomenal global success of *The X-Files* in the mid-1990s and the keenness of commissioning editors to cash in on its appeal, as well as to the approach of a new millennium, with its cultural focusing of attention on 'the end of days'. Certainly, each of the three dramas that emerged – *The Uninvited* (ITV, 1997), *Invasion: Earth* (BBC Scotland with the Sci-Fi Channel, 1998) and *The Last Train* (ITV, 1999) – were fictions of catastrophe and apocalypse that stood in a long tradition of such sf on British television.

Invasion: Earth, for example, was an attempt to recapture the mystery and suspense of the *Quatermass* dramas in terms of its alien invasion narrative of Earth caught in a war between the benign Echoes and the malevolent nDs, together with its apocalyptic climax. The presence, however, of American actor Fred Ward, who played Major General David Reece and the co-production involvement of the US-based Sci-Fi cable channel indicated the new realities of producing big-budget sf TV in a globalised entertainment age. Like *Doctor Who: The Movie*, *Invasion: Earth* was aimed squarely at an international market.

Writer Matthew Graham's six-part *The Last Train* (ITV, 1999) was somewhat different, drawing inspiration from a more locally indigenous British disaster tradition that includes *Survivors*. Disdaining the cliché of nuclear conflict, the series deployed the most recent trend in apocalyptic scenarios – an asteroid collision – as the catastrophic event that wipes out most of humanity. A group of survivors, seemingly representative of multicultural Britain yet still characterised stereotypically (Mick, for example, played by Treva Etienne, is black and a criminal), are preserved when their train from London to Sheffield enters a tunnel at the moment of impact. Frozen cryogenically by the contents of a canister carried by one of the passengers, the survivors regain consciousness and emerge from their tomb almost fifty years after the event. The serial then chronicles the quest they undertake from a shattered Sheffield (clearly a homage to *Threads*) to the catastrophe-survival shelter, ARK. Unlike *The Uninvited* and *Invasion: Earth*, *The Last Train* explores catastrophe intimately and without sentiment, dramatising the difficulties of finding fresh water, food and shelter in a world remade by disaster. This intimacy is developed further as the drama asks, through dialogue, subtext and event, what drives individuals to survive? The answer forms the trajectories of each of the characters as they move across the blighted landscape.

With its more thoughtful juxtapositions of delusion and optimism, tenderness and cruelty, the mundane and the extraordinary, *The Last Train* marked a return to sf TV that at least considered its own cultural milieu. Now, in the twenty-first century, there are hopeful signs that the long famine of indigenous sf TV, only intermittently punctuated in the preceding decade by dramas such as *The Last Train*, has come to an end with a new home-grown BBC *Doctor Who* series launched in 2005, initially starring Christopher Eccleston as the Doctor (later replaced by David Tennant), that included scripts by top British TV dramatist Russell T. Davies. Add to this Gerry Anderson's new CGI version of *Captain Scarlet*, a revival of Nigel Kneale's *The Quatermass Experiment*, transmitted live by the BBC (1st tx. BBC 4, 2 April 2005), plus a big-budget movie version of *The Hitchhiker's Guide to the Galaxy* (dir. Garth Jennings, USA/UK 2005), long planned by the late Douglas Adams, and it seems that interest in the production possibilities of the form is stronger now than it has been for many years.

The appearance of this volume, examining British sf TV's various 'futures past', therefore could not be more timely. While the diverse texts under consideration here fascinate and dazzle with their eclecticism, one thing unites them. Whether utopian or anti-utopian, comedy or catastrophe fiction, they all dare to dream of other possibilities beyond their immediate present, and in that sense sf TV can be seen to constitute its own distinctive mode of cultural criticism. Even though their visions of the future may be wholly pessimistic and dark, all sf TV texts carry within them the seeds of a latent utopianism, because appealing to the dreamer in all of us, they refuse to accept the way things currently are, telling their audience, often to the latter's delight and mystification, that the way things are today is not the way they are always necessarily going to be. Tomorrow is most definitely another day and the future, they dare to tell us, can always be different.

NOTES

1. *Starburst*, *TV Zone* and *Cult Times* are all published by Visual Imagination Limited.

2. I.Q. Hunter (ed.), *British Science Fiction Cinema* (London and New York: Routledge, 1999). The contributors to both this and the current volume are James Chapman, Andy Sawyer, Sue Short, as well as editors John R. Cook and Peter Wright.

3. Texts focusing on iconic series include Manuel Alvarado and John Tulloch, *Doctor Who: The Unfolding Text* (London: Macmillan, 1983) and Chris Gregory, *Decoding The Prisoner* (Luton: John Libby Media, 1997). As well as John Tulloch and Henry Jenkins' *Science Fiction Audiences: Watching Doctor Who and Star Trek* (London and New York: Routledge, 1995), texts focusing on reception studies of sf TV fan communities also include Matthew Hills, *Fan Cultures* (London and New York: Routledge, 2002).

4. E. Glenn, 'Fantasy Flashback: *The Time Machine*', *TV Zone* 17 (1991), pp. 28–30.

5. J. Jacobs, *The Intimate Screen: Early British Television Drama* (Oxford: Oxford University Press, 2000), p. 1.

6. A. Pixley, 'Nigel Kneale Interview – Behind the Dark Door', 1996, www. geocities.com/TelevisionCity/8504/kneal.htm (accessed 21 November 2003).

7. *Quatermass and The Pit*, Episode 6, 'Hob' (1st tx. BBC TV, 26 January 1959).

8. *A for Andromeda* is also of interest on account of its attitudes to gender. For further discussion, see Joy Leman, 'Wise Scientists and Female Androids', in John Corner (ed.), *Popular Television in Britain* (London: British Film Institute, 1991).

9. By 'telefantasy', it is meant popular fantasy TV drama which eschews realism in favour of glamour, escapism or the construction of alternative fantasy realms. British examples might include many of the popular action adventure series produced by ITC (Incorporated Television Company) in the 1960s such as *The Saint* (1962–69), *The Champions* (1968–69) and *Randall and Hopkirk (Deceased)* (1969–70). With its world of secret agents and its construction of an anti-utopia based upon technological surveillance, *The Prisoner* seems to straddle both categories. For further discussion of *The Prisoner* in the context of British action adventure series of the 1960s, see James Chapman, *Saints and Avengers: British Adventure Series of the 1960s* (London and New York: I.B. Tauris, 2002), pp. 49–51.

10. In 2004, a new live action movie version of *Thunderbirds* was produced by Working Title films in association with Universal Pictures, directed by Jonathan Frakes. Anderson had no involvement in its production and refused to endorse the movie.

2

Quatermass and the origins of British television sf

JAMES CHAPMAN

It is difficult today to appreciate the impact made by *The Quatermass Experiment* on British television viewers in 1953. This 'thriller for television in six parts' was the first drama serial to excite the public's imagination to the extent that, according to popular folklore, pubs were emptied on Saturday evenings whilst viewers of a 'nervous disposition' were advised not to watch. It was an immediate success. A further two *Quatermass* serials were made during the 1950s – a belated fourth serial followed in 1979 – and the first three stories were all remade as feature films by Hammer Film Productions.[1] *The Quatermass Experiment* has been described in such terms as 'one of the most significant BBC drama productions of the early 1950s' and 'a landmark both in BBC policy, as a commissioned original TV drama, and in intensity of audience response'.[2] Its significance within the historical development of television drama is that it challenged received wisdoms about the technological and aesthetic possibilities of the medium. It has been claimed by television scholars as representing an important moment in the 'opening up' of the small screen from the 'intimate' to the 'expansive' form of drama.[3] Yet this focus on the formal and aesthetic properties of *The Quatermass Experiment* has tended to obscure the place of the four *Quatermass* serials in the generic lineage of television science fiction. Not only do the *Quatermass* serials exemplify many of the key themes and tropes that constitute TV science fiction; they also represent an important attempt to legitimate sf as a 'serious' genre.[4]

The Quatermass Experiment was neither the first instance of serious sf produced for television nor the first sf serial written specifically for television, but the extent of its popularity and its influence was such that it can reasonably be seen as marking the beginning of sf as a significant television genre. Before *Quatermass* sf had only a sporadic presence on British television. The earliest examples of the genre had been live adaptations of sf literature, such as the Czech writer Karel Capek's *RUR* (1938) — the play that introduced the word 'robot' into the English language — and H.G. Wells's classic *The Time Machine* (1949). The fact that neither of these television plays seems to have made much of an impact was probably due in large measure to the technological limitations of early television, though another factor that needs to be taken into account is the difficulty of adapting literary sf (which is predominantly about ideas) for a visual medium such as television. This, at least, was the verdict of two BBC writers commissioned to survey the field of sf literature in 1962: 'Audiences — we think — are not as yet interested in the mere exploitation of ideas — the "idea as hero" aspect of SF.' The report concluded that 'the vast bulk of SF writing is by nature unsuitable for translation to TV'.[5]

In the early 1950s sf was seen, within television circles at least, as a juvenile genre. Among the biggest ratings successes for American television had been sf series made for what *Variety* termed the 'kidvid' slot, such as *Captain Video* (1949–53), *Tom Corbett – Space Cadet* (1950–55) and *Rocky Jones – Space Ranger* (1953–54).[6] The sf movie serials of the 1930s, such as *Flash Gordon* (1936) and *Buck Rogers* (1939), also enjoyed an afterlife when shown on television in edited form. The first British sf serial was *Stranger from Space* (1951), shown in ten-minute episodes as part of the children's programme *Whirligig*. None of the eleven episodes is known to have survived, but the serial seems to have been a predecessor of Spielberg's *E.T.: The Extra-Terrestrial* (1982) insofar as it followed the adventures of a friendly Martian marooned on Earth who is befriended by a young boy. The foremost British sf hero of the day was undoubtedly 'Dan Dare – Pilot of the Future', the lantern-jawed hero of the flagship comic strip in the boys' paper *Eagle*, launched in 1950, whose outer-space adventures thrilled a generation of British schoolboys. It is interesting to conjecture why Dan Dare was never adapted for television, as American comic strip heroes Buck Rogers and Flash Gordon were in the early 1950s,[7] though there was a serial on Radio Luxembourg (1951–56) where Dan was played by Noel Johnson, who had a suitably heroic pedigree having already played *Dick Barton – Special Agent* on radio for the BBC (1946–51). However, the Dan Dare comic strip was drawn with such a degree of visual imagination by artist Frank Hampson – and, moreover, was in colour – that any attempt to translate it to television would inevitably have disappointed.[8]

Nigel Kneale, who wrote all the *Quatermass* serials, has always claimed not to be a particular enthusiast of sf, remarking that 'I find my occasional sampling of science fiction acutely disappointing; so much of it is the space equivalent of Barbara Cartland, over-written and peopled by very dull characters.'[9] Yet, rather like Terry Nation, another television writer who claimed not to like sf but came to be indelibly associated with the genre through his creation of the Daleks for the long-running series *Doctor Who*, Kneale's sf television scripts have overshadowed his other work, including writing the screenplays for Tony Richardson's film adaptations of *Look Back in Anger* (1959) and *The Entertainer* (1960). Kneale, a short-story writer, had joined the BBC in 1951 and had quickly established a reputation as a skilled adapter for the television medium. He so impressed Michael Barry, the recently appointed head of drama (television), that a year before *Quatermass* Barry was telling his superiors that 'we cannot afford to lose his knowledge of Television built up over nine months'.[10] Kneale's pre-*Quatermass* work included an adaptation of Charles Irving's apocalyptic thriller *Number Three* in 1952. Following the first *Quatermass* serial he adapted George Orwell's *Nineteen Eighty-Four* (1954); he would later write a number of thoughtful and challenging television plays including *The Year of the Sex Olympics* (1968) – a prescient satire of the sort of 'reality TV' that became popular some three decades later – and the chilling supernatural thriller *The Stone Tape* (1972).[11]

From early in Kneale's career as a television writer, he was keen to explore the visual as well as the dramatic possibilities of the medium. The watchword of most television drama at the time was 'intimacy'. Television was an intimate medium both because it was broadcast directly into the home and because the television screen was small. The preferred style of intimate drama was the outcome of both technological and aesthetic determinants: television cameras and receivers were unsuitable for long shots, which lost their scale and definition on the small screen, but were ideal for close-ups, which not only captured the immediacy of live performance but also allowed the producers to economise on sets. It was this style that characterised the so-called 'golden age' of television drama in the 1950s with its spare sets, intense acting and psychologically oriented story lines. Kneale, however, disliked the intimate form of drama, which he regarded as being too wordy, and argued instead for the adoption of film methods, including more extensive use of filmed inserts in otherwise live transmissions. The use of film, he averred, 'adds both physical freedom and atmosphere' and could 'provide a most useful extension of the story beyond the cramped studio sets'. Kneale also disliked the conventional form of television drama (the single play), preferring instead the serial form, in which 'it is possible to tackle a fairly complex idea in detail, using a full range of characters. It gives you time to shape a whole background.'[12]

While popular discourse around *Quatermass* has generally attributed creative agency to Kneale as the writer, Kneale himself was always quick to acknowledge the influence of producer Rudolph Cartier.[13] Cartier was an Austrian who had worked at Germany's famous UFA studio in the late 1920s and early 1930s alongside writers such as Emeric Pressburger and Billy Wilder. He came to Britain as an exile in 1936, worked in the British feature film industry after the Second World War and then joined the BBC in 1950. Cartier, described in an obituary as 'one of the fathers of modern television drama', was an innovator in the use of film inserts to develop story lines rather than just to provide links between live sequences.[14] Cartier and Kneale first worked together on an adaptation of a German anti-war novel, *Arrow to the Heart*, in 1952. It soon became clear that they shared similar views about television drama and were keen to extend the boundaries of the medium. Cartier claims to have told Michael Barry that 'the BBC needed new scripts, a new approach, a whole new spirit, rather than endlessly televising classics like Dickens or familiar London stage plays'.[15] His outlook chimed with that of Kneale, who, when he was commissioned to write the first *Quatermass* script, 'saw it as an opportunity to do something different – an adventure yarn, something that wasn't people talking in drawing rooms'.[16]

There are differing accounts of the origin of *Quatermass*.[17] Cartier later claimed that Kneale 'had all three stories in his mind from the start. We decided to do *Experiment* first because we thought it would give us less trouble with exteriors and things like that.'[18] This is flatly contradicted by Kneale himself, who has always claimed that the first serial came about as an ad hoc response when 'one day in 1953 the BBC suddenly discovered that they had a gap in the schedule, a slot for a serial, and nothing remotely planned'.[19] *The Quatermass Experiment* was written for the Saturday evening serial slot that had previously included adaptations of detective stories and thrillers such as Sir Arthur Conan Doyle's *Sherlock Holmes* and John Buchan's *The Three Hostages* – both of which had been adapted by film critic C.A. Lejeune – as well as original stories for television such as Francis Durbridge's *The Broken Horseshoe*. *Quatermass* can be seen, therefore, within a tradition of other critically lowbrow popular genres serialised for television. Kneale recalled that 'I churned it out fairly fast; in fact, I was still writing it while it was being transmitted. There were six episodes and I was still working on the last one when the second one went out.'[20]

It is evident that *The Quatermass Experiment* was intended from the start as a serious attempt at science fiction. Cartier, in a letter to the Air Ministry requesting technical assistance, described the basic idea of the serial thus:

> I am preparing a 'Science-Fiction' Serial, which will be in six episodes between 18th July to 22nd August. The background of it is in London and it deals with the activities of a fictional establishment called 'The British Experimental Rocket Group', which attempts the first journey into space. I am most anxious to lift this production above the level of strip-cartoons and magazine thrillers, and we have secured technical datae [*sic*] and scientific support from responsible quarters.[21]

The desire to provide a plausible scientific basis for the serial, especially in its depiction of rocketry, links *The Quatermass Experiment* to early 1950s' sf films such as *Destination Moon* (dir. Irving Pichel, 1950, based on Robert Heinlein's *Rocketship Galileo*, 1947) and *Rocketship X-M* (dir.

Kurt Neumann, 1950), which focused on the technology of space flight and, in the former case at least, had a reasonably plausible scenario (the first manned flight to the moon). It may have been these films that Cartier had in mind when he instructed his actors 'not to give away any details of the serial to the Press as we are in strong competition with films in science fiction of this kind'.[22]

The Quatermass Experiment was nothing if not ambitious, especially given the nature of the technical facilities that were available at the time. It was broadcast from the BBC's television studio at Alexandra Palace using what Kneale claimed 'were literally the oldest operational cameras in the world, with fixed lenses and "watch-the-birdie" view-finders, tracking on bicycle wheels'.[23] The entire serial was allocated a budget of £3,500, of which over half went on artists' payments, with £570 spent on sets and £380 on film inserts (exterior shots and special effects shots that were incorporated into the live broadcast by telecine). In order to put this in context, a Sunday night play with a Thursday repeat, running for 90 minutes, typically cost between £2,000 and £3,000.[24] The special effects were accomplished with what can best be described as Heath Robinson ingenuity.[25]

The Quatermass Experiment has been described as 'the first television drama that genuinely gripped the entire nation'.[26] While this is something of an exaggeration – in 1953 approximately only one household in seven had a television set – there is nevertheless ample evidence to indicate that the serial made a considerable and lasting impact on those who saw it. The BBC's Audience Research Department, which conducted qualitative research into the viewing preferences of a cross section of the public, found that *Quatermass* had met with a higher than average 'reaction index' from viewers and concluded that most viewers 'considered it a most unusual, exciting and ingenious serial'. There was some disappointment with the last episode, largely because there was a technical fault during the climax which led to a break in transmission. A minority of viewers disliked the serial, stating that it was either 'too fantastic' or 'too horrific', while some condemned as 'tasteless' the setting of the climax in Westminster Abbey. Overall, however, reaction to the serial was highly positive.[27] There is, further, much anecdotal evidence to support the popularity of the serial: 'Will friends and acquaintances please note that I refuse to answer telephone calls during future instalments of this serial?',

C.A. Lejeune noted in her *Observer* column after watching the first episode.[28] And, significantly, there was immediate interest from the film industry. On 24 August, two days after the last episode of the serial was broadcast, the BBC's assistant head of copyright reported that 'I have had a letter from Hammer Film Productions Ltd. saying that they would be interested in the purchase of film rights in "The Quatermass Experiment".'[29] Hammer had a relationship of sorts with the BBC, having already produced film versions of the radio serials *Dick Barton – Special Agent* and *The Adventures of PC49*, but *Quatermass* would be the first British television serial adapted for the big screen.[30]

It is important to place the popular reception of *The Quatermass Experiment* in context. The intrinsic interest of the serial itself notwithstanding, its timing was exceptionally fortunate. *Quatermass* belongs to the historical moment when television was on the cusp of becoming a genuine mass medium alongside radio and cinema. The first half of the 1950s was the most rapid period of enlargement for both the potential and the actual television audience in Britain. When the television service resumed after the war in June 1946 it was available to about 15,000 homes, mostly in the Greater London area, but the building of new high-power transmitters – at Sutton Coldfield in the West Midlands in 1949, Holme Moss in Yorkshire in 1951, and Wenvoe in South Wales and Kirk o'Shotts in Central Scotland in 1952 – brought a potential 28 million viewers within its orbit. The BBC estimated that by 1953 the television service was available to over 80 per cent of the population. At the same time the size of the actual audience was expanding rapidly, as evidenced by the number of combined 'sound and vision' licences (costing £2): 343,882 in 1950; 763,941 in 1951; 1,449,260 in 1952; 2,142,452 in 1953; 3,248,852 in 1954; and 4,503,766 in 1955.[31] In three years, between 1950 and 1953, therefore, the size of the television audience had increased over sixfold, and it doubled again over the next two years between 1953 and 1955. It is extremely unlikely that *Quatermass* would have made the impact it did if it had been made before 1953. Moreover, it followed a mere two months after the event that, in the words of one commentator, 'symbolizes the point when television surpassed radio as the major mass medium'.[32] On 2 June 1953 over 20 million people had watched the live television coverage of the coronation of Queen Elizabeth II from Westminster Abbey (the majority of them watching in the homes of other people). The coronation would still have been a recent memory for viewers when the last episode of *Quatermass* was broadcast. Peter Hutchings has suggested that some of the impact of *Quatermass* can be attributed to 'a kind of iconoclasm ... a furtive pleasure in seeing the Queen supplanted by a deadly alien monster about to reproduce'.[33] Against this, however, must be set the fact that some viewers were put off by the 'tasteless' climax and that the last episode had the lowest reaction index of the whole serial.

Yet the success of *The Quatermass Experiment* was due to more than an accident of timing, however propitious. The serial tapped into other concerns that were current in 1953. Kneale averred that 'I don't like the term "science fiction", but if we're going to bandy it about, it could be applied just as well to the world we live in ... I try to give those stories some relevance to what is round about us today.'[34] Most obviously, the serial can be seen in relation to the discourse of scientific and technological advancement that was a major theme of post-war sf. The war and post-war years saw a number of highly significant developments in the fields of physics, chemistry and medicine in which British scientists (popularly known as 'boffins') made important contributions. The British engineer Frank Whittle had developed a working jet engine in 1941; Sir John Cockcroft and Ernest Walton won the Nobel Prize for Physics in 1951 for their pioneering research in nuclear disintegration (popularly known as 'splitting the atom'); Cambridge bacteriologists Ernst Chain and Howard Florey, along with Sir Alexander Fleming, were awarded the Nobel Prize for Medicine in 1945 for their work in developing penicillin; and in 1953 the British biophysicist Francis Crick and the American James Watson discovered the 'double helix' structure that is the basis of DNA.

Kneale is supposed to have taken the first name of his fictional Professor Bernard Quatermass from the British radio astronomer Bernard Lovell, who designed the pioneering radio telescope and observatory at Jodrell Bank. Quatermass is the archetypal 'boffin'.[35] He conforms to the popular image of the boffin that historian Kenneth O. Morgan describes as 'the typically British combination of intellectual rigour and romantic amateurism that characterized much of British science in the post-war period'.[36] Quatermass, played in the first serial by Reginald Tate, is head of the British Experimental Rocket Group and has designed a manned space rocket which, as the first episode begins, is returning from its first flight. The fictional device of Britain having its own space programme – also a feature of contemporaneous films such as *Spaceways* (dir. Terence Fisher, 1952) and *The Net* (dir. Anthony Asquith, 1953) – can be interpreted as an assertion of Britain's world status. Hence the excited radio reporter in the second episode of *Quatermass* who proudly announces that 'three valiant Britons' have made the first expedition into space – correcting himself with the qualification 'or British subjects' when he remembers that one of the trio is a German scientist. *Quatermass*, in this context, belongs to a narrative of national achievement and progress that it shares with films like *The Sound Barrier* (dir. David Lean, 1952) in which it is a British test pilot who first flies at the speed of sound in a British-designed jet plane (when in reality the sound barrier had already been broken by American pilot Chuck Yeager in 1947).[37]

The fact of Britain's decline as a world power, strikingly obvious in hindsight, was less apparent to contemporaries. The early 1950s was a period of considerable optimism for the future. Britain had survived the war with her overseas empire substantially intact (it is too often forgotten that the granting of independence to India in 1947 and Palestine in 1948 were the last major acts of decolonisation for a decade). The Festival of Britain in 1951 'made a spectacular showpiece for the inventiveness and genius of British scientists and technologists'.[38] Incidents such as the escape of the frigate HMS *Amethyst* from the Yangtze river in China (July 1949) and the valiant defence of the 'Glorious Gloucesters' at the Battle of the Imjin River in Korea (April 1951) drew favourable comparison with heroic feats during the Second World War. The year of *The Quatermass Experiment* witnessed the successful ascent of Mount Everest by a British-led expedition and the coronation of a young queen that contemporaries were quick to herald as the advent of a new 'Elizabethan' age. Even more symbolically, perhaps, the wartime leader, Sir Winston Churchill, was back in Downing Street. There seemed good reason for believing that Britain was still the great power she had been before the Second World War.

'I'VE ALWAYS BEEN WORRIED THERE MIGHT BE SOMETHING WE COULDN'T COPE WITH' Professor Bernard Quatermass (Reginald Tate) and team prepare to confront a nightmare from space in *The Quatermass Experiment* (1953)

Much of the impact of *The Quatermass Experiment* arises from its rupturing of this mood of post-war complacency. As Quatermass himself remarks: 'I've always been worried there might be something we couldn't cope with.' The Quatermass rocket may symbolise British technological prowess, but the experiment goes horribly wrong as the returning rocket goes off course and crashes on Wimbledon Common. (Ironically, the exterior of the rocket is represented by film stock shots of a German V2 rocket, which in 1944 had brought its own form of destruction to London.) It transpires that the rocket has come into contact with an alien organism that has killed two of the astronauts and has infected the third, Victor Carroon, who begins to turn into a plant-like life form which threatens to wipe out the human race by spreading its deadly spores. The orthodox interpretation of 1950s' sf and horror is to interpret the 'monster' as a metaphor for the 'beast' unleashed by the atomic bomb, against which there was no conventional defence. In this respect *Quatermass* can be linked to films such as *The Beast from 20,000 Fathoms* (dir. Eugene Lurie, 1953) and *Godzilla* (dir. Inoshiro Honda, 1955) – in which prehistoric monsters woken from hibernation by atomic tests lay waste to New York and Tokyo, respectively – as well as anticipating British 'creature features' such as *Behemoth the Sea Monster* (dir. Eugene Lurie, 1959) and *Gorgo* (dir. Eugene Lurie, 1961). *Quatermass* posits a more imaginative means of destroying the monster than the military or scientific solutions provided by most creature features (*Gorgo* excepted): Quatermass uses a tape recording of the other astronauts, whose knowledge and memories Carroon has absorbed, to awaken the monster's last vestige of human feeling and thus cause it to destroy itself.

At the same time, however, *The Quatermass Experiment* was different from filmic sf, if only because technological determinants required its makers to focus on characterisation and ideas rather than visual spectacle. This was a matter of necessity, as Kneale recognised, 'because there was no other choice, you simply couldn't launch into a load of special effects, because there weren't any'.[39] A key scene in the fourth episode (as described in the script) makes an ironic comparison between film and television sf. Carroon, on the run from the authorities, hides in a cinema which is screening an sf film called *Planet of the Dragons*. The 'film within a film' – referred to in internal production documentation as 'the "Hollywood" picture' [40] – involves a space lieutenant and a space girl who find true love whilst battling against (unseen) monsters on a distant planet and seems deliberately parodic of the juvenile style of sf from which *Quatermass* sought to differentiate itself. Moreover, the film is being shown in 3-D – the year 1953 marked the height of Hollywood's short-lived flirtation with 3-D film-making in an attempt to lure back declining audiences – which requires cinemagoers to wear special spectacles. The experience is uncomfortable for one member of the audience ('I dunno which is worse – with them on or with them off. Get an 'eadache or be driven loopy tryin' to watch it.') and the scene thus suggests that the experience of cinema spectatorship is inferior to watching in the comfort of one's own home.[41] Cartier felt that television was a more effective medium for this sort of story on the grounds that special effects looked less risible on the small screen:

When the viewer was watching these 'horrific' TV productions of mine, he was – I like to think – completely in my power, and accepted the somewhat far-fetched implications of the plot (such as the man who turned into a vegetable) without a murmur, while in the cinema, there was usually a titter of false laughter whenever one of these scenes came up.[42]

Given the popular success of *The Quatermass Experiment*, it was inevitable that a sequel would follow. *Quatermass II*, broadcast in the autumn of 1955, was part of the BBC's response to the arrival of Independent Television – a strategy which had also, notoriously, involved killing off Grace Archer, a leading character of the popular radio serial, on 22 September, the day ITV began broadcasting. Unlike the first serial, *Quatermass II* was given a regular time slot (8 p.m.) and all episodes were telerecorded to enable a repeat screening. The budget for the whole serial was £7,500, over twice that of the first *Quatermass*. It was broadcast from the BBC's Lime Grove studios, technically better equipped than Alexandra Palace, and made more extensive use of film inserts than its predecessor, particularly involving location work at the Shell Haven oil refinery on the Thames estuary. Quatermass was played this time by John Robinson, a late replacement for Reginald Tate, who had died shortly before the serial was due to be broadcast.

Quatermass II aroused as much public interest as its predecessor.[43] Its first episode, watched by an estimated 58 per cent of the adult television audience – though with the caveat that in the autumn of 1955 only 188,000 households were able to receive ITV – had a higher reaction index than the first episode of *The Quatermass Experiment*, and 77 per cent of the sample said they intended to watch the rest of the serial. The majority of viewers found it 'intensely thrilling and most exciting', though again there were some 'who objected strongly to this serial on the grounds that it was too horrific, especially for Saturday night viewing when children would probably be watching. In addition a small number dismissed it as quite absurd and altogether too stupidly far-fetched.'[44] Even with competition from ITV, however, the audience for *Quatermass II* was larger than it had been for *Experiment*, if only because the number of homes with television sets had doubled in the last two years. Despite its popular success, however, there is evidence that *Quatermass II* was less well regarded within the BBC itself. Cecil McGivern, the controller of television, put on record his view that it 'is not nearly as good as the first "Quatermass" serial' and that the first episode 'had a lot of far too complicated dialogue, incidents which were improbable even with reference to a serial which is based on improbability … and *far* too little action'. 'The programmes are being "shot" with considerable skill by Rudolph Cartier,' McGivern added, 'but what he is shooting is just not good enough.'[45] Michael Barry replied: 'I have been pleased with the present serial which, in my opinion, is developing more smoothly and with more maturity than the first "Quatermass", which seemed to me very rough.'[46]

Kneale, who evidently was shown the controller's memorandum by Barry, responded by citing favourable press reviews of the serial, noting the reaction from the film industry ('A firm bid for the script of the new serial was made as soon as it was read, a week *before* production commenced – by the same company who made the recent Quatermass film') and rebutting the criticism of the dialogue with the claim that fans of the serial 'ranged from the Oliviers to children and persons of imperfect English'. His reply to McGivern also explained the rationale of *Quatermass II*:

> I have tried to make this serial as effective as its predecessor, but in quite a different way: a logical extension. Given the publicly-expected components of the dogged professor, rocketry and Things from space, in terms of (substantially) live television, the possibilities are not infinite; but I eventually worked out a story that seemed more than mere repetition. The 'gimmick' this time, of course, is that an invasion of the earth by Things is one year under way by the time the story begins. Instead of a normal world with one sinister element moving in it, as before, we have one normal protagonist (Quatermass) moving in an increasingly abnormal world.[47]

While Kneale seems to have felt constrained both by the technical limitations of television and by the conventions of the genre – the success of *The Quatermass Experiment* inevitably meant that viewers would carry certain expectations of the sequel – it is clear that he was concerned to vary the formula as much as those constraints allowed.

Quatermass II – Kneale disliked the numeral but admitted 'I couldn't think of a better title'[48] – explores different sf themes and tropes from the first serial. *Experiment* had been an example of the alien invasion narrative in which a 'thing' from space threatens the world with destruction but is itself destroyed through either the ingenuity and resourcefulness of humans (represented by the boffin Quatermass) or, as in the case of H.G. Wells's *The War of the Worlds* – published in 1898 and filmed by George Pal in 1953 – by fortunate accident. It is a trope that still persists in recent examples of both filmic and television sf such as the movie blockbuster *Independence Day* (dir. Roland Emmerich, 1996) and BBC Scotland's *Invasion: Earth* (1998). *Quatermass II*, however, is more readily located within a generic lineage that emerged only in the 1950s: the paranoid sf thriller. Its most obvious generic reference point is *Invasion of the Body Snatchers* (dir. Don Siegel, 1956) – which it predated by a year – in so far as it concerns the attempted colonisation of Earth by aliens who are able to take over the minds and bodies of human beings. It also anticipates the Quinn Martin television series *The Invaders* (1967–68), which was based on the similar premise of an alien invasion by stealth. Quatermass stumbles upon the plot by accident when he is called in by Captain Dillon, head of an army radar tracking station, to investigate a shower of meteorites that have against all probability landed in close formation. A reconstruction from remaining fragments reveals the meteorites to be hollow, from which Quatermass surmises that they are in fact capsules containing alien creatures which breathe ammonia (those who come into contact with the capsules are affected by ammonia gas and subsequently are 'taken over') and which, it transpires, are building colonies on Earth.

Invasion of the Body Snatchers – in which the aliens arrive in mysterious 'pods' – has typically been interpreted as an allegory of American Cold War paranoia and the McCarthyite 'witch-hunts' of the early 1950s. *Quatermass II* obviously cannot be read in quite the same way – there was, after all, nothing really comparable to McCarthyism in Britain – though it does share similar themes, of secrecy, phobia, mistrust of outsiders and the sense that nothing is quite what it seems. While tracking the meteorites, Quatermass comes across a top-secret government installation in a security area patrolled by sinister armed guards, who seize the meteorite fragments. Quatermass is puzzled because the installation seems to have been modelled on his own design for a moon colony. His efforts to investigate are thwarted when the committee responsible turns out to have been taken over by the aliens (they bear a telltale mark on their skin), and so Quatermass has to infiltrate the plant himself. There is a sense in which Quatermass himself is more of an outsider than he had been in the first serial. Whereas in *Experiment* Quatermass had the assistance of Scotland Yard (albeit that his relationship with Inspector Lomax was somewhat uneasy to begin with), in *Quatermass II* the various people who help him – Captain Dillon, a senior civil servant, an MP, a public relations man and a journalist – meet sticky ends (all except Dillon, who has to survive as he is the fiancé of Quatermass's daughter Paula). Quatermass learns that far from being a food processing plant, as everyone supposes, the installation is in fact a colony housing a large amoeboid creature which is growing in size by conjoining with the creatures in the meteorite capsules. He has to win the trust of the initially suspicious construction workers who, when they learn the truth, storm the plant. Kneale said that 'the idea was contemporary to the fifties. During that time Government bodies were building early warning radar bases, germ warfare factories, mysterious isolated laboratories, all of which were hidden from the public in inaccessible places.'[49] Kneale probably had in mind such installations as the Atomic Weapons Research Establishment at Aldermaston, Berkshire, which later became a focus of the anti-nuclear movement. *Quatermass II* expresses anxieties about the growth of a secret state – 'This is a free country in time of peace', Quatermass protests as he is escorted off-site by armed guards – and, with its narrative of cover-ups and quasi-military installations, anticipates Chris Carter's highly successful *The X-Files* (Fox Television, 1993–2002) by some four decades.

The underlying paranoia that characterises *Quatermass II* suggests a society less at ease with itself than in *Experiment*. This is apparent from the beginning when the failure of the 'Quatermass II' nuclear-powered rocket signals an end to the British attempt to conquer space. Quatermass recognises the blow to national self-confidence this represents: 'It won't be easy to accept we're no longer part of the race.' [50] *Quatermass II* pre-dated the Suez Crisis by a year, but all the same may be seen as an early example of the narrative of national impotence (Quatermass, metaphorically, fails to get his rocket 'up') that some commentators have detected in British sf from the mid-1950s.[51] Quatermass's confidence is so shattered that he begins to question his own sanity: upon seeing the installation which so clearly resembles his own plan for a moon colony, he says to himself, 'I think I'm going mad.' There is also a suggestion of social unrest – a theme that would become ever more prominent in the later *Quatermass* serials. The notion of Britain as a consensual society is shattered by the climax of the fifth episode, where an uprising of workers – a politically highly charged theme if ever there was one at the height of the Cold War – leads to a pitched battle for control of the plant. The workers have been shaken from their cosy complacency by Quatermass, who is forced to align himself with a marginalised group in order to save the day.

Quatermass and the Pit, which duly followed three years later, is generally regarded as the best of the *Quatermass* serials.[52] It was allocated a significantly larger budget – £2,560 per episode – and was a more polished production than the previous two. It was broadcast live from the BBC's Riverside Studios and introduced yet another new Quatermass in the person of André Morell.[53] The third *Quatermass* serial made even more extensive use of film – some 45 minutes in total – and succeeded in integrating them into the broadcast to the extent that Kneale claimed 'a surprisingly satisfactory number of expert colleagues failed to spot exactly *which* 45 minutes'.[54] This can probably be explained by the fact that most of the film inserts are not exteriors as in *Quatermass II* (except for the opening of the first episode) but are either special-effects shots or crowd scenes filmed indoors at Ealing Studios (recently acquired by the BBC). 'On the technical side,' Kneale averred, 'it went about as far as possible towards exploding the "intimacy" fallacy. Huge sets, long shots, crowd scenes were the order of the day.'[55] That said, however, much of the power of *Quatermass and the Pit* derives from its highly atmospheric use of a handful of claustrophobic sets.

Quatermass and the Pit achieved the highest audience of any of the serials – reflecting again the increase in the television audience in Britain throughout the 1950s – with the BBC estimating some 11 million viewers for the last episode on 26 January 1959. But, according to the London office of the US-based Nielsen Ripley organisation, which monitored viewing habits for the commercial networks, in those areas which received both BBC and ITV more households were tuned in to *Keep It in the Family* on ITV.[56] So far as qualitative evidence of reception is concerned, the BBC's Audience Research Department found that *Quatermass and the Pit* had a similar reaction index to *Experiment* but was down slightly on *Quatermass II*. There were some complaints that 'the story had got off to a disappointingly slow start', though even so viewers tended to remain with the serial. Interestingly, given that the first two serials had been criticised by some for their horrific and frightening content, the first episode of *Quatermass and the Pit* disappointed some viewers on the grounds 'that the bloodcurdling events foreshadowed in the trailer had not, alas, come to pass'. Many viewers watched the serial largely because they had seen the others, 'which were remembered with pleasure'.[57]

Kneale described *Quatermass and the Pit* as 'a race-hatred fable'.[58] There is a greater sense of topicality than in the previous serials in so far as *Quatermass and the Pit* was written shortly after the race riots that occurred in Notting Hill, London, in the summer of 1958, and the story takes place against a background of social unrest including, as a radio news bulletin announces, 'a week of racial disturbances' in Birmingham. This was a time of increasing immigration to Britain from the Commonwealth, especially from the West Indies. In June 1958 it was estimated that the black population of Britain numbered 180,000, and, while the situation in Britain can never be compared to the institutionalised racism of the apartheid regime in South Africa, there was nevertheless an informal segregation, with the majority of black immigrants settling in particular areas such as Brixton in London and the St Paul's area of Bristol.[59] The inclusion of a black workman in the group of construction workers who feature at the beginning of the first episode is indicative of the sort of manual job that most black immigrants were obliged to take. The scenes of violent public disorder and mass hysteria at the end of the serial, as people affected by irrational forces turn on anyone whom they perceive as different, can readily be interpreted as an allegory of the race riots of 1958.

Yet the race-hatred parable of *Quatermass and the Pit* is far more subtle and complex than such a straightforwardly reductionist reading of the narrative as allegory would allow. The story involves the discovery during excavation work in London of a mysterious capsule, which the army assume to be an unknown German secret weapon from the Second World War but which Quatermass suspects is an alien spacecraft that crashed on Earth millions of years ago. The capsule contains two kinds of skeletal remains: ape-like creatures with unusually large cranial cavities, and large insect-like creatures that putrefy when the capsule is opened and they come into contact with the atmosphere. Quatermass and palaeontologist Dr Matthew Roney deduce from the evidence that the insect skeletons are the remains of Martians who evacuated their own planet when it became uninhabitable and who attempted to preserve their own species by tampering with the physiology of the creatures they found on Earth. Quatermass uses a 'spectral oscillator' invented by Dr Roney to record images from the past and is presented with a harrowing picture of what happened to the Martians. It is surely not too fanciful to speculate that Quatermass's description of 'a race purge … a cleansing of the hives … a ritual slaughter to preserve a fixed society' would in 1958 have been understood by many as a reference to the Holocaust.

There is certainly no ambiguity about the conclusion of the serial. At the end of the final episode, following the outbreak of irrational violence that has almost destroyed London – and to which he himself nearly succumbs – Quatermass makes an impassioned television broadcast that is delivered directly to camera:

> If another of these things should ever be found, we are armed with knowledge, but we also have knowledge of ourselves and of the ancient, destructive urges in us that grow more deadly as our populations increase and approach in size and complexity those of ancient Mars. Every war crisis, witch-hunt, race riot, purge, is a reminder and a warning. We *are* the Martians. If we cannot control the inheritance within us, this will be their second dead planet.

The most didactic scene in any of the Quatermass serials, this conclusion was not to the liking of Michael Barry, who complained that it was 'an extremely pompous & in some ways inconclusive end'.[60] While it does not, admittedly, provide a clear resolution to the narrative, the scene as filmed does make for a very powerful and provocative ending to the serial.

Quatermass and the Pit is unusual for sf in that it looks to the past rather than to the future and suggests that an alien invasion has taken place some 5 million years ago. It also bridges the traditional divide between sf (concerned with the scientific and the rational) and horror (delving into the supernatural and the irrational). It posits an intriguing, if disturbing, answer to the evolutionary question of the 'missing link' between apes and men. As a deeply sceptical government official puts it: 'You realise what you're implying – that we owe our human condition to the intervention of insects.' It is little wonder, faced with this hypothesis, that the government prefers to believe the army's explanation of a German secret weapon. At the same time, however, *Quatermass and the Pit* also draws upon occult imagery and motifs that defy scientific rationalism. Quatermass and Roney find the sign of the pentacle on the Martian spacecraft and deduce that it is the inherited 'race memory' of the Martians that explains why so many different human societies throughout the ages have visualised the demonic in the same way as a horned beast. The Martians had a form of telekinetic power that explains phenomena such as ghosts and second sight. In its linking of science and the supernatural, *Quatermass and the Pit* anticipates Kneale's *The Stone Tape*, which supposes that ghosts are the result of psychic residue and can be exorcised through a process analogous to wiping a tape. It is a combination of scientific and occult knowledge that finally saves the day. With a fiery apparition of a horned beast appearing over London (not seen but described by an airline pilot), Roney remembers that iron and water are the devil's traditional enemies and destroys it by throwing a wet steel cable into the inferno, killing himself in the process.

It is clear from the topical references throughout, and the closing speech in particular, that *Quatermass and the Pit* is set against an even more insecure world than *Quatermass II*. The Cold War looms more prominently than in the previous serials: an early reference to deadlock in nuclear disarmament talks in Geneva provides the background to a subplot that involves placing nuclear missiles on the moon. 'The present state of world politics leaves no doubt about that – whoever plants those missiles can police the Earth', declares the pompous Colonel Breen. Quatermass, however, resists the appropriation of his research for militaristic purposes: 'We are on the verge of a new dimension of discovery. It's the great chance, leave our vices behind us, war first of all. Not to go out there dragging our hatreds and our frontiers with us.' To this extent *Quatermass and the Pit* needs to be seen in the context of mounting public concern over nuclear proliferation in the late 1950s, which culminated in the founding of the Campaign for Nuclear Disarmament (CND) in February 1958 by Bertrand Russell and Canon L. John Collins. Quatermass is dismissive of what he calls 'the dead man's deterrent' – the idea that pre-programmed missiles will destroy an aggressor even if Britain has already been annihilated – and there is no doubting that the serial, if not directly advocating disarmament, is sceptical of the notion of 'mutually assured destruction' (MAD) that underscored nuclear strategy during the Cold War.

At one point in *Quatermass and the Pit*, Colonel Breen tells the professor: 'You're a tired old man and you need a long rest – that's not just my view, either.' It is tempting to see this as Kneale's comment on the future of Quatermass at a time when Kneale was about to seek new challenges in the film industry. Quatermass was indeed to have the long rest prescribed for him, for it would be a full twenty-one years before a new *Quatermass* serial was aired (a belated film version of *Quatermass and the Pit* had followed some nine years after the television original). Kneale worked on the script of *Quatermass IV* in the late 1960s, and in 1973 it was announced that it was to be made by the BBC.[61] In the event, however, the BBC decided against it, reportedly on the grounds that the estimated cost of £200,000 was deemed too expensive, and the serial was shelved. It was picked up in the late 1970s by Euston Films, a subsidiary of Thames Television, which announced that it would produce a four-part serial, now simply entitled *Quatermass*, at a cost of £1.2 million.[62] Euston was responsible for some of the most successful ITV series of the 1970s and early 1980s, including *Special Branch*, *The Sweeney*, *Van der Valk*, *Danger UXB*, *Minder* and *Reilly – Ace of Spies*, and had also dabbled in feature film production in the form of the two *Sweeney* spin-offs. According to Verity Lambert, who became chief executive of Euston Films in 1979:

> *Quatermass* came to us in the shape of four scripts which had been commissioned by the BBC and which had been turned down by

them as being too expensive for them to make. It was very expensive – I think it was the most expensive thing we had attempted at Euston Films at that point. And we felt that the only way we could justify the expense was to make sure that we could re-edit it into a film which could possibly have theatrical release as well as have a four-parter.[63]

Quatermass was produced by Ted Childs (producer of both *Sweeney* films) and directed by Piers Haggard (whose previous credits included the occult 1970 horror film *Blood on Satan's Claw* and the BBC's Dennis Potter serial *Pennies from Heaven* in 1978). It starred Sir John Mills as Quatermass and the cast included Simon MacCorkindale and Barbara Kellerman, both of whom had film careers, suggesting that Euston had international sales in mind. As Lambert indicated, a 102-minute feature film version was prepared at the same time, though in the event the planned theatrical release never materialised.[64]

Quatermass was broadcast on the ITV network in the autumn of 1979 but failed to achieve anything like the impact of the 1950s' serials. The largest audience was for the first episode (12.4 million) but even so it failed to register in the weekly top twenty.[65] The critical reception was lukewarm at best.[66] There are a number of possible explanations for its relative failure. Its scheduled broadcast was delayed by a technicians' strike that took ITV off the air for several weeks in the autumn of 1979 and meant that the serial went out at short notice and with inadequate publicity when the service resumed on 24 October. Although it was a far more polished production than its predecessors, due to being made entirely on film and with a substantially larger budget, *Quatermass* rather lacks the immediacy of its predecessors. Ted Childs felt that it 'was perhaps too downbeat a story for a popular audience' and that 'the punters were used to a fairly high standard of technical representation from American television – you know you had had *Star Trek* and then there had been movies like *Star Wars* and *Close Encounters of the Third Kind*. And we just couldn't afford that.'[67] *Quatermass*, which like the previous serials was made for adult audiences (it was broadcast at 9.10 p. m. on Wednesday evenings), was outside the mainstream of television sf as represented by the BBC's long-running *Doctor Who* (which reached the peak of its popularity in the late 1970s) and by American imports such as *Battlestar Galactica* (1978–80) and *Buck*

Rogers in the 25th Century (1979–81). All those series, significantly, were shown on Saturday evenings around teatime, suggesting that sf was considered essentially a children's genre within the television industry. Kneale, for his part, simply felt that the themes of the serial had dated in the decade since he wrote it and that 'Quatermass had had his day'.[68]

That said, however, *Quatermass* is not without its points of interest and has, arguably, been unfairly maligned in comparison to the earlier serials. Far from being a poor relation to its predecessors, *Quatermass* is a worthy successor that can be seen as a compendium of their various themes. It returns to the idea of space exploration (*Experiment*), again posits an invasion by stealth (*Quatermass II*) and again makes use of both scientific and occult motifs (*Quatermass and the Pit*). In particular its narrative of social disintegration – a characteristic of 1970s' futuristic cinema such as *A Clockwork Orange* (dir. Stanley Kubrick, 1971), *Soylent Green* (dir. Richard Fleischer, 1973), *Sleeping Dogs* (dir. Roger Donaldson, 1977) and *Mad Max* (dir. George Miller, 1979) – suggests that Quatermass's prophetic warning at the end of *Quatermass and the Pit* has come true. The tone is set by an anonymous voice-over narration at the start of the first episode: 'In that last quarter of the twentieth century, the whole world seemed to sicken. Civilised institutions, whether old or new, fell as if some primal disorder was reasserting itself. And men asked themselves: why should this be?' *Quatermass* pictures a Britain of the future (it is set approximately in the year 2000) in which order has collapsed: cities are urban wastelands with barricades and violent street gangs, while Wembley Stadium has been turned into a gladiatorial arena where gangs converge to fight each other. The two principal gangs are known as the 'Blue Brigade' and the 'Badders' – an obvious reference to violent anarchist groups of the early 1970s such as the Red Brigades and the Baader–Meinhof Group – and the privatised police force (referred to as 'Pay Cops') is shown to be both brutal and corrupt. The government is represented as ineffectual and indifferent: 'They call it urban collapse – then it's nobody's fault', remarks Dr Kapp (MacCorkindale), an idealistic scientist who represents a younger version of the now elderly Quatermass. In its scenes of urban violence and gang warfare, *Quatermass* is particularly reminiscent of *A Clockwork Orange*: it begins with the professor, on his way to a television studio, being mugged by a curiously well-spoken gang not unlike Alex and his 'Droogs' in Kubrick's film. It also anticipates the apocalyptic thriller *Mad Max 2* (dir. George Miller, 1981) in linking social disintegration to a fuel shortage: there are references to Britain's North Sea oil supply (which came online in the 1970s) having dried up and petrol rationing has been introduced. Quatermass, now retired and living in Scotland, is shocked by what he sees in the city and is unable to comprehend the depths to which society has plunged. All he can say – repeatedly – is 'Why?'

The narrative of social disintegration is linked thematically to the narrative of national decline. No longer a frontrunner in the space race (as she had been in *Experiment*), Britain has to watch from the sidelines while the United States and the Soviet Union attempt the first link-up in space. Quatermass, now deeply jaundiced about the whole space project, describes this bitterly as 'a symbolic wedding between a corrupt democracy and a monstrous tyranny'. He recognises that Britain has lost her global role and blames this on the superpowers: 'Two superpowers full of diseases – political diseases, economic diseases, social diseases. And their infections are too strong for us, the small countries, for when we catch them we die.' An American commentator refers to 'that Third World you're so keen on joining'. In one scene – a visual reference to *Quatermass II* – Quatermass and Kapp drive through a derelict refinery and Quatermass muses that North Sea oil was 'going to put everything right', suggesting that the vision of national prosperity and energy self-sufficiency sold to the British public in the 1970s had not been realised.

While the theme of social decay is the most interesting aspect of the serial, the main storyline concerns Quatermass's search for his missing granddaughter, who has run away to join a mysterious sect known as the Planet People. These are young people who have 'dropped out' of society and who believe that they will find refuge on another planet through meditation and transference. The Planet People converge on ancient sites such as Ringstone Round (a stone circle rather like Stonehenge), where they are suddenly vaporised by an intense white light. Quatermass and Dr Kapp investigate, discovering that the appearance of the light coincides with an energy transmission from an unknown source that destroyed the US–Soviet space station. It transpires that the young people are in fact being 'harvested' by aliens – for what purpose it is never explained – who visited the Earth thousands of years ago and left subterranean beacons (ley lines) to direct them to particular locations. Here there is an obvious link to *Quatermass and the Pit* through the device of an alien threat from the past and the combination of the scientific and the supernatural. Quatermass is unable to convince the Planet People of the danger they are in – they distrust all 'science men' – and the authorities are equally sceptical. Quatermass is even more of an outsider than he had been in the previous stories: shunned by establishment and counterculture alike, his only allies are Kapp and a small group of scientists who represent rationality in an increasingly anarchistic world. Quatermass and Kapp set a trap for the aliens by creating the impression of a large gathering of young people but setting off an atomic bomb. The nuclear deterrent of which Quatermass had been so sceptical in *Quatermass and the Pit* is now literally a dead man's deterrent: Quatermass apparently suffers a heart attack and, in a gloomily annihilistic climax, dies along with Kapp and Hettie, his granddaughter. Kneale never reveals who or what the aliens are; his interest seems to have been more in exploring the conflict of age versus youth. He later made clear where his own sympathies were: 'I tried to have the older generation saving the young people, but I'm not sure if the young people were worth saving. They weren't that interesting, and they were a bit out of date: flower children instead of punks.'[69]

The relative disappointment of the final *Quatermass* suggests that Kneale was correct in believing that 'Quatermass had had his day'. Perhaps it was for this reason that he chose to kill off the professor at the end of the story.[70] It was largely a matter of changing historical context. Quatermass originated in the 1950s and the themes that inform the serials – the role of the scientist in society, the ideological background of the Cold War, the decline of British power – are rooted historically in that decade. Yet if the cultural relevance of Quatermass has passed, the historical significance of the original *Quatermass* serials is incontestable. For one thing, they exerted an enormous influence on the future trajectory of sf as a television genre. The thematic similarities to both *The Invaders* and *The X-Files* have already been noted; the influence of *Quatermass* can also be identified in the BBC's own *A for Andromeda* (BBC TV, 1961), *Doctor*

Who (BBC TV, 1963–89; 1996; 2005–), *Doomwatch* (BBC TV, 1970–72) and *Survivors* (BBC TV, 1975–77).[71] The real historical importance of *Quatermass*, however, is that the serials demonstrated the possibilities of sf written specifically for television that dealt with wider political, social, scientific and ethical issues. *Quatermass* was neither juvenile nor risible – dangers always inherent in the genre – and proved that sf, intelligently treated, could win both popular and critical acclaim. It is for this reason that *Quatermass* may rightly be said to represent the origins of sf as a significant British television genre.

NOTES

The research for this essay would not have been possible without the kind assistance of the staff of the BBC Written Archives Centre, Caversham Park, Reading. My thanks also to Alma Hales for facilitating the loan of tapes of *Quatermass II* from the BBC Film and Video Archive and to Dr Ian Hunter for providing a copy of *The Quatermass Conclusion*.

1. *The Quatermass Experiment* was broadcast in six episodes between 18 July and 22 August 1953, *Quatermass II* in six episodes between 22 October and 26 November 1955, and *Quatermass and the Pit* in six episodes between 22 December 1958 and 26 January 1959. The film adaptations by Hammer were *The Quatermass Experiment* (USA: *The Creeping Unknown*, dir. Val Guest, 1955), *Quatermass 2* (USA: *The Enemy from Space*, dir. Val Guest, 1957) and *Quatermass and the Pit* (USA: *Five Million Years to Earth*, dir. Roy Ward Baker, 1967). The fourth serial, called simply *Quatermass*, was broadcast in four episodes between 24 October and 14 November 1979. An edited feature-length version of the last serial was prepared for overseas theatrical distribution under the title *The Quatermass Conclusion*.

2. Catherine Johnson, 'Exploiting the Intimate Screen: *The Quatermass Experiment*, Fantasy and the Aesthetic Potential of Early Television Drama', in Janet Thumim (ed.), *Small Screens, Big Ideas: Television in the 1950s* (London: I.B. Tauris, 2002), p. 181; Charles Barr, 'Broadcasting and Cinema 2. Screens within Screens', in C. Barr (ed.), *All Our Yesterdays: 90 Years of British Cinema* (London: British Film Institute, 1986), p. 215.

3. Jason Jacobs, *The Intimate Screen: Early British Television Drama* (Oxford: Clarendon Press, 2000), p. 117.

4. An indication of the 'low' cultural status still attached to sf is that the serials are glossed over in the 'official' history of the BBC by Asa Briggs, whose only comment on the ground-breaking *Quatermass Experiment* is that it 'was the first of many ventures in serialized science

fiction'. Briggs also seems to confuse the story lines of the second and third serials, writing that 'in the third series [*sic*] the Professor, operating in a Ministry of Science that was dominated by "Zombies" (a key word of the period), discovered "new depth in himself".' See the fourth and fifth volumes of his *History of Broadcasting in the United Kingdom: Sound and Vision 1945–55* (Oxford: Oxford University Press, 1979), p. 640, and *Competition 1955–1974* (Oxford: Oxford University Press, 1995), pp. 423–4. Most critical discussion of *Quatermass* is to be found in cult television and sf magazines: Stephen R. Bissette, 'The Quatermass Conception: Nigel Kneale and the Birth of Television Terror', *Video Watchdog* 12 (July/August 1992), pp. 32–46; John Brosnan, 'Quatermass', *StarBurst* 15 (1979), pp. 5–8; Andrew Pixley, 'Grave Situation: Quatermass Enters', *TV Zone* 106 (September 1998), pp. 39–43; Andrew Pixley, 'The Martian Inheritance: We are the Martians', *TV Zone* 110 (January 1999), pp. 36–41; and Dave Rolinson and Nick Cooper, '"Bring Something Back": The Strange Career of Professor Bernard Quatermass', *Journal of Popular Film and Television*, 30/3 (Autumn 2002), pp. 158–65. See also Roger Fulton (ed.), *Encyclopedia of TV Science Fiction* (London: Boxtree, 2000), pp. 451–7.

5. BBC WAC T5/647/1: 'Science Fiction' by Alice Frick and Donald Bull, 17 April 1962.

6. See David Weinstein, 'Captain Video: Television's First Fantastic Voyage', *Journal of Popular Film and Television* 30/3 (Autumn 2002), pp. 148–57.

7. Following on from the success of *Captain Video*, ABC ran a TV series of *Buck Rogers* in 1950–51. Two different actors played Buck: Ken Dibbs and Robert Pastene. It was transmitted live and no surviving kinetoscope tele-recordings appear to exist. There was also an independently produced TV series of *Flash Gordon* shown on the Dumont TV network in the USA in 1954, with Steve Holland playing Flash Gordon. (These are not to be confused with the old 1930s' film serials, which were re-edited and shown as TV films on US TV in the 1950s.)

8. See Alastair Crompton, *The Man Who Drew Tomorrow* (Bournemouth: Who Dares Publishing, 1985). An Anglo-American animated series of *Dan Dare*, using state-of-the-art CGI effects, was produced by Foundation Imaging in 2001.

9. Quoted in Julian Petley, 'The Quatermass Conclusion', *Primetime* 9 (Winter 1984–85), p. 22.

10. Quoted in Johnson, 'Exploiting the Intimate Screen', p. 183.

11. On Kneale's career, see Richard Dalby, 'Nigel Kneale: Creator of "Quatermass"', *Book and Magazine Collector*, April 2002, pp. 26–35; Jonathan Jones, 'My God, It's Horrible', *Guardian* G2, 30 June 1999, pp. 12–13; and Julian Petley, 'The Manxman', *Monthly Film Bulletin* 662 (March 1989), pp. 90–93. On *The Year of the Sex Olympics*, see the review by John R. Cook, *Film International* 4 (2003), pp. 44–7, and his essay, 'The Age of Aquarius', in this volume.

12. Nigel Kneale, 'Not Quite So Intimate', *Sight and Sound* 28/2 (Spring 1959), pp. 86–8.

13. The term 'producer' in television at this time is more akin to that of the director in so far as it was the producer who supervised the production on the floor, chose camera angles, and so forth.

14. Laurence Staig, *Independent*, 14 June 1994, p. 14. See also obituaries in the *Guardian*, 11 June 1994, p. 32; *Daily Telegraph*, 9 June 1994, p. 19; and *The Times*, 10 June 1994. For an overview of Cartier's career, see Lynda Miller and Julian Petley, 'Rudolph Cartier', *Sight and Sound* 59/2 (Spring 1990), pp. 126–29.

15. Quoted in Miller and Petley, 'Rudolph Cartier', p. 126.

16. Quoted in Paul Wells, 'Apocalypse Then! The Ultimate Monstrosity and Strange Things on the Coast... An Interview with Nigel Kneale', in I.Q. Hunter (ed.), *British Science Fiction Cinema* (London: Routledge, 1999), p. 50.

17. It seems that the title *The Quatermass Experiment* was decided upon relatively late in the day. Internal production documentation in the BBC Written Archives (BBC WAC T5/418) indicates that the serial was variously known as *The Unbegotten* and *Bring Something Back* (referring to the send-off by one of the astronaut's wives).

18. Quoted in Miller and Petley, 'Rudolph Cartier', pp. 127–8.

19. Quoted in Wells, 'Apocalypse Then!', p. 50.

20. Ibid. It is evident from production documentation in the BBC Written Archives that the serial was made quickly. In one memo Cartier wrote: 'Owing to the time pressure which the production of the new Serial will involve, and as it is an unusual semi-scientific subject, it would be appreciated if rehearsals could be located centrally within easy reach of the British Museum Reading Room and University.' BBC WAC T5/418: Rudolph Cartier to Betty Bulling, 27 May 1953.

21. BBC WAC T5/418: Rudolph Cartier to C. Moodie (Air Ministry Information Division), 12 June 1953. Cartier's letter was a request for three high-altitude flying suits 'so that we can give our viewers authenticity for "space suits" as far as possible'.

22. BBC WAC T5/418: Memorandum by Mrs Nest Bradney (Publicity Officer), 17 June 1953.

23. Kneale, 'Not Quite So Intimate', p. 86.

24. Jacobs, *The Intimate Screen*, p. 112.

25. The titles were done by sprinkling 'dri-kold' powder onto a metal tray through a stencil which had the lettering cut out. The tray was then heated with a blowtorch so that the powder evaporated. When the film of this process was run backwards, it gave the impression of the titles emerging from a cloud of steam to become visible on a black background. (The titles were further enhanced by the use of 'Mars – Bringer of War', the first suite of *The Planets* by Gustav Holst, which adds a foreboding sense of doom to the opening of each episode. 'Mars' was retained for *Quatermass II*, though *Quatermass and the Pit* had

specially composed title music.) The monster in the last episode of *The Quatermass Experiment* was a glove puppet, worked by Kneale himself, shot against a photographic blow-up of the interior of Westminster Abbey.

26. Daniel O'Brien, *SF: UK – How British Science Fiction Changed the World* (London: Reynolds & Hearn, 2000), p. 60.

27. BBC WAC T5/418: Viewer Research Report VR/53/421, 2 September 1953.

28. *Observer*, 26 July 1953, p. 11.

29. BBC WAC T5/418: G.M. Turnell to Michael Barry, 24 August 1953.

30. For production histories of the Hammer adaptations, see Tom Johnson and Deborah Del Vecchio, *Hammer Films: An Exhaustive Filmography* (Jefferson NC: McFarland, 1996).

31. Briggs, *Sound and Vision 1945–1955*, p. 221.

32. Andrew Crisell, *An Introductory History of British Broadcasting* (London: Routledge, 1997), p. 75.

33. Peter Hutchings, '"We're the Martians Now": British sf Invasion Fantasies of the 1950s and 1960s', in I.Q. Hunter (ed.), *British Science Fiction Cinema* (London: Routledge, 1999), p. 38.

34. Kneale, 'Not Quite So Intimate', p. 88.

35. For a discussion of the characterisation of the scientist in the *Quatermass* serials, see Joy Leman, 'Wise Scientists and Female Androids: Class and Gender in Science Fiction', in John Corner (ed.), *Popular Television in Britain: Studies in Cultural History* (London: British Film Institute, 1991), pp. 108–24.

36. Kenneth O. Morgan, *The People's Peace: British History 1945–1990* (Oxford: Oxford University Press, 1992), p. 109.

37. On *The Sound Barrier* and *The Net* in the context of postwar techno-logical advancement, see Michael Parris, *From the Wright Brothers to Top Gun: Aviation, Nationalism and Popular Cinema* (Manchester: Manchester University Press, 1995), pp. 173–6.

38. Morgan, *The People's Peace*, p. 110.

39. Quoted in Petley, 'The Quatermass Conclusion', p. 23.

40. BBC WAC T5/418: Rudolph Cartier to Richard Greenough (designer), 5 June 1953.

41. It might be argued that both television and film versions of *The Quatermass Experiment* make ironic references to the limitations of the other medium. At the climax of the film, for example, the monster appears during an outside broadcast (OB) from Westminster Abbey by the BBC. The OB producer orders the broadcast to be stopped in order that viewers are not frightened. Charles Barr interprets this in terms of the film – an early X-certificate 'horrific' effort from Hammer – showing what television could not (Barr, 'Broadcasting and Cinema 2. Screens within Screens', p. 215). Might it also be seen as an ironic reference to the break in transmission during the original television broadcast?

42. Rudolph Cartier, 'A Foot in Both Camps', *Films and Filming* 4/12 (September 1958), p. 10.

43. Public interest can be gauged from the viewers' letters held by the BBC Written Archives Centre (BBC WAC T5/2540). There were several enquiries regarding the ending – some viewers were left uncertain from the last episode whether Quatermass made it back to earth after travelling to the aliens' asteroid base – and one sublime letter from a lady who was unable to see the conclusion of the serial: 'On November 21st I go over to Dublin to enter an Anglican Convent. I began watching your serial "Quatermass II" and find, to my great distress, that I will miss the final installment [*sic*] … The thought of spending the rest of my life wondering what really happened annoys me so much that I couldn't help writing. We can receive no letters in the Convent so this is my only hope.' Cartier obliged by providing a synopsis of the last episode, even though usually 'it is against our regulations and principles to reveal the end of a serial to private individuals'.

44. BBC WAC T5/2540: Audience Research Report VR/55/529, 9 November 1955.

45. BBC WAC T5/2540: Cecil McGivern to Michael Barry, 31 October 1955.

46. BBC WAC T5/2540: Michael Barry to Cecil McGivern, 8 November 1955.

47. BBC WAC T5/2540: Nigel Kneale to Cecil McGivern, 5 November 1955.

48. Quoted in Richard Holliss, 'TV Zone', *StarBurst* 58 (June 1983), p. 40.

49. Ibid.

50. There is contemporary significance in the fact that the 'Quatermass II' test that results in a nuclear explosion takes place in Australia. The British nuclear programme first became public knowledge following atomic tests at Woomera in northern Australia in 1952. The first British hydrogen bomb – many times more powerful than the atom bomb – was exploded at Christmas Island in the Pacific in 1957.

51. See Hutchings, 'We're the Martians Now', pp. 33–47, and David Pirie, *A Heritage of Horror: The English Gothic Cinema 1946–1972* (London: Gordon Fraser, 1973), pp. 29–33.

52. See, for example, reviews of the video release of *Quatermass and the Pit* (BBC Enterprises) by Julian Petley in the *Monthly Film Bulletin* 662 (March 1989), pp. 93–4, and Jeffrey Richards, 'The Demon from Outer Space', *Daily Telegraph*, 26 July 1988, p. 10.

53. An internal production document for *The Quatermass Experiment* reveals that Morell had been in the frame for the first serial: his name has been crossed out and Reginald Tate's written in. BBC WAC T5/418: Rudolph Cartier to 'Press Officer, Television', 23 June 1953.

54. Kneale, 'Not Quite So Intimate', p. 86.

55. Ibid., p. 88.

56. *Variety*, 18 February 1959, p. 18.
57. BBC WAC T5/2302: Audience Research Report VR/58/706, 7 January 1959.
58. Kneale, 'Not Quite So Intimate', p. 88.
59. Morgan, *The People's Peace*, p. 202.
60. BBC WAC T5/2306/1: Michael Barry to Rudolph Cartier, 20 December 1958.
61. Jack Bell, 'Quatermass IV', *Daily Mirror*, 22 November 1972; Richard Last, 'Quatermass and the Horrors of the Earth', *Daily Telegraph*, 3 September 1973.
62. Richard Last, 'Come-back for Quatermass', *Daily Telegraph*, 11 September 1978; Kenneth Hughes, 'Quatermass Reaps a Horror Harvest', *Daily Mirror*, 25 August 1979; Penny Junor, 'Quatermass on the Road to Urban Collapse', *Evening News*, 31 August 1979.
63. Quoted in Manuel Alvarado and John Stewart, *Made for Television: Euston Films Limited* (London: British Film Institute, 1985), p. 85.
64. The feature film version had the more resonant title of *The Quatermass Conclusion*. Ironically, it was the feature film that for many years was the only commercially available version of this story by dint of its release by Thames Video in 1989. In 2003 Clear Vision Video issued both *Quatermass* and *The Quatermass Conclusion* on video and DVD.
65. Alvarado and Stewart, *Made for Television*, p. 202.
66. See the reviews on the British Film Institute microfiche for *Quatermass*: Clive James, 'Monster's Return', *Observer*, 29 October 1979, and 'Sorry, Quaterfans!', *Observer*, 4 November 1979; Judith Cook, 'Quatermass Ain't What It Used to Be', *Western Mail*, 10 November 1979; and Richard Last, '"Quatermass" Ends in Mumbo-Jumbo', *Daily Telegraph*, 15 November 1979. The most positive reviews came from Martin Jackson of the *Daily Mail*, 25 October 1979 and 15 November 1979.
67. Quoted in Alvarado and Stewart, *Made for Television*, p. 87.
68. Wells, 'Apocalypse Then!', p. 56.
69. Ibid.
70. One American commentator wrote that Quatermass's death 'made me feel bad, the way a Sherlock Holmes fan would reading "The Falls at Reichenbach" (Bruce Eder, 'Scaring Us With Science', *Village Voice*, 18 August 1987, p. 77). Conan Doyle had famously killed off Sherlock Holmes in 'The Final Problem' (wherein he is presumed dead after an encounter with his arch foe Professor Moriarty at the Reichenbach Falls), only to resurrect him in 'The Empty House'. Kneale did much the same thing when he resurrected the professor for a BBC radio serial *The Quatermass Memoirs* in 1996. Quatermass was played by Andrew Keir, who had previously played the role in the film version of *Quatermass and the Pit*. Meanwhile in 2005 Professor Quatermass found himself resurrected in much younger form (as played by actor Jason Flemyng) for a one-off revival of *The Quatermass Experiment*, which was transmitted live by BBC 4 on 2 April 2005.

71. *A for Andromeda* and its sequel *The Andromeda Breakthrough* used several tropes common to the Quatermass serials: contact with an unknown alien presence, government cover-ups and the ethics of scientific advancement (in this case the knowledge, provided by aliens, of how to create artificial life). *Doomwatch* was the first 'green' sf series concerning a group of scientists working for the Department for the Observation and Measurement of Science. *Survivors*, by Terry Nation, was a post-apocalyptic drama in which 95 per cent of the human race have been wiped out by a plague. The character of Doctor Who was not dissimilar to Professor Quatermass, a possessor of advanced scientific knowledge with a highly ethical streak. During his third incarnation (played by Jon Pertwee) the Doctor, marooned on Earth, acted as scientific adviser to the British division of UNIT (the United Nations Intelligence Taskforce), where he was called on to defeat attempted alien invasions of the planet. The fourth Doctor adventure, 'The Seeds of Doom' (1976), features a vegetable organism that grows to gigantic size. In the seventh Doctor story, 'Remembrance of the Daleks' (1988), the appearance of Daleks in London in 1963 prompts one character to remark 'I wish Bernard were here.'

3

Tardis at the OK Corral:
Doctor Who and the USA

NICHOLAS J. CULL

In the summer of 2000, a group of leading British film and television professionals compiled a list for the British Film Institute of the one hundred most significant British television programmes of all time. The third item on that list was BBC TV's long-running science fiction serial *Doctor Who*.[1] This acclaim and the enduring affection of British audiences suggest that *Doctor Who* offers the cultural historian a valuable window on British popular culture during the years it initially played on television: 1963 to 1989. At the most basic level, the programme shows the influence of the Second World War. The Doctor's struggles against the Daleks and other totalitarian invaders served as a stage on which to relive Britain's historical stand against Nazi Germany.[2] Yet the story of the programme's rise and fall and passing references within the unfolding story line illuminate a second influence: post-war Britain's encounter with the United States. The character of the Doctor may have defined himself against the Daleks and won but in many ways the programme as a whole defined itself against the United States and lost. Yet America could also be a model, an inspiration and a market. *Doctor Who*'s complex relationship with the United States, and its expression in the equivalent series *Star Trek* (NBC, 1966–69; 1987–2005), raise issues within the wider development of British television and British culture and illuminate international questions of American media power.

THE USA AND THE ORIGINS OF *DOCTOR WHO*

Doctor Who was profoundly shaped by the United States. As the home of post-war science fiction, America inevitably provided the cultural model for a British science fiction serial such as *Doctor Who*. By the same token, there were elements in American science fiction that the programme's creators took pains to avoid. The origins of *Doctor Who* lie in the spring of 1962, when BBC executives, eager to revive flagging ratings, commissioned their script department to scour contemporary science fiction in search of suitable material to adapt as a serial. The Corporation's commercial rival, ITV, had just begun to screen the lively American import *The Twilight Zone* (CBS, 1959–64), and a number of science fiction short stories of its own. The first Script Department report, completed in April 1962, stressed the American domination of the genre, noting that 'sf is overwhelmingly American in bulk' and that the 'subtlest exponents ... are a group of American writers'. The sub-genre of satirical science fiction seemed entirely American. As the BBC hoped to develop programming in cooperation with the eventual writer, they soon found the field of candidates 'boiling down to a handful of British writers'. The report dismissed some of the older, dated, writers, including C.S. Lewis, and noted that most suitable British novels – the report mentioned John Wyndham's *The Midwich Cuckoos* (1957) – had already been snapped up for film adaptation.[3]

A second report in July 1962 took the plunge and nominated five American novels as possible sources for a British-based serial. These were Poul Anderson's *Guardians of Time* (coll. 1960); Eric Frank Russell's *Three to Conquer* (1956); Clifford Simak's *Eternity Lost* (1949); Katherine MacLean's *Pictures Don't Lie* (1951) and C.L. Moore's *No Woman Born* (1944). Anderson's tale of a time-travelling police force struggling to protect the course of history seemed particularly appropriate for adaptation.[4] When, in early 1963, the BBC drama department began to draw up plans for a Saturday evening science fiction serial, it was the script department's synopsis of Anderson's novel that set the producers thinking about a time-travel scenario; allusions to H.G. Wells came later in the process.[5]

American science fiction also served as a negative model for the BBC through the dreaded Hollywood B-movie. The script department stressed that it was looking for stories that did not feature 'Bug Eyed Monsters... or Tin Robots (since the audience must always subconsciously say "my goodness, there's a man in there and isn't he playing the part well")'. The report noted that these sorts of difficulties had already contributed to the failure of recent commercial television adaptations of three short stories, "Little Lost Robot" written by Isaac Asimov in 1947; "The Yellow Pill" by Rog Phillips from 1953, and "The Dumb Martian" published by John Wyndham in 1952.[6]

The desire to avoid the 'Bug Eyed Monster' emerged as a particular obsession of the man who became the driving force behind the development of *Doctor Who*, Sydney Newman. Newman was a Canadian who had worked with the National Film Board and gone on to make his name in television drama at CBC (Canadian Broadcasting Corporation). In the late 1950s, he had moved to Britain and energised the drama output of ABC (Associated British Company) with programmes such as *Armchair Theatre* (1956–74) and *The Avengers* (1961–9).[7] As a Canadian, Newman was used to both borrowing from and defining his work in contrast to 'the giant next door'. This process continued in *Doctor Who*. He had a horror of mindless monsters lumbering around for their own sake in American 1950s B-movies. He wanted the adventures of *Doctor Who* to be consistent with both historical and science fact (which was also, of course, the claim of numerous B-movies). He ensured that the crew of the Doctor's time/space machine included a science and a history teacher and hence aligned the programme with the BBC's historical public service mission to educate. Yet he also represented a dynamic North American approach to broadcasting. The young woman he selected to produce *Doctor Who*, Verity Lambert, also knew the American scene; she had cut her teeth in New York as assistant to the producer and talk-show host David Susskind. One of the early writers, John Lucarotti, had worked in the United States and Canada. Lucarotti was already adept at the art of appropriation, having written CBC's answer to Walt Disney's *Davy Crockett* (1954–55), the 1957–58 frontier adventure: *Radisson*. Lambert had the sense to recognise the value in bending Newman's ban on bug-eyed monsters and presided over the arrival of the Daleks. From their entrance, the success of the programme seemed assured.[8] It soon became apparent to the producers of the programme that the closer the Doctor came to bug-eyed monsters and outer-space adventures, the better the ratings. *Doctor Who* had found his niche as a British character living American B-movie adventures.

BRITISH ADVENTURES IN AMERICA'S WORLD

Although the Doctor was supposed to be an alien, his manners and adventures were deeply embedded in the stories that British people told themselves about themselves, the most obvious being the emphasis on law and order symbolised by the outward form of his time/space machine – the Tardis – as a London police telephone box. The character asserted national values and acted out national mythology at a time of great uncertainty. Much of this uncertainty stemmed from the dominance of the United States and the decline of Britain. Since the end of the Second World War, Britain had been learning to be, in movie terms, a supporting actor in the American drama. *Doctor Who* was escapism and this was part of what Britain needed to escape from. More especially, *Doctor Who* adventures played directly into Britain's strategies for coping with American power. Britain's elite had long comforted itself that while America had strength, Britain had character and wisdom; as a jokey poem circulating among British diplomats in Washington during the Second World War had it: 'In Washington Lord Halifax/ Once whispered to Lord Keynes:/ "It's true *they* have the money bags/ But *we* have all the brains".[9] *Doctor Who*'s adventures provided perhaps the most sustained and widely seen expression of the national belief in the triumph of brains over brawn. Unlike John Wayne, the Doctor (like the British policeman) never carried a gun but somehow always 'muddled through'.

As Britain struggled to create a space for itself in America's world, the writers of *Doctor Who* could not avoid addressing American issues. Five months into its first season, the script editor of *Doctor Who* proposed a six-part adventure in which the Doctor (William Hartnell) would visit the American Civil War.[10] In the event, this became a tiny segment in a Dalek adventure 'The Chase' (transmitted in the summer of 1965), during which the Doctor and his companions witness Lincoln delivering the Gettysburg Address. This was the Doctor's only 'straight' visit to America: it soon became apparent that the writers of *Doctor Who* could only approach America through humour.

During the same adventure, he landed on top of the Empire State Building and encountered a stereotyped American tourist, and took part in a slapstick-style chase through Hollywood in the 1920s. In the summer of 1966, the *Doctor Who* team spent an entire adventure spoofing the Western. In 'The Gunfighters', the Doctor found himself in Tombstone caught up in the events around the gunfight at the OK Corral. The only other adventure with so overt a comic tone had been 'The Romans' in early 1965, which degenerated into a satire of the Hollywood epic. Sydney Newman was unimpressed by the Wild West digression. In an angry note to the Head of Serials he noted:

> [T]he entire attack was misconceived. Somehow or other *Dr. Who* audiences, as proven from many past successes, always want to believe in the particular life-and-death situation that *Dr. Who* and his companion find themselves in. The Mickey-taking aspects of this particular one I think alienated all except the most sophisticated.[11]

The BBC's audience research unit bore out Newman's view. The adventure produced the lowest levels of viewer satisfaction in the programme's original 26-year run.[12]

Although it would not be until his ill-starred 1996 reincarnation that the Doctor would return to to the United States, the serial, like many other British television programmes of the era, featured occasional American characters and a low level of sparring with American culture. These included the usual British stereotypes of the gruff American general or hapless tourist.[13] 'Tomb of the Cybermen' (1967) featured an American space captain, Captain Hopper (George Roubicek), who, after delivering a party of archaeologists to a distant planet, played little part in the action. As the story neared its climax, he popped back to offer his support but declined to follow the Doctor (by this time played by Patrick Troughton) into the tomb of the title. There was a national twist to the sarcastic response of the Doctor's companion, Victoria: 'It's comforting to know we have your superior strength to call on should we need it.' In the 1968 adventure 'The Mind Robber', the Doctor is threatened by a character clearly meant to satirise the American tradition of costumed super heroes: The Karkus. The Doctor and his companions find themselves in a realm where fictional characters have come to life. He is generally able to defeat them because of his familiarity with great literature.

Unfortunately the muscle-bound Karkus is a lowbrow strip cartoon character extracted from the memory of one of his assistants, Zoe, and the Doctor nearly gets crushed.

By the 1970s, *Doctor Who* seemed more comfortable with an American presence. In the 1971 adventure 'The Claws of Axos', the Doctor (now played by Jon Pertwee) is assisted by an American agent called Bill Filer (Paul Grist). In the first episode, Filer is teased about having come to help the British Army capture the Master (the programme's arch villain) single-handed. He quips back: 'No... I think that was Errol Flynn.' In 1984, the show acquired its first regular American character, a graduate student named Peri (played by British actress Nicola Bryant), who served as the Doctor's companion until 1986 and endured teasing about her use of American idiom. The script took occasional pot shots at the United States, as in 'The Mark of the Rani' (1985), in which the Doctor discovered that the entire American Revolution had been the result of an evil alien woman's mischievous brain experiments. By this stage, the producers of *Doctor Who* set one adventure each year in an overseas location and planned to film the story 'The Two Doctors' for 1985 in New Orleans. Budget concerns required a rapid rewrite to shift the location to Seville.

Doctor Who allowed British characters to move in American space. This happened literally with the Doctor visiting the moon ('The Moonbase', 1967) two years before Neil Armstrong, or in adventures like 'The Ambassadors of Death' (1970), which had British astronauts returning from Mars with the Union Jack flag on their spacesuits. It also happened at a wider level. *Doctor Who* provided a canvas on which British writers could explore science fiction and maintain the 'Hammer Studios tradition' of horror and fantasy. The Doctor's air of happy-go-lucky improvisation was matched by the programme's shaky sets and improvised monsters. For some, the production values were all part of the fun but they ensured that the programme would look pretty silly when compared to the 1969 off-season guest in *Doctor Who*'s Saturday teatime slot: *Star Trek*.

DOCTOR WHO AND THE CHALLENGE OF *STAR TREK*

Star Trek, like *Doctor Who*, had transatlantic elements in its genesis. *Star Trek*'s creator, Gene Roddenberry, was a fan (and eventually a friend) of the great British sf novelist, Arthur C. Clarke. He also loved C.S. Forrester's *Hornblower* naval adventure novels and imagined his science fiction series as 'Hornblower in space'. Of course, as a writer of TV Westerns he also had the American concept of a Western-style '*Wagon Train* to the Stars', and by taking the punchier Afrikaans equivalent to a wagon train he acquired the title *Star Trek*. But his central character, Captain Kirk (William Shatner), drew on British influences. Roddenberry variously saw Kirk as not just Hornblower but Hamlet, Holmes and even such real-life heroes as Sir Frances Drake, Sir Walter Raleigh and doomed Antarctic explorer Robert Falcon Scott. Like these characters, Roddenberry imagined Kirk as a character flawed by a 'predilection for action over administration, a temptation to take the greatest tasks onto himself'. The series premiered in the USA on 8 September 1966 and, although it only lasted three seasons on NBC network television, it prospered in syndication.[14] *Star Trek* followed very different plot trajectories from *Doctor Who*. For all Roddenberry's belief in a universe built on 'infinite diversity in infinite combination', the voyages of the Starship *Enterprise* were in many ways expansionist: integrating and coordinating newly discovered worlds into the intergalactic federation. Captain Kirk therefore seemed like an all-American hero. *Doctor Who*, by contrast, tended to the conservative (with a small 'c') as well as the defensive. He worked like a cosmic knight errant ensuring that history would take its assigned course: that old civilisations would be preserved, evil contained and disputes resolved. Thus each programme fitted the national imagination of the culture that produced and embraced it.[15]

America's growing interest in science fiction (seen in *Star Trek* and *Lost in Space* [CBS, 1965–68]) had already touched *Doctor Who*. In 1967, the writer who had created the Daleks, Terry Nation, moved to the USA and began a futile bid to relaunch the Daleks in a wider market.[16] The Doctor therefore faced the challenge of *Star Trek* bereft of the creatures that had been his greatest ally in the quest for British ratings. The producers played up the role of the Cybermen as substitutes and hoped for the best. But *Doctor Who* was experiencing wider problems. The second Doctor (Patrick Troughton) was not as popular as the first. Audiences detected 'stale and predictable plots'. 'Why', one viewer complained in 1969, 'must all other space-beings be baddies or monsters – cannot Dr. Who meet a friendly alien?'[17]

FIGHTING EXTERMINATION   The third Doctor (Jon Pertwee) confronts his old enemy, the Daleks, just as *Doctor Who* the series had to fend off the American threat from *Star Trek* in the early 1970s.

At times, even the production team despaired. During the making of 'The Mind Robber' in 1968, the script editor Derrick Sherwin complimented the episode's writer, Peter Ling, noting that he was 'quite certain that this [adventure] is going to be one of the few winners. This isn't a load of old cobblers...'[18] *Star Trek* offered much: complex ideas, occasional love interest, aliens from the friendly to the psychopathic, planets in various technicolor hues and astonishing special effects. *Doctor Who* suddenly seemed tame.

The BBC audience research unit soon noted unfavourable comparisons to the American show. One viewer commented that the 1970 season of *Doctor Who* was 'hardly an adequate substitute for *Star Trek* and by comparison rather childish'.[19] In 1970, the producers of *Doctor Who* retrenched, shifting to colour and stories set on Earth, which allowed the budgets to go further. They also increased the action content of the programme: a stunt team called Havoc featured regularly in the cast, playing either marauding aliens or the gallant British soldiers trying to fight them off. The new incarnation of the Doctor, Jon Pertwee, was skilled in the extraterrestrial martial art of Venusian akido (a nod to Mr. Spock's Vulcan neck pinch). The 1972 adventure 'The Curse of Peladon' even seemed compatible with the *Star Trek* universe as the Doctor worked to help a primitive planet enter the Galactic Federation. But *Doctor Who* also knew how to capitalise on its history. From 1972, the Daleks once again became an annual feature of the serial, and in 1973 a special tenth anniversary adventure brought together all three of the Doctors to date.[20] *Doctor Who* seemed safe, and when Tom Baker took over the role in 1975 audience numbers climbed to unprecedented levels.

In 1970, the BBC promoted the second season of *Star Trek* in the primetime adult slot of 7.10 to 8 p.m. on a Tuesday night. The programme commanded an impressive 19 per cent of the national audience. British audiences recognised that this was more than the 'American trash' that they complained of in other quarters.[21] In its turn, *Star Trek* increased the market for TV science fiction in 1970s' Britain. *Doctor Who* veterans Barry Letts and Terrance Dicks collaborated with John Lucarotti on a six-episode adult space drama called *Moon Base 3* (BBC TV, 1973). The British media mogul Lew Grade, who had spent much of the previous decade paying Gerry Anderson to make science fiction television programmes with the American market in mind, invested several million pounds in Anderson's *Space: 1999* (ITC, 1975–77). Meanwhile the creator of the Daleks, Terry Nation, devised two successful adult science fiction programmes for the BBC: the first, *Survivors* (1975–77), dealt with life after a future plague. The second, *Blake's 7*, ran from January 1978 to December 1981 and was a space adventure in which a group of freedom fighters stole a spaceship not unlike the Starship *Enterprise* and resisted an evil interplanetary empire that just happened to have the same name as the good empire of *Star Trek*: the Federation.

The second challenge to *Doctor Who* came in the form of George Lucas and *Star Wars*. The release of *Star Wars* in Britain in the winter of 1977–8 presented a threat of a completely new order.[22] Not only were the effects astonishing when set against the bargain-basement monsters of *Doctor Who* but also the film proved that science fiction could be big business. The revenues generated by *Star Wars* enabled Lucas to develop the necessary infrastructure to make similar future projects look even more wonderful, through his special-effects subsidiary Industrial Light and Magic. Paramount Studios had been thinking about a new *Star Trek* series since 1975 and now the success of *Star Wars* and also Steven Spielberg's *Close Encounters of the Third Kind* (USA, 1977) encouraged them to bring *Star Trek* to the big screen in a series of films from 1979.[23] *Star Wars* also produced a coterie of small-screen imitators such as *Battlestar Galactica* and *Buck Rogers in the 25th Century*.[24] Though not as successful in the United States, *Buck Rogers* proved a hit in Britain. In 1980, ITV scheduled it against *Doctor Who* and effectively recaptured the Saturday teatime slot. *Doctor Who* eventually responded by moving to weekday evening slots on BBC 1 for season nineteen (January–March 1982).[25] The shift worked well in the short term but the challenge from America remained.

Graham Williams, the producer of *Doctor Who* when the *Star Wars* boom hit Britain, responded to the American challenge by falling back on the time-honoured British response that brains and character could win through. He later recalled:

> I was up against it, because my boss was saying, 'What are we going to do about *Star Wars* coming out, and *Star Trek* coming back?' And my point was that we didn't have the money or the expertise to do it. Neither did *they* have our – I thought it was British – television strength, which is in building and creating – writing, acting, directing – character and pretty quirky character at that. Again, all this, as you see, added up to the humour and that sort of treatment. If we didn't go for the hardware, we had to go for something. And we went for character.[26]

The producers believed they had a winning formula and they began to prove it in the export market. The BBC had been exporting *Doctor Who* since December 1964, when Canada became the first customer.[27] By 1972, the programme was playing 27 countries from Australia to Zambia.[28] The success of *Star Wars* and on-going life of *Star Trek* in domestic syndication in the USA, created an obvious American market for *Doctor Who*. In the 1977–8 season, the programme finally began to play across the United States. By 1984, with the global audience for the programme now stretched across

54 countries, 112 American stations (mainly public broadcasting stations) carried *Doctor Who*.[29]

By the late 1970s, British television was well established in the United States. Two programmes devised by *Doctor Who*'s creator Sydney Newman had led the way: *The Avengers* and *The Forsyte Saga* (BBC TV, 1967). Mobil corporation sponsored British costume drama in the *Masterpiece Theatre* strand (1971–) long hosted by Alistair Cooke, and programmes like *The Prisoner* (ITC, 1967–8), *Monty Python* (BBC TV, 1969–74), the *Benny Hill Show* (ITV, 1969–89) and even *Are You Being Served?* (BBC TV, 1972–83) acquired a cult following. As Jeffrey Miller has noted, these British programmes prospered because they were unlike the usual American television, or, in the phrase he borrows from the *Monty Python* team, they were 'something completely different'.[30] The same was true of *Doctor Who*. The programme's quirky, witty approach drew audiences eager for a change from the usual thrust of American science fiction.[31] However, American entrepreneurs were swift to recognise the potential for marketing the serial along exactly the path established by *Star Trek*: fan organisations and series of increasingly large-scale conventions followed. In November 1983, 7,000 fans attended a convention held in Chicago to celebrate the twentieth anniversary of the serial. American newspapers and magazines ran stories with obvious punning titles like 'Why the Doctor is in'. British fans grumbled about American commercialisation.[32]

The programme's producer from 1980, John Nathan-Turner, relished *Doctor Who*'s American success. When casting the new Doctor, he selected Peter Davison, who was already well known in the United States for his role in BBC's nostalgic veterinary drama *All Creatures Great and Small* (BBC TV, 1978–80; 1988–90). Nathan-Turner also redesigned the Doctor's entourage to maximise its appeal to the target audience, including a twenty-something Australian air hostess, and two teenagers. With an eye to American fans, he encouraged cast members past and present to participate in conventions.[33] The programme also spoke to fans on both sides of the Atlantic by paying an increasing amount of attention to series continuity. *Doctor Who* became ever more self-referential and 'about' *Doctor Who*. Yet the strategies adopted to deal with a transatlantic market in science fiction television were not necessarily mutually compatible. Character and humour could disrupt series continuity, especially when that humour was at the expense of the series. From 1979, *Doctor Who* had sought out guest stars and played with the audience's recognition of their identities outside the series: the *Monty Python* comedian John Cleese appeared in the final episode of 'City of Death' (1979) as an art critic in the Louvre gallery who mistakes the Doctor's time/space machine – the Tardis – for a sculpture. John Nathan-Turner spoke of *Doctor Who* becoming like the legendary British variety programme *The Morecambe and Wise Show* (BBC TV, 1968–77), with guest stars popping up to demonstrate what 'good sports' they were. The fans hated this.[34] Moreover, the entire strategy placed *Doctor Who* on a collision course with the wider audience's desire to suspend disbelief that Sydney Newman had noted at the time of the disastrous 1966 comedy-western debacle. There was an obvious market for a British antidote to American science fiction but this could be more conveniently met by overtly satirical programmes which did not have *Doctor Who*'s history, 'national treasure' status or need to work as a plausible thriller. The former *Doctor Who* script editor Douglas Adams moved into precisely this territory with his radio, television and eventual novel series: *The Hitchhiker's Guide to the Galaxy*. Meanwhile *Doctor Who* drifted ever lower in the ratings.

LOST IN SPACE: *DOCTOR WHO* IN THE ERA OF TRANSATLANTIC CO-PRODUCTION

At the end of the 1989 season as audiences nose-dived, the BBC ended *Doctor Who*. The series lived on in the 1990s in radio adventures, spin-off novels and web-based fan culture. An enterprising group of independent filmmakers even produced its own spin-off videos featuring characters and creatures from the show.[35] Old episodes appeared on video and became a staple of BBC/Flextech satellite television channels such as UK Gold. But competition from the USA seemed too intense to allow a British challenge in the form of new television episodes. America had learned to serve its science fiction with enough multicultural inflection to please the most discerning international audience. *Star Trek: The Next Generation* premiered in the United States in 1987. It presented a wiser vision of the future than the expansionist world of Captain Kirk. Its stories avoided

American 'gung ho' heroics. Indeed the star was a British character actor, Patrick Stewart. The show had all *Doctor Who*'s eclecticism and humour and effects were light-years away from anything the BBC could attempt alone. A big budget response would require American co-production funds and these seemed available only for *Masterpiece Theatre*-style classic costume drama.

As the *Star Trek* franchise prospered, diversified and begat competitors, Britons still went into space but only in quirky comedies such as Nick Park's first Wallace and Gromit film *A Grand Day Out* (1992), or in out-and-out satires like *Red Dwarf*, Rob Grant and Doug Naylor's long-running space spoof for BBC North, which premiered in 1988. A tale of a mixed-race working-class lad from Liverpool, addicted to lager and curry, who finds himself stuck in a spaceship along with a cat which has evolved into a zoot-suited African American, plus a campy American-accented robot and an officious hologram of his deceased British colleague, *Red Dwarf* fitted 1990s' Britain in a way that *Doctor Who*, with its cosy paternalism and emphasis on intellect, could not. Humour (much of it at the expense of American science fiction), transatlantic characters and low-tech effects had won the day. This show had plenty to say about changing conceptions of Britishness and the sort of national roles forced on Britain by the tastes of American audiences and co-producers. In the 1997 episode 'Beyond a Joke' the crew even visited a holographic rendering of the BBC Classic Serial/PBS *Masterpiece Theatre* idea of Britain: 'Jane Austen World' and introduced the Bennett girls from *Pride and Prejudice* (1813; BBC TV adaptation, 1995) to curry. Meanwhile, explicit anti-Americanism surfaced in the BBC/Channel Four co-production of Dennis Potter's final work, *Cold Lazarus* (1996). This dystopian science fiction drama included a prolonged attack on international corporate domination of the British media. The target was clearly Rupert Murdoch, but the villains in the programme were portrayed as Americans.[36] In reality, the outlook was not wholly bleak. The advent of the niche Sci-Fi cable channel in the United States helped the cause of British science fiction by providing a new outlet for classic British material and creating a possible partner for major co-productions. In 1998, the Sci-Fi Channel and the BBC collaborated on *Invasion: Earth*, featuring Hollywood regular Fred Ward as an American general leading NATO resistance to an alien invasion of Scotland.

In the mid-1990s, the future of *Doctor Who* became tied to this world of international co-productions and corporate domination. As Hollywood plundered classic television for film ideas, *Doctor Who* seemed ripe for exploitation. During the early 1990s, the right to produce *Doctor Who* had been held by a British company called Dalentry. Its plan for a film was to match the technical skills of a team of *Doctor Who* designers from the BBC with financial support from the French company Lumière and musician Bryan Ferry. *Star Trek*'s Leonard Nimoy was to be the proposed director of the project and it had been hoped that Alan Rickman would play the Doctor.[37] By 1994, since the Dalentry production seemed to be stalled, the BBC sought an alternative partner and concluded a surprise transatlantic deal with Steven Spielberg's Amblin entertainment. Spielberg reportedly favoured casting *Monty Python* star Eric Idle in the role for a film and television series.[38] Corporate wheels turned and the project ended up as a BBC co-production with Universal Studios (Canada) for the Fox television network: a $5 million *Doctor Who* television film, which, if successful, would lead to five more. *Doctor Who*'s future now lay in American hands.

The *Doctor Who* television movie premiered in the United States in mid-May 1996 and in Britain a week later (BBC 1, 27 May 1996). The writer/co-producer Matthew Jacobs had a personal link to the serial. His father had played Doc Holliday in the OK Corral adventure and Jacobs had visited the set to watch progress.[39] Given the negative audience reaction to this episode, it was hardly a good omen. But Jacobs took some care to respect the origins of *Doctor Who*. He opened with the Doctor's last BBC incarnation (Sylvester McCoy), who in due course regenerated into the British actor Paul McGann. But much else had changed. The Doctor was adrift in San Francisco and the plot now reflected American interest in action and romance and plot preoccupations familiar from *Star Trek*. For the first time, the Doctor kissed a woman and spoke about his family. As though providing an Oedipal explanation for his persistent interest in the planet, the Doctor explained that his mother had come from Earth. The intermarriage between aliens and humans was a major feature of *Star Trek*, providing the background to such characters as Spock and Deanna Troi, but it had not hitherto attracted the interest of *Doctor Who* writers. Like the Klingons in *Star Trek: The Next Generation*, the

Daleks, who were heard off-screen in the prologue, had softened to suit the post-Cold War era. In this case, it destroyed their accepted characteristics. The Daleks here are sufficiently legally minded to execute the Master for his crimes. They allow their arch-enemy the Doctor to drop by and pick up the pieces for return to his home world and are sufficiently bad at the one thing they do best – extermination – to leave enough of the Master intact for him to return to life.

There were other traces of American science fiction. Jacobs used technical language borrowed from *Star Trek*, speaking of the Tardis having a 'cloaking device', and gave the Doctor's old adversary, the Master, abilities that reflected (and required similar effects to) the T1000 Terminator in James Cameron's *Terminator 2* movie (USA, 1991). There were moments of compensation, however. When a traffic cop confronts the Doctor, his American companion explains the Doctor's eccentricity simply by saying 'he's British'.[40] Viewers in Britain had mixed reactions to the film; many enjoyed it, but it was audiences in the United States that mattered. The American screening had attracted only 8.5 million viewers and had come seventy-fifth in the ratings. Plans for future adventures starring Paul McGann evaporated forthwith.[41]

American themes had never been lucky for *Doctor Who*: the lure of Hollywood had removed the key writer Terry Nation in the late 1960s, and two former Doctors, Patrick Troughton and Jon Pertwee, had collapsed and died while on American tours.[42] In the later 1990s, American reaction to an already Americanised television movie killed plans to revive the programme. *Doctor Who* remained a pawn in the transatlantic media game. For the BBC, its third biggest export after *Teletubbies* (BBC TV, 1997–2002) and *Pride and Prejudice* was just too lucrative an asset to neglect. Newspaper reports on future revivals repeatedly returned to the need to find a Doctor who appealed to American tastes. Hot favourites included *Star Trek: The Next Generation*'s Patrick Stewart and black American stars Denzel Washington and Laurence Fishburne.[43] In 2004, however, the BBC announced that the British actor Christopher Eccleston had been cast as the Doctor for a new series made by BBC Wales. His companion was the British starlet Billie Piper, suggesting a nod in the direction of *Buffy the Vampire Slayer* (Warners/UPN, 1997–2003). The writer/executive producer Russell T. Davis made no secret of his admiration for the creator of *Buffy*, noting 'Joss Whedon raised the bar for every writer – not just genre/niche writers, but every single one of us.'[44]

In the spring of 2005, *Doctor Who* returned to British television in one of the most successful relaunches of a series ever seen. New audiences and old tuned in by the million to see old monsters and new. Themes that marked the programme as a product of its time included an unprecedented acknowledgement of the Doctor's sexuality and a marked emphasis on female agency. Strong female characters abounded and almost all the episodes were either resolved by female intervention or concluded with a female character in the position of power with responsibility for the future. While the programme's Britishness was present, there was a sense that this was British with an eye to international marketability. National icons, including people (Charles Dickens), places (the London Eye and Big Ben tower) and events (the London Blitz), figured prominently. America and Americans appeared in the story. Later episodes featured a dashing bisexual American time-traveller and reformed conman named Captain Jack Harkness (played by Glasgow-born but Illinois-raised actor Jack Barrowman) as a companion of the Doctor. The sixth episode, 'Dalek' (1st tx. BBC 1, 30 April 2005), saw the Tardis materialise beneath the salt flats of Utah in the near future, where a crazed American Internet billionaire named Henry Van Statten (played by Corey Johnson) has imprisoned the last surviving Dalek as part of a museum of alien relics. In a direct comparison between an American and a Dalek, the American seemed much worse and the Doctor said as much.

The series played strongly in Canada and Australia, joined the line-up on the BBC Prime satellite channel and sold swiftly to New Zealand, South Korea, the Netherlands and Italy but failed initially to win a US screening. The Sci-Fi Channel reportedly considered the show 'too British'. The immediate future of the resurrected programme seemed secure, however, as Scottish actor David Tennant took over the role in the closing seconds of the first season. At the same time, it remains to be seen exactly how America – the cosmic force that influenced the birth and early development of *Doctor Who*, as well as shaped the original programme as a source for competitors and a market – would impact in the longer term upon the fortunes of the reborn series.

NOTES

This chapter has been developed from presentations given at the British Cinema and Television Research Group, De Montfort University, and at the British Council 'British Travellers' conference at Warwick (December 1997). The author is grateful to the participants at these events for their comments; to James Cod from the BBC Written Archives Centre in Caversham for his help in recovering the necessary documents; and to Karen Ford, Niall McKeown, Phillip Lindley and Todd Swift for their comments on the essay at various stages of development; and to Paul Cohen for stimulating *Doctor Who* conversations. Press cutting research has been greatly helped by Roger Anderson's excellent *Doctor Who* cuttings page at www.cuttingsarchive.org.uk/.

1. *Doctor Who* was a science fiction serial aimed at a family audience which ran on BBC TV from 1963 to 1989. Episodes were typically 25 minutes long and broadcast early on Saturday evenings. The programme concerned the adventures of an alien traveller who, together with human companions, roamed the Galaxy in a time/space craft called the Tardis, which looked like a London police telephone box. When the first actor to play the part retired in 1966, the writers announced that the Doctor had the power to regenerate into a new form. In 2005, the format was successfully revived by head writer/executive producer Russell T. Davies for a new updated BBC TV series (Series 1 1st tx. BBC 1, 26 March–18 June 2005). The Daleks, invented by Terry Nation, were the doctor's best-known enemy. For the poll of British TV, see *Sight and Sound*, October 2000, p. 3.

2. This reading is noted in John R. Cook, 'Adapting Telefantasy: The *Doctor Who and the Daleks* Films', in I.Q. Hunter (ed.), *British Science Fiction Cinema* (London: Routledge, 1999) and discussed in Nicholas J. Cull, 'Bigger on the Inside… Dr. Who as British Cultural History', in G. Roberts and P.M. Taylor (eds), *The Historian, Television and Television History* (Luton: University of Luton Press, 2001), pp. 95–112.

3. BBC Written Archives Centre, Caversham Park (hereafter BBC WAC), T5/647, Donald Bull/Alice Frick, 'Science Fiction', April 1962. In 1964 the *Doctor Who* team considered hiring John Wyndham to write for the programme. See Whitaker to Lambert, 7 September 1964.

4. BBC WAC T5/647, John Braybon/Alice Frick, Report: Science Fiction, 25 July 1962.

5. BBC WAC T5/647, Discussion of Science Fiction Series, 26 March 1963.

6. BBC WAC T5/647, John Braybon/Alice Frick, Report: Science Fiction, 25 July 1962.

7. For Newman's career, see *Toronto Star*, 31 October 1997.

8. BBC WAC T5/647, BBC WAC C.103, Sydney Newman to Jeremy Bentham, 13 April 1984; '*DR. WHO*: Preliminary Notes for a Promotion meeting', Donald Wilson, 30 July 1963.

9. David Dimbleby and David Reynolds, *An Ocean Apart: The Relationship between Britain and America in the Twentieth Century* (London: Hodder & Stoughton, 1988), p. 180.

10. BBC WAC T5/647, Whitaker to Lambert, Proposals for Doctor Who, 14 April 1964.

11. BBC WAC T5/1249/1, Newman to Head Serials, 23 May 1966.

12. BBC WAC C.103, Samantha Beere, *Doctor Who* Audience Research Data, 1963–1989, Broadcasting Research Information Services Report (hereafter Beere 1989), pp. 11–13.

13. *The Tenth Planet* (BBC TV, 1966) and *Silver Nemesis* (BBC TV, 1988).

14. For quotations and an account of the programme's origins, see Stephen E. Whitfield and Gene Roddenberry, *The Making of Star Trek* (New York: Ballantine, 1968), esp. p. 28. The *Doctor Who* team produced a parallel mix of TV history and plot background in Terrance Dicks and Malcolm Hulke, *The Making of Doctor Who* (London: Pan, 1972). See also Yvonne Fern, *Gene Roddenberry: The Last Conversation* (Berkeley: University of California Press, 1994), pp. 35–6, 66, 67, 78.

15. One of the original creators of *Doctor Who* had even suggested that the Doctor might be revealed to be a scientist who had 'opted out' and now tried to stop scientific progress when he encountered it. BBC WAC T5/647, '*Dr. Who*' General Notes on Background and Approach, undated but *circa* April 1963.

16. Adrian Rigelsford, *The Doctors: 30 Years of Time Travel* (London: Boxtree, 1994), p. 61. Nation moved to the USA again in 1980, without substantial success.

17. BBC WAC R9/7/97, Audience Research Report on *The Krotons*, 6 February 1969.

18. BBC WAC T5/2, 532/1, Sherwin to Ling, 15 July 1968.

19. BBC WAC C.103, Beere 1989, p. 7.

20. Louis Marks wrote the return adventure, 'Day of the Daleks'; however, the script editor, Terrance Dicks, enlisted Terry Nation to approve the Dalek dialogue. BBC WAC T65/15/1, Nation to Dicks, 20 July 1971.

21. BBC WAC R9/7/104, Audience Research Report on *Star Trek*, 1 June 1970. Anti-American spleen can be found in the report on the rowdy children's show *The Banana Splits* of 6 March 1970, which was variously described as 'cheap nasty American vulgarity' and 'American trash'.

22. It should also be said that Britain seemed to have much more of a presence in the abstract *Star Wars* world of princesses and swordfights than the overtly American world of *Star Trek*, more especially given the use of British studio facilities, British stars (including Peter Cushing, who had played *Doctor Who* in two spin-off movies in the mid 1960s) and numerous British character actors, some of whom (including Darth Vader's 'body', Dave Prowse) had appeared in *Doctor Who*.

23. For an account, see Joel Engel, *Gene Roddenberry: The Myth and the Man Behind Star Trek* (New York: Hyperion, 1994), pp. 165, 180–86.

24. *Battlestar Galactica* ran in the United States for one season in 1978, with

a sequel season as *Galactica* in 1980. *Buck Rogers in the 25th Century* ran for two seasons in 1979–80 and 1981.

25. BBC WAC C.103, Beere 1989, p. 8.

26. John Tulloch and Manuel Alvarado, *Doctor Who: The Unfolding Text* (London: Macmillan, 1983), pp. 178–9.

27. BBC WAC T5/647/1, brochure and Dennis Scuse (General Manager, TV) to Head of Serials, 21 December 1964. Export had required changes to the programme, including a shift away from low light levels in spookier scenes, which had created technical difficulties for tape transfer.

28. Dicks and Hulke, *The Making of Doctor Who*, p. 8. The Doctor at the time, Jon Pertwee, reported being pulled over by a Moroccan traffic policeman, who then recognised him and let him go.

29. *Time*, 9 January 1984, p. 53.

30. Jeffrey S. Miller, *Something Completely Different: British Television and American Culture* (Minneapolis: University of Minnesota Press, 2000).

31. This aspect of *Doctor Who* appreciation is noted by British and Australian fans in John Tulloch and Henry Jenkins, *Science Fiction Audiences: Watching Doctor Who and Star Trek* (London and New York: Routledge, 1995), pp. 122–3, 165–7.

32. *Time*, 9 January 1984, p. 53; and *USA Today*, 28 August 1985. On American 'commercialisation' of *Doctor Who* see Tulloch and Jenkins, *Science Fiction Audiences*, pp. 160–63; and Camille Bacon-Smith, *Enterprising Women: Television Fandom and the Creation of Popular Myth* (Philadelphia: University of Pennsylvania Press, 1992), p. 15.

33. Tulloch and Alvarado, *Doctor Who: The Unfolding Text*, esp. p. 242.

34. For fan hatred of Nathan-Turner, see *The Stage*, November 1988; Tulloch and Jenkins, *Science Fiction Audiences*, ch. 6.

35. For coverage of Doctor Who spin-offs including the BBV (Bill and Ben Video) productions, see 'Regenerate', *Daily Telegraph*, 5 August 1999.

36. For background, see John R. Cook, *Dennis Potter: A Life on Screen* (Manchester University Press, Manchester, 1998) pp. 301–16.

37. 'BBC faces £14m law suit after *Dr. Who* film plan scrapped', *Guardian*, 15 February 1997; '*Dr. Who* Design Team Sues BBC over Film Rights', *The Times*, 24 August 1998.

38. '*Dr. Who*'s Flying Circus', *Mail on Sunday*, 22 May 1994.

39. Philip Segal, introduction to Matthew Jacobs, *Doctor Who: The Screenplay* (London: BBC Books, 1996), p. vi.

40. *Doctor Who* (BBC/Universal, 1996).

41. *Daily Mirror*, 26 July 1996.

42. *Sunday Times*, 29 March 1987; *Daily Telegraph*, 21 May 1996.

43. *Sunday Times*, 19 September 1999; *Independent on Sunday*, 29 August 1999.

44. www.bbc.co.uk/cult/news/drwho/2004/08/10/13635.shtml (accessed 24 September 2004).

4

Countering the counterculture:
The Prisoner and the 1960s

SUE SHORT

Produced between 1966 and 1967, *The Prisoner* (1st tx. ITV London 1 October 1967–4 February 1968) emerged during a period of radical social transformation. The 1962 Cuban missile crisis had marked the height of Cold War tensions; humankind was about to take a giant leap with the first moon landing; civil rights and anti-Vietnam War demonstrations in the United States signalled a new confidence in the power of protest and a developing counterculture was making its presence felt in music, art and ideology. *The Prisoner* arose out of these cultural circumstances and, with a central theme exploring the conflict between individuality and conformity, it can be seen to share many of the anti-establishment feelings of the decade. However, as closer analysis reveals, the series responds to the period, and the counterculture in particular, with an interesting degree of caution.

In evaluating the programme as both product and critique of the 1960s, this chapter reveals how *The Prisoner* communicates many of the concerns voiced by the era's political dissenters, yet also identifies how the series distances itself from the liberalism characterising the so-called 'hippy' era. Loaded with paradoxes, *The Prisoner* sets forth a treatise on the rights of the individual to be free, yet condemns such activities as promiscuity and drug taking for their demoralising and delusional effects. As such, it appears to have pre-empted the criticisms that have tended to be made only recently of a period in modern history generally prefixed by the terms 'swinging' and 'psychedelic' – thus offering an interesting commentary on the times just as they were changing.

The programme's central premise consists of one man's bid for freedom from a conformist society intent on 'breaking' him, yet the subject is no student radical or political activist existing on the fringes of straight society but a secret agent working for the British government. However, as the show's pre-title sequence reveals, this agent has attempted to resign from his job and is subsequently drugged and kidnapped by unknown agents and taken to a mysterious location known only as 'The Village'. Each episode in the series details the efforts made by this protagonist, played by Patrick McGoohan, and referred to only as 'Number Six', to escape from the strange society in which he has been placed, yet successive failures force him to examine its structure more closely, to determine how it is organised and maintained and repeatedly to defy its various methods of control.

The Village's seaside setting, the stilted upper-class speech codes used by the majority of its population, and specific features such as the Labour Exchange and Citizens' Advice Bureau, all provide it with a curious 'British' quality, yet its exact location remains obscure and the various nationalities of its inhabitants add to the notion that it could, in fact, be anywhere. Despite the Cold War rhetoric upheld by so many conventional spy narratives of the time, *The Prisoner* avoids ascribing a specific geographic identity to its fictional society and thus refuses to align it with any single nation. Consequently, rather than depict the dictatorial policies of the Village authorities as emblematic of the Eastern bloc, the series urges viewers to look beneath the façade of Western democracy. In asking audiences to assess the Village as a microcosm of any advanced industrial nation – one which employs a quaint parochialism to conceal the machinations of a harsh totalitarian state – it initiates a mode of questioning that is at odds with a programme seemingly designed for mere entertainment. Indeed, in terms of what television had previously offered, *The Prisoner* transformed the medium's potential to convey complex, even radical ideas, in an innovative and searching manner.

Situated in what appears to be a holiday resort, 'residents' are both imprisoned and indoctrinated, mouthing platitudes to one another that express nothing of what they really feel. The gaily coloured costumes worn by these inhabitants fail to conceal the misery of their expressions and they appear to be devoid of the individual or collective will necessary to effect change. Ranged against them is the full arsenal of the anti-utopian tradition: each resident is depersonalised and numbered, in a manner reminiscent of Yevgeny Zemyatin's *We* (1924); mass observation of the kind found in George Orwell's *Nineteen Eighty-Four* (1949) covertly monitors activity, including the use of television as a means of surveillance; and drugs are used to manipulate perception and memory, recalling Aldous Huxley's *Brave New World* (1932). Yet perhaps the most obvious influence is the work of Franz Kafka, particularly his preoccupation with revealing the repressive means by which an anonymous power preserves social order.

As with Kafka's writing, the series mixes the absurd and the abysmal in the bizarre world of the Village, and Number Six's continual fight with the authorities there, like so many of Kafka's protagonists, demands to be read as a symbolic rather than literal attempt to preserve both sanity and integrity in the face of continual manipulation. Sinister control techniques used by the Village authorities range from hypnosis and aversion therapy to the employment of increasingly fantastical devices – such as machines able to screen subconscious thoughts and an all-seeing robot security force known as 'Rover'. Like Swift's Gulliver, whose travels abroad highlight the foibles of his own world and the people in charge there, Number Six's experiences in the Village are a distorted, satiric vision of the very world from which he has attempted to resign – a place that is both nightmarish and strangely familiar.

The Prisoner not only questions how authority is exercised over people but also demonstrates how such power conceals itself. Indeed, the true radicalism of the series lies in locating such concerns within a seeming utopia – a sunny seaside setting where people have the appearance of carefree holidaymakers – in order to ask questions about the nature of freedom and individuality within a supposed democracy. Because coercive measures are used to restrict individual freedom and maintain the status quo, the Village can be seen to represent the very totalitarianism and bureaucracy that an idealistic generation was rebelling against in the 1960s. However, Patrick McGoohan was somewhat removed from this generation and their beliefs, as was the character he played. Recognition of the key role McGoohan had in devising the series is vital to understanding its intentions, for while *The Prisoner* offers a radical critique of contemporary democracies, it also dramatises McGoohan's own discontents, on both a personal and a professional level, with the world at large, with targets that extend beyond the 'establishment' itself and which can even be seen to operate in its defence at times. Accordingly, the entire series can be attributed not only to McGoohan's 'genius' but also to his ego.

In many ways, the show's premise of a man attempting to resign from his job reflects the level of dissatisfaction experienced by the actor himself. McGoohan was bored with playing John Drake, the lead character in the popular series *Danger Man* aka *Secret Agent* (ITC, 1960–67) and wanted to create a new twist on the spy genre. He was also in the unique position of having a powerful foothold in his established role with the commercial TV production company ITC (Independent Television Corporation), one he was able to exploit when pitching his idea for *The Prisoner* to ITC managing director Lew Grade. An unprecedented amount was invested in the series (£75,000 per episode) and an unusual degree of trust placed in McGoohan. With a willing financier eager to retain his services at seemingly any cost, McGoohan's concept can be seen as the ultimate vanity project – one whose existence can largely be attributed to the unique position he found himself in.

It is not surprising, therefore, that the themes examined in the programme have been understood as the product of its star-auteur. Indeed it is perhaps all too easy to idealise McGoohan's role in the series and to forget the vital parts played by producer David Tomblin and script editor George Markstein – who devised the series' founding idea of a secret location where spies are not only debriefed but forcibly detained in the interests of state security. Yet it is McGoohan who pitched the idea to Grade; McGoohan who headed the company responsible for bringing it to fruition; McGoohan who wrote and directed a number of key episodes; and, of course, McGoohan who played the lead role with such unforgettable intensity. The corresponding attempt by one man to exert his will on the shaping of a series can thus be seen to complement Number Six's equivalent effort to assert his individuality and resist coercion.

That compromises were made in getting McGoohan's vision on screen, including extending the series' original concept of seven episodes in order to make the show more appealing for syndication, proves the extent to which all creative ventures must yield to the demands of commerce, no matter how bankable their lead. Nevertheless, McGoohan exercised a degree of control that was and remains remarkable. In fact, stories that have surrounded production of the series make McGoohan sound at times like one of the petty authoritarian dictators that were so frequently caricatured in the series, thus lending a particular irony to the show's central theme of individuality versus society. Even the character he plays serves as a cipher for his own personality. Not only does Number Six share McGoohan's birthday but biographical elements are also used in the penultimate episode, 'Once Upon a Time' (1st tx. ITV London, 28, January 1968), to outline Number Six's past.[1] Furthermore, both men share the same fundamental mission, for they attempt to assert individual will against officialdom, to retain identity and integrity in the face of conformity and commercialism, and in a sense both men invariably fail. According to most accounts, McGoohan became obsessed with the project, hiring and firing at will, causing Markstein to leave after the thirteenth episode (thereby exercising full artistic control at the expense of the show's continuity) and generally succumbing to megalomania in delivering the episodes promised.[2]

In addition to lambasting the British electoral and educational systems as working to create a contrived consensus and criticising the medical establishment for similarly helping to induce conformity, the series thus has an extra-textual resonance in exposing the flaws of any individual with too much power at his disposal. While McGoohan, like Number Six, set out to criticise the world at large, he ultimately showed how easily good intentions may become corrupted. It is in this sense also that the series can be seen to comment on the 1960s as a period in which social criticism and ideals were at their highest yet equally susceptible to compromise and corruption. As a character dubbed 'the Colonel' comments in the episode 'Checkmate' (1st tx. ITV London, 3 December 1967): 'We all eventually join the enemy against ourselves.' A re-examination of the values and themes explored in the programme makes this seemingly inevitable fact all the more explicit and can even be interpreted as a deliberate acknowledgement, on McGoohan's part, of how easily we may lose our way in attempting to maintain specific ideals.

Chris Gregory, author of the book *Be Seeing You…: Decoding the Prisoner* (1997), perceives the conflict faced by both McGoohan and his fictional alter ego as emblematic of the period, and reads particular significance in the fact that 'As McGoohan was making *The Prisoner*, The Beatles were recording their masterwork *Sgt Pepper's Lonely Hearts Club Band* (1967).' In Gregory's view, 'The figure of McGoohan as an individual against the establishment was one with which many young people identified, just as they did with Jagger, Dylan, Lennon or Jim Morrison.'[3] However, McGoohan was not only considerably older than these quintessential angry and rebellious young men; his beliefs were not in keeping with the values of the burgeoning countercultural movement with which each singer was, in various ways, associated. In fact, although *The Prisoner* takes issue with the notion of government and mainstream society, it is also hostile to the 'alternative' lifestyles being promoted at the time.

One such criticism concerns recreational drug use. While Timothy Leary was urging a generation to 'tune in, turn on and drop out' of conventional society by taking LSD, McGoohan depicted drugs as dangerous and debilitating. Hence although drugs were invested with transgressive potential by the 'hippy' counterculture of the 1960s – perceived as a means of breaking through the hegemonic notion of a singular reality – they are critically viewed in the series as a means of social control, utilised by the powers that be to gain acquiescence from potentially disruptive subjects.

The history of the emerging drug culture of the 1960s is perhaps important to note here, for subcultural experimentation with drugs such as LSD was clearly a subversion of their intended use within clinical psychology as a means of straightening out the abnormal mind.[4] *The Prisoner*'s depiction of drugs in the Village, where they are administered to quell 'deviant' behaviour and elicit co-operation, returns us to these origins. The scenes that take place in the Village hospital are by far the most disturbing images of the series, featuring shots of jittering bodies in darkened corridors and shock treatments being administered to unfortunate residents. The implications are reminiscent of Ken Kesey's landmark countercultural novel *One Flew Over the Cuckoo's Nest* (1962), which uses a mental hospital – termed 'the Combine' – as a metaphor of totalitarian society, where aberrant individuals are similarly processed and contained.

In Kesey's symbolic hospital, drugs are used to impede the mental functioning of inmates and thus ensure the smooth running of the ward. However, for the book's narrator, Chief Bromden, 'madness' provides insight. He experiences hallucinatory scenes that expose the mechanical workings of both the 'Big Nurse' in charge of the ward and the symbolic world she controls. As witness to 'crazy horrible things too goofy and outlandish to cry about and too much true to laugh about', he watches patients being dissected by robot workers at night – a surreal reflection of the dehumanising processes that go on during the day.[5] The inspiration for such 'visions' would ironically help to extol the virtues of drug use within the burgeoning counterculture, for although state-controlled drugs are critiqued in the novel for limiting the individual's capacity for resistance, they were also partly responsible for the book's creation. Kesey worked at Menlo Park hospital and experimented with the medication there – including LSD – while writing the novel. After the book's success, he became a founding member of the Merry Pranksters – a prominent element of psychedelic culture who toured North America in a converted school bus celebrating the effects of LSD in what were termed as 'Acid Tests' or 'Happenings'. Accordingly, despite appearing to denounce the use of mind-altering drugs in his novel, Kesey ultimately became one of their greatest advocates.

Just as Kesey used the profits from his novel to finance his countercultural experimentation, so McGoohan capitalised on the success of *Danger Man* to create *The Prisoner* – his own equivalent 'experiment'. Moreover, just as Kesey was very much in control of the 'acid' dropped on the bus and of where the Pranksters went and what they did when they got there,[6] so McGoohan exercised comparable control over his own 'vehicle', behaving in a manner that was far from communal, egalitarian or easy-going. Yet while drugs were the hip new currency of Kesey's self-appointed governorship, deemed intrinsic to wresting consciousness from straight society's grip, such thinking was anathema to McGoohan, whose denunciation of narcotics in *The Prisoner* is both absolute and irrevocable.

The Village, like Kesey's fictional Combine, relies on drugs to maintain control over its citizens, yet the series dismisses any potentially liberating or enlightening effects that psychotropics might offer. Instead drugs are portrayed as an obstacle to Number Six's liberty, draining his energy, distorting his perception, and even threatening his sanity. However, drugs are presented as only one means of mental manipulation in both the Village and the Combine and both texts describe the more extreme techniques used to drain people of their individuality. By referring to such barbaric procedures as lobotomies and electroshock therapy, both McGoohan and Kesey question the methods used to treat actual 'mental' patients at the time. They also appear to draw on the work of radical 1960s' psychologist, R.D. Laing, who criticised mental health practices as a covert means of social control. Indeed *The Prisoner* takes these ideas to an extreme by portraying human victims of Pavlovian behavioural conditioning experiments, with some 'patients' killed in the bid to ensure conformity.

The extent to which people can be controlled is a crucial theme in Kesey's and McGoohan's work and there are remarkable similarities in the conclusions they reach. Both *One Flew Over the Cuckoo's Nest* and *The Prisoner* are essentially about imprisonment and individuality, questioning the degree to which genuine freedom is ever achievable. In the novel, Kesey's seemingly irrepressible protagonist, Randle P. McMurphy, is a free-spirited nonconformist transferred from jail to a mental hospital for what he thinks will be an easier life. What he learns instead is that the regime in hospital is designed to crush a man's spirit, to turn inmates against one another and to preserve the established order at all cost. Although he endeavours to fight the system, he is ultimately defeated.

The Prisoner is equally allegorical in questioning what constitutes lack of freedom. Life in the Village seems easy enough. Few residents are seen to work, accommodation and meals are provided, and a wealth of leisure time is available. Indeed they seem to be on a permanent vacation. However, as the series reveals, while this existence may seem carefree, it is strictly monitored and controlled and is therefore the equivalent of an elaborate prison. In the opening episode, 'Arrival' (1st tx. ITV London 1 October 1967), the newly arrived Number Six watches as a procession of Villagers freeze at a single command from Number Two – the individual ostensibly in charge of events. The action serves two purposes. Primarily, it enables the detection and removal of a presumed transgressor from the crowd, yet it additionally warns the newcomer of the consequences of breaking the Village's rules. It is a nightmarish moment, designed to indicate the triumph of social engineering at work, yet it fails as a deterrent for, like R.P. McMurphy, Number Six is a rebel intent on fighting the system at virtually any cost. Unlike McMurphy, however, whose troublesome mind is ultimately lobotomised, there are limits to what those in charge are prepared to do to gain Number Six's cooperation. Since his mind is considered a unique commodity, which they cannot risk damaging, he is protected from the Village's more barbaric methods of coercion. He therefore assumes a position of relative superiority to the other residents, and this crucially enables him to retain his sense of self. By contrast, the majority of his fellow inmates are portrayed as docile sheep and he derisively refers to them, on more than one occasion, as 'a row of rotten cabbages' ('Free For All', 1st tx. ITV London, 22 October 1967; 'The General', 1st tx. ITV London, 5 November 1967). The drugged stupor evident in so many close-ups of their faces makes the series' critique clear: in McGoohan's view, drugs are a social pacifier, rather than the perceptual stimulant advocated by Kesey, Leary and others.

Other aspects of the series seem to oppose emerging counter-cultural trends, suggesting that it is not governmental power itself that is expressly targeted in *The Prisoner* but a laissez-faire attitude to both sexual and psychedelic experimentation – an attitude consid-ered by conservative groups at the time to be both misguided and potentially damaging to the social order. That the show seems to concur with this conservative stance is perhaps one of its greatest ironies. Ian Rakoff, an editorial assistant on the programme and author of *Inside The Prisoner*, has described the series as 'A journey to save an individual from moral decline into the anonymity of the melting community. It was the battle of the 1960s.... At the heart of it is the question: what boundary can or should exist between the individual and authority.'[7]

McGoohan has never elaborated on the enigmatic qualities of the series, yet his own ethical principles were clearly invested in *The Prisoner* and can be seen to condemn specific freedoms rather then champion them, voicing concern against what has frequently been dubbed the 'permissive society' of the 1960s. Indeed, in a rare disclosure, McGoohan explicitly states that it is the prospect of living

BETWEEN AUTHORITARIANISM AND ANARCHY   The enigmatic
Number Six (Patrick McGoohan) in *The Prisoner*.

in a libertarian society that truly alarms him, asserting: 'I've always
been obsessed with the idea of prisons in a liberal democratic society.
I believe in democracy but the inherent danger is that with an excess
of freedom in all directions we will eventually destroy ourselves.'[8]
Hence far from simply condemning the machinations of a repressive
Orwellian regime and despite the dystopian elements so apparent in
the series, it is the consequence of having too much freedom that
clearly concerns McGoohan. It is small wonder, then, that *The Prisoner*
is such a puzzle, given that it rails against both authoritarianism and
potential 'anarchy' in equal measure.

In the series, the latter possibility seems to be implicitly connected with the counterculture and it is not only drugs and the
mind-expanding claims being made for them that are condemned in

successive episodes; the concept of 'free love' – another shibboleth of the 'flower power' generation – is also called into question. Changing attitudes towards marriage and fidelity, encouraged in part by the newly available contraceptive pill, were responsible for a shift away from traditional mores regarding sexual behaviour. In an extreme move against this cultural shift, *The Prisoner* adopts a puritan stance towards sexuality, made manifest in its hero's rejection and explicit distrust of women. This antipathy is marked throughout the series and seemingly legitimated by the fact that, from the very first episode, women are frequently used as pawns by the Village controllers, pretending to collaborate with Number Six in order to deceive him. A clear distrust of women results, as stated in 'Dance of the Dead' (1st tx. ITV London, 26 November 1967) when he tells a female Number Two: 'Never trust a woman.' In 'It's Your Funeral' (1st tx. ITV London, 17 December 1967), when a female resident questions why he is so cautious, he replies acerbically: 'Many times bitten, forever shy.' Even Alison (Jane Merrow), the young woman to whom Number Six is closest (and who is even shown to have a telepathic connection to him in 'The Schizoid Man', 1st tx. ITV London, 29 October 1967) eventually betrays him to the authorities, while the demented Sonia (Justine Lord) in 'The Girl Who Was Death' (1st tx. ITV London, 21 January 1968) claims to love him even as she tries to kill him – thereby justifying his distrust of women in general.

There are additional reasons for this aversion towards women and towards the suggestion of any romantic or sexual dalliances that lie outside the text of *The Prisoner*, and within McGoohan's own value system. McGoohan's moral principles were so strong that he famously refused to play James Bond when offered the part because of the permissive sexual behaviour of the character, and he repeatedly defied any attempt to provide John Drake with a love interest on the grounds that this would be unsuitable for a family audience.[9] Yet, as refreshing as this moral stance may seem in terms of moving away from representing women as mere sex objects, *The Prisoner* reiterates stereotyped female behaviour nonetheless, particularly the notion of duplicity. Although women are occasionally placed in powerful positions (there are three female Number Twos in the course of the series), such appointments only prove the degree to which they cannot be trusted. The first of these characters rises from her initial status as maid and ostensible assistant to Number Six in 'Free For All' to maniacal controller of the Village – revealing that she never truly had his interests at heart. The seemingly solicitous 'Mrs Butterworth' (Georgina Cookson) is similarly shown to be deceptive when she is unveiled as the new Number Two at the close of 'Many Happy Returns' (1st tx. ITV London, 12 November 1967). Yet the most fearsome female Number Two (Mary Morris) appears in 'Dance of the Dead', for in suggesting that Number Six is either insane or dead, she tries to undermine his self-belief at its very core.

If not explicitly treacherous or dehumanising, female characters are depicted as damsels in distress who bring out the Prisoner's more chivalrous side, such as the suicidal Number Seventy-Three (Hilary Dwyer) in 'Hammer into Anvil' (1st tx. ITV London, 10 December 1967), or Cathy (Valerie French) in 'Living in Harmony' (1st tx. ITV London, 14 January 1968). At other times, however, he appears to have no such concern for hapless females, even when they are as much victims of the Village authorities as himself. For example, in 'Checkmate', the lovelorn 'queen' (Rosalie Crutchley) is hypnotised into believing that she loves Number Six and consequently follows him everywhere (thus unwittingly providing his captors with knowledge of his every move). Although she lacks any control over the situation, this is inconsequential to Number Six; her devotion earns only his animosity and her increasingly pathetic attempts to be with him are met with continual rejection. Even when she is reduced to tears, the Prisoner's only response is to remark coldly: 'I'm waterproof.'

Co-star and friend Alexis Kanner has commented on this apparent aversion towards women as a tendency exhibited by the star himself, describing McGoohan as 'a man who has always been difficult around actresses and females'. [10] While this comment is obviously conjectural, women in the series are nevertheless repeatedly represented as untrustworthy. As Chris Gregory has pointed out: 'There are two texts of *The Prisoner* – the series itself and the story of its production … in both texts McGoohan is cast as the supreme individualist.'[11] Within the series, women are clearly represented as a threat to this individualism; yet, rather than stemming from any overt misogyny, Number Six's apparent hostility towards women may simply have been introduced by McGoohan to avoid having any romantic encounters, thus preserving his own ethical standpoint regarding sexual mores.

McGoohan's Catholic background doubtlessly influenced his views against portraying sexual intimacy on screen.[12] Indeed he is said to have planned to join the priesthood before pursuing acting. Yet he evinces another kind of moral leadership in *The Prisoner*, upholding particular values such as the sanctity of marriage. Significantly, despite various female plans to ensnare him, Number Six kisses only his fiancée (in 'Do Not Forsake Me, Oh My Darling', 1st tx. ITV London, 7 January 1968) and here another actor plays the part, Number Six's mind having been temporarily placed in another man's body – a strategy that allowed production to continue while McGoohan filmed *Ice Station Zebra* (dir. John Sturges, USA, 1968). This sole reference to a fiancée seemingly proves the Prisoner's heterosexuality while explaining his lack of interest in other women as a mark of his unimpeachable character.

Given *The Prisoner*'s stance on drug use and its marked avoidance of sexual relations, it seems clear that the rebellion launched by Number Six is far removed from that promoted by the 'hippy' movement. Yet it is not simply with regard to drugs and sex that the series opposes the attitudes of the emergent counterculture; it also strikes a blow at the heart of the decade's peace movement. In fact, despite the pacifist stance adopted throughout the series, the final episode, 'Fall Out' (1st tx. ITV London, 4 February 1968), appears to satirise this ideal as an untenable ideological position. A violent revolution breaks out in the Village, with Number Six at its head, culminating in the deployment of what appears to be a nuclear weapon. The fact that innocent people are likely to be annihilated in the process is scarcely considered, and by selecting the Beatles song 'All You Need is Love' as the soundtrack to scenes of violence, including Number Six and his new-found cohorts machine-gunning their way through military guards, the significance of the series' ethical U-turn is ironically highlighted. Not only is it the sole contemporary pop tune to be played throughout *The Prisoner* but its context appears to question the very tenets of 1960s' pacifism, not to mention the pacifism that McGoohan had, up until this moment, equally striven to uphold in the series.

McGoohan has later remarked of the scene: 'There comes a time when rebellion is necessary.'[13] Yet what is particularly notable is that aiding Number Six, with a machine gun of his own, is a character specially written for the last instalment, an archetypal 'hippy' youth referred to as Number Forty-Eight (Alexis Kanner). In fact, Number Forty-Eight seems to have been developed in order to question the efficacy of the countercultural movement as a whole. The character is introduced at the beginning of the episode and asked to stand trial (alongside another alleged dissident) before the Village President. Number Six, his individuality and authority seemingly recognised, observes proceedings from a throne. Although proclaimed by the President as 'the voice of rebellious youth', Number Forty-Eight says nothing of any consequence and is deemed to represent an 'impure' revolt. Dressed in Carnaby Street chic, complete with Sergeant Pepper-style jacket, Buddhist bell and top hat, all he achieves is to cause momentary mayhem amid the assembly by performing a rendition of the spiritual 'Dry Bones' by way of his defence.[14] That the charge against him is read by a masked figure labelled as an 'Anarchist' is itself replete with irony, and in being accused of such crimes as 'total defiance of the elementary laws which sustain our community, questioning the decisions of those who voted to govern us' and 'unhealthy aspects of speech and dress not in accordance with general practice', the counterculture is clearly invoked as an undesirable force. However, it is also seen as incoherent and immature, prompting the President in charge of proceedings to label Number Forty-Eight and the generation he represents as 'uncoordinated youth rebelling against nothing it can define'.

The point is further elaborated at the episode's conclusion, in which, having supposedly escaped the Village through violent means, the youth formerly known as Number Forty-Eight thumbs a lift along a motorway, first in one direction, then the other, revealing in one sense his freedom to go anywhere while also underlining his utter aimlessness and, by extension, that of the counterculture he symbolises. According to Rakoff, the part was based on Mark Davies, a young man working in production on the series, who

> exuded brotherly love and peace. He made no bones about being right up to date, doing drugs and being hooked on macrobiotics. His dress, his walk and his talk were all quintessentially of the period, of the moment. On sunny days, Mark would take his lunch break out on the back lot, ploughing his way through *The Glass Bead Game* (1943) by Herman Hesse, or reading his favourite

science fiction author, Alfred Bester, accompanied by rice balls
with tofu.[15]

McGoohan was apparently fascinated by Davies yet seems to have
adopted only the most superficial aspects of his appearance when
devising Kanner's part. As Rakoff observes: 'In the production,
Kanner's supposed embodiment of the spirit of the moment seemed
an uncomfortable contrivance. It was all "yeah, man", with hair
cropped unfashionably short.'[16] Whether McGoohan deliberately set
out to parody 'hippiedom' with the inclusion of Number Forty-Eight,
or simply failed to address the complexities of the movement he
embodies, remains unclear. In a televised interview given to Warner
Troyer in 1977, McGoohan describes the point of Kanner's character
as symbolising how 'It's easy for us to go astray in youth and he was
astray and he's trying to get everything together again.'[17] To what
degree Number Forty-Eight is 'astray', as McGoohan contends, is not
specified, yet the character's lack of direction and purpose is seemingly intended to describe not simply youth but the counterculture
that his speech and dress so clearly evoke.

Why a direct reference to this movement was left until the final
episode raises a number of questions and may be cynically read as a
hurried attempt by McGoohan to instil greater contemporary relevance
to the programme in its final moments. Steven Paul Davies suggests
that such relevance was always a concern, stating that 'McGoohan
was making his series during the summer of love, acid, Carnaby St.
fashion and The Beatles. These were changing times and he knew it.
McGoohan felt that he should contribute something to this cultural
revolution.'[18] As we have seen, however, his 'contribution' is largely
critical of these changing times. A comment made by McGoohan
in 1996 affirms a sense of promise let down by the aimlessness
he perceived in the countercultural movement, reflecting: 'If only
youth had a leader, I think we would have had a great revolution
which might have changed the face of the earth for a while but
they didn't have a leader.'[19] In truth, there were various leaders and
spokespersons, though McGoohan would not have approved of any
of them, and Number Forty-Eight seems intended to undermine
the revolutionary spirit acknowledged in this later comment. The
character lacks eloquence, is crudely drawn and singularly unworthy

of admiration. He is an adolescent compared to Number Six and is patronisingly told by him, after an energetic yet incoherent outburst against the system: 'Don't wear yourself out.' However, he is not dismissed entirely and Number Six notably adopts his speech codes – similarly referring to the President as 'dad' – before enlisting the young man's help in staging his revolt. By arming 'rebellious youth' with a machine gun the need for decisive action is registered, yet by moving towards violence *The Prisoner* subverts its own pacifist ideals for reasons that remain unclear.

It is a conclusion that seems designed to provoke audiences, particularly as it contradicts the ethical stance upheld previously in the series, for, despite occasional fistfights with guards, Number Six's behaviour is civilised and restrained. At McGoohan's insistence, guns are eschewed, a fact highlighted in the Western episode, 'Living in Harmony'. Here, Number Six's refusal to carry a gun was seen as sympathetic to anti-Vietnam War sentiments in the USA – which seemingly led to the episode being banned by CBS. Although the official reason given for the ban was the use of drugs in the episode, this makes no sense when drugs are (negatively) alluded to throughout the series. In fact, it is particularly inexplicable in this instance as experimentation with drugs is shown fatally to limit the individual's ability to distinguish fantasy from reality.[20] The likelier explanation is that it is the pacifist stance of the story that caused such concern. A plot as recognisably 'American' as a Western, in which a character refuses to draw a gun, clearly makes a definitive statement about the US presence in Southeast Asia, and as the Vietnam War was already attracting considerable dissent at the time, a symbolic refusal to be enlisted in combat was hardly a message American networks wished to promote.

Given such apparent sympathies, the decision to reverse the pacifist stance of the series in its last instalment is odd indeed. Perhaps the use of force in 'Fall Out' is an admission of the fact that violence is sometimes necessary. Perhaps it is intended to indicate that every ideal, no matter how well intentioned, is open to eventual corruption. With hindsight, the use of violence chillingly anticipates the definitive end to the psychedelic 1960s in the Manson murders and the assassination of Martin Luther King. More conservatively, it might be read as a warning against individuality on a mass scale, suggesting that the likely effect this would have on society is complete dissolution. Or it may simply have been motivated by frustration and fatigue on the part of McGoohan, rather than any attempt to capture or criticise the spirit of the age, prompted by the simple desire to end things with a bang.

In deliberately breaking with the pacifism of the series, 'Fall Out' may have had no clearer purpose than to bring a decisive end to an increasingly problematic production. Yet what is most perplexing, if not revealing, is that McGoohan seemingly betrays his own principles in order to provide audiences with a memorable climax. Even in refusing to supply the Bond-style villain expected of him, the episode is all too reminiscent of a Bond scenario – complete with secret underground chamber and military personnel whose central function is merely to be killed. Although violent revolution is ultimately shown to be ineffectual, with the episode's last moments confirming that despite the implied destruction of the Village, nothing has really changed, its inclusion remains discomfiting, for while it may highlight the futility of using force to achieve one's end, it also seriously compromises Number Six's (and also McGoohan's) integrity. Indeed the central message of 'Fall Out' is that as moral individuals struggling to maintain our integrity in the face of compromise and collusion, we have no greater enemy than ourselves.

This is the point at which audiences baulked; when the show's greatest mystery – the question of who is the Number One running the Village – is revealed to be a man resembling Number Six himself. It was an answer audiences were seemingly unprepared for, particularly as it failed to resolve the questions raised in the series in any straightforward manner. The fleeting shot of the contorted face of Number Six's alter ego was understandably perplexing to viewers. Rather than offering any external enemy, it invites a more symbolic reading, asserting that underneath the veneer of civilisation – represented by Number Six – there lies the primal egotistical adversary that we are all, in essence, in conflict with; ready to betray our nobler instincts simply to get ahead. Ironically, it is this revelation that prompts the Prisoner towards violence, his anger unleashed in the missile launch and ensuing break-out from the Village. In many ways, this response is the ultimate denial. Even when confronted with the truth – that Number One is within himself – Number Six still believes that there is another place he can escape to, that returning to his former life will effectively free him from the constraints he has faced, or allow him to evade the issue of his own responsibility. It is this inability to face the truth of his situation that ultimately restricts his freedom because he is unwilling to accept that the Village is vaster than it seems, or that he will always have himself to contend with.

As a supposed 'everyman', Number Six was always a difficult character to fathom: a rebel in a suit who resigned (as he states in 'The Chimes of Big Ben' 1st tx. ITV London, 8 October 1967) due to 'a matter of conscience', he is also very much a 'square' whose adoption of Number Forty-Eight's speech codes comes across more as parody than sympathy. Neither Number Six's lifestyle nor his attitude conforms to the countercultural values of the period. Formerly a government agent of sufficiently high rank to afford a flat in central London – enjoying a lifestyle that includes a servant and in which his prized possession is a Lotus 7 sports car – there is little to indicate that Number Six wishes to abandon the trappings of the material world he so evidently enjoys. (Indeed, the Village authorities test the purity of his revolt by offering him a million pounds in travellers' cheques – which he duly pockets before meeting Number One.) He remains an establishment figure, even in the Village, recognised by the ruling elite as someone special; someone who is even asked to serve as their new leader in 'Fall Out'. While he declines this offer and heads for 'home', the fact that his front door opens automatically in the same way as his residence in the Village restates the somewhat defeatist message that the Prisoner, and by extension we ourselves, can never truly escape.

Previous episodes presage such a conclusion in having falsely led Number Six 'home' on a number of occasions, yet by having him repeat the process the show reiterates the extent to which we are all prisoners of our own making, seemingly compelled to perpetuate the same mistakes through force of habit, a refusal to learn, and an inability to conceive of alternatives. As the series demonstrates, Number Six had a number before he ever entered the Village and sufficient reason to suspect his former employees of being no different to the Village authorities, yet he returns to this life nonetheless as if 'programmed' to do so – revealing that he was more conditioned than he seemed. In effect, the point made is that we are not only our own worst enemies but also our own warders.

Perhaps this was too philosophical an idea for audiences in the 1960s, too problematic in suggesting that, rather than attempt to externalise an enemy, we should look more introspectively at our own values and behaviour. Certainly such a contention makes a great deal of sense in reminding us that we are all responsible, as moral agents, for our actions, yet that there is also a need to look beyond ourselves to the world at large, to believe that change is possible and to strive to make a difference. It is this recognition, after all, that propelled an entire generation towards protest and activism in the name of social change. As Yippie activist Abbie Hoffman has commented: 'The lesson of the 60s is that people who cared enough to do right could change history.'[21] By working to end racial segregation, raising environmental awareness, campaigning for global tolerance and promoting both women's rights and the gay liberation movement, the decade's activists effectively changed not only people's consciousness but the world itself.

By contrast, there is an insistent note of hopelessness in *The Prisoner*'s cyclical narrative. It ends as it begins, with Number Six driving his car under thundery skies, reiterating the sense in which nothing has altered, or is capable of altering. Against a historic backdrop of intense social transformation, this stasis seems remarkably conservative, and here again *The Prisoner*'s ethos, its cautious view of the possibilities for social progress, if not outright rejection, dramatically conflicts with that of the 1960s' counterculture. Daniel O'Brien has argued that the show's cyclical ending can be read as a metaphor of British society – 'absurd, hypocritical, complacent and corrupt'[22] – a reading that encapsulates the pessimism of the series and its bleak stance on the potential for change. While the sheer numbers of activists working together for a common cause defined the political movements of the 1960s, *The Prisoner* does not share this collectivism. Despite the invigorating energy with which Number Six defies the Village authorities, he has no opposing ideology with which to counter them and seems equally hampered by a lack of affinity with others. The suspicion (and derision) with which Number Six views other residents prevents the possibility of collective resistance, and it is notable that his greatest display of concern for their welfare is made in 'It's Your Funeral', when he prevents an assassination plot organised by select residents. While he acts to avoid reprisals, his actions also preserve the status quo. In fact, it is small wonder that potential rebels distrust him, believing him, as in 'Checkmate', to be working against them. Even when he joins forces with other dissidents, most notably in 'Fall Out', he seems to do so entirely for his own benefit, and in resorting to violence he demonstrates how easily idealism founders in the face of opposition.

Estranged from the prevailing optimism of the decade, and for all his ostensible defiance, the Prisoner betrays a pronounced cynicism about the prospects of achieving change. His resignation may be read as the equivalent of 'dropping out', yet ensuing events reveal the impossibility of escaping either the rat race (the London to which he repeatedly returns) or the Village (which is finally seen as the world itself). Although seemingly rebellious, he ultimately does what is expected of him, seemingly caught on an eternal treadmill because of an inability to relinquish his former beliefs. Profoundly 'unmutual', Number Six trusts no one and is distrusted, in turn, by everyone except the authorities he despises. In truth, he never envisages an alternative way of life to the comfortable existence he led before his resignation, and this is why he is unable to be free. As Gary Gerani observes, the series suggests that 'we are all prisoners made content with the comforts of our prosperous liberal democracy, so long as we don't press too hard for answers, push too much for absolute freedom.'[23] *The Prisoner* dramatises what happens when we do 'press too hard' and reveals that Number Six has been a prisoner all along. He may appear to be the quintessential anti-authoritarian figure yet is seemingly afraid of change. A rebel in a suit with a fancy sports car, the Prisoner relies on no one but himself but has nowhere new to go, proving how elusive genuine freedom is when new options are not taken.

The counterculture provided a number of such options, including 'dropping out' of mainstream society altogether, yet many dropped back in again when the going got tough, such as Yippie co-founder Jerry Rubin, who worked on Wall Street in the 1980s, or the activist mentioned in Joan Didion's memoirs who eventually joined the Bank of America's management programme.[24] However, these instances do not mean that the movement itself failed, only that the political and commercial need for conformity takes its prisoners where it can. Ultimately, *The Prisoner* shares a common spirit with the groups that McGoohan seemed so uncertain of: questioning authority, defying convention, experimenting with established art forms and inviting people to think for themselves. Like the counterculture itself, the series should be remembered for what it attempted as much as for what it achieved. In this respect, *The Prisoner* stands unique in British television science fiction and fantasy, retaining an enigmatic quality that increases with the passage of time and continuing to broach issues that are scarcely even considered today. As Number Six states defiantly: 'I will not be pushed, filed, stamped, briefed, debriefed, or numbered. My life is my own.' The series may finally cast doubt upon this last assertion but it remains inspirational nevertheless, like the decade from which it emerged.

NOTES

1. See Steven Paul Davies, *The Prisoner Handbook* (London: Pan–Macmillan, 2002), p. 147 and Alain Carraze and Helene Oswald, *The Prisoner: A Televisionary Masterpiece* (London: Virgin Press, 1990), p. 228.
2. Davies, *The Prisoner Handbook*, pp. 45–52; Ian Rakoff, *Inside The Prisoner: Radical Television and Film in the 1960s* (London: Batsford, 1999), pp. 41–60.
3. Chris Gregory, *Be Seeing You…: Decoding The Prisoner* (Luton: University of Luton Press, 1997), p. 22.
4. Jay Stevens's *Storming Heaven: LSD and the American Dream* (London: Paladin, 1989) documents the historical development of LSD, including its initial use within institutional psychology.
5. Ken Kesey, *One Flew Over the Cuckoo's Nest* (London: Picador, 1973), p. 84.
6. See Tom Wolfe's *The Electric Kool-Aid Acid Test* (1968; London: Black Swan, 1992), which chronicles the Merry Pranksters' travels.
7. Rakoff, *Inside The Prisoner*, p. 158.
8. McGoohan, quoted in Gary Gerani and Paul H. Schulman, *Fantastic Television* (New York: Harmony Books, 1977), p. 121.
9. Gerani and Schulman, *Fantastic Television*, p. 124.
10. Kanner, quoted by Rakoff, *Inside The Prisoner*, p. 171.
11. Gregory, *Be Seeing You…*, p. 32.
12. Rakoff, *Inside The Prisoner*, p. 94.
13. Carraze and Oswald, *The Prisoner*, p. 7.
14. Gregory interprets the song's significance as reference to 'a nation of skeletons, human beings without souls' – and thus the Villagers themselves (*Be Seeing You…*, p. 167).

15. Rakoff, *Inside The Prisoner*, p. 41. Hesse's *The Glass Bead Game* (1943) contains many elements found in *The Prisoner*, including the name Joseph Serf, adopted by McGoohan as directorial credit for two episodes, while the moral quandary presented in the book – which asks when it is right to stop playing the game and act – is a consistent motif within the series, particularly its finale. Such intertextuality suggests some familiarity at least with contemporary countercultural literature, even if familiarity does not necessarily imply sympathy. I am indebted to Lesley Stevenson for pointing out these aspects in Hesse's novel.
16. Rakoff, *Inside The Prisoner*, pp. 75–6.
17. Warner Troyer, interview with Patrick McGoohan for TV Ontario (TVO) in March 1977, available on www.the-prisoner-6.freeserve.co.uk (accessed 1 April 2004).
18. Davies, *The Prisoner Handbook*, p. 157.
19. McGoohan, quoted by Davies, ibid., p. 158.
20. See Rakoff, *Inside The Prisoner*, p. 41.
21. www.gis.net/~lsaver/Abbie Hoffman.html (accessed 1 April 2004).
22. Daniel O'Brien, *SF: UK: How British SF Changed the World* (London: Reynolds & Hearn, 2000), p. 101.
23. Gerani and Schulman, *Fantastic Television*, pp. 122–3.
24. Joan Didion, *The White Album* (London: Flamingo, 1993), p. 288.

5

The age of Aquarius: utopia and anti-utopia in late 1960s' and early 1970s' British science fiction television

JOHN R. COOK

> This is the dawning of the age of Aquarius
> The age of Aquarius...
> Harmony and understanding
> Sympathy and trust abounding
> No more falsehoods or derisions
> Golden living dreams of visions...[1]

On 27 September 1968, the American 'tribal love-rock' musical *Hair* opened in London one day after the abolition of theatrical censorship in Britain. Under the Licensing Act of 1737 and subsequently the Theatres Act of 1843, the Lord Chamberlain had hitherto been required to give prior approval to the performance of plays on the London stage. Now, with his censorship powers having been abolished under a new Theatres Act which had come into law just the day before, there appeared to be no longer any limits to theatrical expression.[2]

The London production of *Hair* was the first beneficiary of this new freedom, with its famous scene in which the entire cast, male and female, appeared nude on stage, emerging from beneath a vast sheet. This could never have been allowed to happen under the old licensing powers of the Lord Chamberlain. As Tom O'Horgan, the director of the London production of *Hair*, stated to the press at the time: 'We couldn't have done the play the way we're doing it prior to this time without drastic modifications'.[3] Just as in the song, it seemed for a moment to be the dawning of a new age – the Aquarian age of 'harmony and understanding', tolerance and permissiveness of which the hippy cast of *Hair* sang. Sweeping away the old, the promised future of 'golden living dreams and visions' seemed to have arrived, and it was here and now in the late 1960s.[4]

As mediated through the 1960s' counterculture in musicals such as *Hair*, the idea of the Age of Aquarius signified the dawning of a new world order – the end of one era and the beginning of another. Astrologically, it describes one of 12 successive 2150-year periods, which correspond to the 12 signs of the zodiac. The previous age, roughly equating with the period since the birth and death of Christ, was now coming to an end; it had been the Age of Pisces. While this Piscean age had been characterised by wars, riots and other forms of civil and ethnic strife propelled by blind faith in religion and political ideology, the new Aquarian age promised a positive future of idealism, enlightenment and an altogether more rational, empirical attitude towards dealing with the various problems besetting the planet.[5] The hippies saw themselves as the children of this new Age of Aquarius, rebelling against the older, more uptight generation of their parents, which represented the Pisceans.

More precise definitions of the Aquarian age are typically hard to come by, and among the counterculture at this time discourses of rationality and permissiveness often seemed to contradict each other and clash; however, one did not need to be a flower child to perceive that in the 1960s Western society and culture appeared to have entered a new era. From John F. Kennedy's 'New Frontier'[6] earlier in the decade to Harold Wilson's mid-1960s' Labourite vision of the 'white heat' of technology,[7] there was a general feeling, even among an older generation of 'Pisceans', that a new future had arrived – a science fiction kind of future – and that it belonged principally to the young.

In Britain the young had been the principal locus of future hopes since as far back as the end of the Second World War and the establishment of the welfare state. Throughout the 1950s there had been tremendous cultural focus on the 'free milk' generation – the first generation to grow up under the new welfare state which had not had to face the twin privations of economic depression and war – and the progress into early adulthood of this new breed of 'welfare

Briton' had been scrutinised closely in newspaper articles, television programmes and books.[8] By the late 1960s, however, this interest had acquired a distinct technological spin – future generations were going to be different not only because they had never had to know the hardships of economic poverty and war, but because they would be entirely familiar and at ease with the coming technological world of the space age: the future of rockets, computers, plastics and all the myriad electronic gadgets and marvels of 'Tomorrow's World'.[9]

The period's bold promise of an imminent technological utopia, to be commandeered by the young, can be seen reflected in some of the most popular British science fiction TV programming of the time. In 1968, following the success of *Thunderbirds* (1965–66) and *Captain Scarlet and the Mysterons* (1967–68), Gerry Anderson's Century 21 production company launched *Joe 90* (1968–69) – a 'Supermarionation' puppet series in which the hero was no longer an adult (as with Jeff Tracy and his sons in *Thunderbirds* or Captain Scarlet) but a mirror image of the show's core audience: a nine-year-old boy.

The premise of the show illustrates the technological utopia point well. 'Joe 90' of the series' title is Joe McClaine (voiced by Len Jones), the adopted nine-year-old son of Professor Ian 'Mac' McClaine (Rupert Davies), who is a brilliant electronics engineer. Mac has created a new super-machine which can record the brain patterns of one person and transfer them to another. When he shows his invention to Shane Weston (David Healy), head of the London office of the World Intelligence Network (WIN), a CIA-style organisation dedicated to maintaining the balance of power, Shane realises the machine's potential to create a new, powerful form of secret agent who would be able to use the skills and experience of any living person in order to accomplish any mission. Weston recommends Joe to be this new super-agent on the grounds that no one would suspect a young boy as a spy.

In this way, nine-year-old Joe becomes special agent 'Joe 90' – outwardly a normal schoolboy but inwardly WIN's most deadly secret agent, equipped with supercomputer amounts of brainpower that allow him direct access to all the world's knowledge in order to fight against the enemies of peace and freedom. At the beginning of each mission, Joe is shown seated in a special chair that rises up within a revolving circular cage, whilst 'psychedelic-style' electronic noises

PSYCHEDELIC SECRET AGENT? Young Joe prepares to expand his consciousness in *Joe 90*.

and lights swirl all around him. This is the curiously named BIG RAT (short for Brain Impulse Galvanoscope Record And Transfer) – the machine that transfers the brain patterns of one person to another. Once the transfer is complete, Joe dons a special pair of 'electrode glasses' when out in the field to activate the brain patterns transferred to him in his father's lab and so trigger the knowledge he needs to accomplish a particular mission. Thus equipped, he has the capability of becoming, as illustrated over the 30 half-hour episodes of the series, an astronaut, a test pilot, a brain surgeon and even in one episode ('The Unorthodox Shepherd', 1st tx. ITV, 22 December 1968), president of the World Bank!

Joe 90, of course, is principally designed as a wish-fulfilment fantasy for late-1960s' schoolchildren, but as such, it helps underscore some of the general cultural tendencies of the period. Through the character of Joe, his brain hardwired at the start of each episode into the BIG RAT supercomputer, the young are shown to be literally at one with technology. His neural downloading of vast amounts of electronically stored data interestingly prefigures our own contemporary technological utopia of the Internet and the dream of instantaneous access to a global storehouse of information and knowledge via computer. Joe is a child of the future: a metamorphosis literally encapsulated within the series' title in the sense that no longer is he simply a nine-year-old boy but instead his status and capacities have been multiplied tenfold to transform him into agent 'Joe 90', his name an appealing futuristic echo of the then distant year of 1990.[10]

While earlier science fiction texts had worried about the effects of brain tampering and, as in John Wyndham's *The Midwich Cuckoos* (1957), the dangers of an Aryan-like future of 'star children' (in both senses of the phrase), by 1968 young Joe, with his blonde hair, preternatural calm and ability to transform both himself and the world around him through the enhanced neural powers of information technology, is held up as the acme of *homo superior*. Fittingly for a TV series aimed at enthusing children, only the young, it is implied, can solve all the current problems of the world and make it a better place. Their minds are more available to new possibilities, and it seems no coincidence that in a series of this period Joe's hard-wiring to his supercomputer is accompanied by 'psychedelic'-style lights and noises, suggesting that the 'doors of perception' may indeed be opening in his case.[11] Yet it is not drugs or any other kind of chemical or physical stimulus that are doing the opening here but rather the miracles of modern computer technology, indicating that in this new world into which the child audience is growing up, it will be brainpower, not brawn, that will resolve all problems and shape the future.

Premiered in the same year, 1968, as the Aquarian dreams of the hippies on stage in *Hair* and in the cinema, director Stanley Kubrick's *2001: A Space Odyssey*, with its own final vision of a 'star child' as the embodiment of all the hopes of mankind in the coming space age, *Joe 90* expressed for its child audience equivalent kinds of 'golden living dreams and visions' of futuristic possibility, appropriate to the then general utopian Zeitgeist. It was a theme that later, 'live action' British science fiction television series aimed at children would specifically go on to refine and develop.

Thus in *The Tomorrow People* (Thames Television for ITV, 1973–79), the metaphor of the new generation as *homo superior* is made literal in the figures of the aptly named 'Tomorrow People', who represent the next stage of human evolution. As embodiments of the rising generation, they have evolved to acquire special powers, including the abilities of telepathy and telekinesis. Most strikingly of all, they can also 'jaunt' – that is, teleport themselves instantaneously from place to place around the universe. Hence, akin to Joe in *Joe 90*, these are young people marked out as 'different' on account of their extra-special powers. Like Joe, they rely for their strength on information technology, in this case on TIM (voiced in the series by Philip Gilbert), a talking 'biotronic' supercomputer, one of whose functions, as with Joe and BIG RAT, is to allow its charges access to all the world's information and knowledge via connection to state information networks, in order that the *homo superiors* may success-fully fight off all kinds of threats to Earth on behalf of the rest of humanity.

In the case of the Tomorrow People, however, their special powers are used to protect the Earth from alien threats on behalf of the Galactic Federation – a peaceful 'United Nations' of space similar in kind to the Federation in *Star Trek* (NBC, 1966–69). As a super-computer constructed by leading 'Tomorrow Person' John (Nicholas Young), with the help of the Galactic Federation, TIM has the role of assisting the *homo superiors* in this fight from their secret base – appropriately called the 'lab' – in a disused tunnel of the London Underground.[12]

Standing firmly in an sf/fantasy tradition of *homo superiors* that takes in, at one end of the spectrum, Wyndham's *The Midwich Cuckoos* and, on the other, popular fantasy action shows such as *The Champions* (ITC,

1968–69),[13] *The Tomorrow People* was actually inspired by two figures whom the show's creator, Roger Damon Price, had encountered in the course of his TV career in the early 1970s. The first was Dr Christopher Evans (1931–79), a leading psychologist and computer scientist of his day, who also had a long-standing interest in science fiction. In 1969 and 1970, Evans edited two anthologies of psychological sf/horror short stories titled *Mind at Bay* and *Mind in Chains*, which featured contributions from many leading writers of these genres, including Brian Aldiss, J.G. Ballard and M.R. James. *Mind in Chains* also included a contribution from Evans himself (co-written with Jackie Wilson) called 'The Dreams of the Computer'. As tellingly suggested by his choice of titles, Evans's dual interests in computer science and psychology had led him to become fascinated by the possibility of there being large areas of the human brain that humans currently could not access, and that if they only could, perhaps through the assistance of computer technology, this would inspire nothing short of a revolution in human consciousness and human progress.[14]

Having met Evans in the course of working on a documentary on him, Roger Price became intrigued with Evans's ideas and would eventually credit him as 'scientific adviser' on *The Tomorrow People* series. The other inspiration for *The Tomorrow People* came on 15 June 1972, when Price met rock star David Bowie on the set of the Thames TV music show *Lift Off with Ayshea*, on which the latter was performing 'Starman' from his famous sf-styled album of that year, *The Rise and Fall of Ziggy Stardust and the Spiders from Mars*. Bowie and Price afterwards became engaged in a long conversation on science fiction. As numerous of the singer's fan sources have since assiduously attested, the Bowie song 'Oh You Pretty Things' (from his 1971 album *Hunky Dory*) became a key influence on *The Tomorrow People*.[15] Certainly, the fourth verse and chorus of the song map directly on to the series, whilst at the same time graphically illustrating the general cultural theme of the period, of the young as somehow intrinsically 'different' and 'better' than their elders:

Look at your children
See their faces in golden rays
Don't kid yourself they belong to you
They're the start of a coming race…
…Homo sapiens have outgrown their use…

...Let me make it plain
You gotta make way for the homo superior...[16]

In *The Tomorrow People*, the transformation of young people into 'the coming race' of *homo superior* is literally dramatised in the process of 'breaking out'. This is when a particular young person first becomes aware of their special powers and starts to 'hatch' as one of the Tomorrow People, usually around their early teens. The shock of realisation that they are different from those around them can be very painful, sometimes fatal, for the individuals concerned and so the role of the established Tomorrow People who have already 'broken out' is to identify all such cases and make immediate contact, helping to guide and advise these fledgling *homo superiors* successfully through the process.

In the drama, individuals often first become aware of their difference from ordinary *homo sapiens* (or the 'Saps' as they are rather scathingly labelled in the series) when they develop telepathy and their minds start to be flooded with the thoughts of those around them. It is at this point that the Tomorrow People, monitoring telepathic signals from their base, realise a new person is trying to 'break out'. If the existing Tomorrow People cannot make telepathic contact or reach these new *homo superiors* in time, these individuals can die due to the extreme shock and physical strain associated with 'breaking out'.

The process is well illustrated in episode one of the very first *Tomorrow People* story ('The Slaves of Jedikiah') when Carol, an established Tomorrow person (played by Sammie Winmill), makes contact with Stephen (Peter Vaughan-Clarke), a hitherto ordinary 14-year-old schoolboy who has started to hear strange voices in his head and thinks he is going mad. The manner in which Carol talks him through the process, persuading him he is not mad but that in fact he is simply becoming aware of previously untapped capacities within himself, illustrates how much the original series' concept owed to Christopher Evans and his theories of the human 'mind in chains':

CAROL   Stephen – look at me. Look carefully into my eyes. Now
    do you trust me?
STEPHEN   Yes.

CAROL   Good. Now I want you to do something. Just try and relax
and imagine that your mind is a fist. A great big fist, clenched
tight. Now let it open, slowly. No – don't let other thoughts come
into your head. Just think of the fist opening very slowly, like a
flower.

STEPHEN   I can feel you, right here inside my head. What's
happening?

CAROL   You're becoming one of us.

STEPHEN   Who's us?

CAROL (echoing)   The Tomorrow People. The Tomorrow People…[17]

In keeping with Evans's theories, the mind is a clenched fist,
unaware of its vast reserves of untapped potential. If humans are
to progress successfully on to the next stage of evolution, they must
learn to open their minds and to free their consciousness, like a
flower opening itself out to the sun. The young are best placed to
make this leap forward since they are not encrusted with the doubts,
habits and disillusioned cynicism of the adult world. As Stephen starts
to make his own leap of faith with the help of Carol, a series of
black-and-white images are superimposed on screen – images which,
in subsequent episodes of *The Tomorrow People*, will be replicated in
the opening titles and which, together with the early synthesiser
theme tune by Dudley Simpson, are perhaps the most hauntingly
memorable aspect of the series. In accordance with Carol's advice,
the sequence begins with a clenched fist slowly opening to expose
to the screen an upturned palm, and then, with this symbolic freeing
of consciousness, a barrage of still images follow one after the
other, appearing out of the middle distance and rushing towards
the viewer in ever-quickening succession: a close-up of a flower; a
space telescope shot of a far-distant galaxy; four figures silhouetted
against a mysterious lunar landscape; the faces of Stephen and his
fellow Tomorrow People; an unborn baby in the womb, and so on.
As the last image seems explicitly to acknowledge, this rushing effect
is similar to the famous 'star gate' sequence in Stanley Kubrick's *2001:
A Space Odyssey*, in which astronaut Dave Bowman (Keir Dullea) was
propelled headlong through space and time for his own eventual
cosmic rendezvous with his 'star child'.

Freeing the mind to open itself up to its hidden potential will, it is
implied, produces an accelerated form of consciousness appropriate

to the modern world of industrial progress and the emerging space age. As Carol puts it to Stephen in this opening episode with respect to the past century of rapid technological advance: 'In the last 100 years, everything has speeded up. The world has changed out of all recognition. And human beings have changed with it.' She goes on: 'Perhaps every child is a Tomorrow Person but doesn't realise it. Or is too frightened to.'

Even more so than *Joe 90*, *The Tomorrow People* is thus cleverly basing its central appeal on a potent form of fantasy identification on the part of the watching child audience. By telling its viewers that any of them could potentially be a 'Tomorrow Person', the series is reassuring each individual child that he or she is special and different. Children are held up as important because – in contrast to the adult generation, including, satisfyingly for the target audience, current authority figures like parents and teachers – they represent the next stage of progress as they will literally be the people of tomorrow. Just like Joe in *Joe 90* with his sharper brainpower and enhanced ability to assimilate vast amounts of information in order to resolve international problems, the young are shown to be innately superior to current adults and ultimately, it is suggested, only they will have the capacity to change the world. As Carol puts it to Stephen in the very first episode, if more and more Tomorrow People manage to 'break out', then 'we can take over – stop wars and put the world in order'. Stephen is incredulous: 'Us children?' he asks. Carol's response is significant: 'Oh, yes. You see – we're mankind's only hope of survival. We're peaceful…'

These, then, are the children of the Aquarian age – the tomorrow people who will bring the Piscean era of wars, strife and race riots to a close, ushering in a new epoch of peace, rationality and enlightenment through an expanded form of consciousness and a sense of global connectedness and mutual interdependence. It was a concept that seemed to strike a chord with young audiences of the 1970s as the original *Tomorrow People* series went on to run for six years, becoming the most popular children's science fiction series Thames TV had produced. In celebrating the potential uniqueness of every child, it also, appropriately for its Aquarian ethos, embraced ethnic and cultural difference, featuring a range of black and Far Eastern actors among its group of *homo superiors* at a time when role models for children from ethnic minorities were few and far between on British television. One such character, Elizabeth (played by Elizabeth Adare), joined the cast in the second season in 1974 and stayed to the very end of the series in 1979, so aware was she of her position as a role model for black British youth.[18]

By that time, however, the Aquarian ideals of emancipated progress towards a utopian future which had underscored the original creation of the series back in the early 1970s seemed tired and out of date in the era of punk rock, strikes and the incipient dawn of Thatcherism. The series had long since gone into decline, as evidenced by increasingly desperate gimmicks such as casting momentarily famous teenage pop stars as Tomorrow People (Mike Holloway of the band Flintlock) and employing laughable special effects due to reduced production budgets, until the final four-part story in 1979, 'War of the Empires', featured a group of aliens called the Sorsons that resembled nothing other than giant walking sink plungers and whose catchphrase, on landing on Earth, was wilfully unoriginal: 'Take me to your leader!' Given such a context, it was perhaps symbolically fitting that it was a strike (by ITV technicians) which finally brought production of the original 1970s' series to a shuddering halt in 1979.[19]

In the early 1970s, however, the metaphor of the young 'breaking out' in order to forge their own identities, separate and distinct from the existing world of adults, was a potent one. The series presented its young audience with a vision of empowerment: it said it was alright to feel separate and different from the world around you and it reassured that there were others of one's peer group who had gone through what you would go through and who would look after you and see you through the changes you were going to experience. In that sense, it seems no coincidence that in the drama 'breaking out' to become a Tomorrow Person occurred to characters in their early teens, for on this level what the series seemed to be offering was a studied metaphor for early adolescence, one that may in turn account for its level of success among young audiences during this period.

As the hippies in *Hair* had demonstrated in abundance, sex was of course a fundamental part of the liberation of humanity promised by the Aquarian age, but on heavily regulated British television of the period this aspect of the possible utopian future had to be treated with a great deal of circumspection. This was especially the case with TV science fiction, which, as with shows like *The Tomorrow People*, had a tremendous appeal to children and early teenagers. In turn, this tended to foster misleading assumptions among many working in television during this time that science fiction was a genre *only* of interest to those groups. Hence, even when working on supposedly 'adult-orientated' science fiction shows, producers of popular series, particularly on commercial television, had to be very careful not to push the boat out too far with regard to the depiction of sex, as well as violence, lest they find themselves disbarred from access to the youth audience that was often a crucial component for ratings success.

When, for example, after *Joe 90* and a final ill-fated puppet series, *The Secret Service* (Century 21/ITC, 1969), Gerry Anderson's Century 21 production company eventually got the green light to make a live action TV science fiction show aimed at adults, *UFO* (Century 21/ITC, 1969–70), it sometimes found it difficult to balance its desire to gesture in a more 'adult' way at the possibilities of personal and sexual liberation in the new technological utopian future that seemed to be just around the corner, with the then current boundaries of mainstream television acceptability. Reusing many of the props, costumes and much of the cast from the Anderson-produced 1968 British sf feature film *Doppelgänger* (aka *Journey to the Far Side of the Sun*), *UFO* anticipates a science fiction future that is only ten years away from the date of production – over images of spacecraft and moonbases in the opening titles, the caption '*1980*' repeatedly flashes up on screen. Earth is under attack from marauding UFOs, piloted by aliens from a dying planet who need to harvest human body parts in order to prolong their own lifespans. It is the job of secret military organisation SHADO (Supreme Headquarters Alien Defence Organisation), from its base beneath the 'Harlington–Straker' film studios on the outskirts of London, to repel these invaders and minimise public awareness of the danger.

Yet what might at first seem a dark proto-*X Files* (Fox Television, 1993–2002) narrative of government secrecy in the face of an alien threat is at the same time mediated by the sheer seduction of its late-1960s' vision of the imminent technological utopia to come, as exemplified by its striking sets, props and costumes. For this is a world

DRESSED TO KILL   The female operatives of Moonbase in *UFO*.

of 'groovy' hairstyles (female Moonbase operatives wear futuristic purple wigs; SHADO commander Ed Straker, played by Ed Bishop, has dyed blond hair cut in a tapered style); Nehru jackets worn over poloneck sweaters; sleek futuristic cars with powered gull-wing doors and built-in car phones; lavish studio sets awash with state-of-the-art computers and other high-tech equipment; plus the aforementioned Moonbase – an impressive complex on the lunar surface from which interceptor craft are launched to provide the first line of defence against the invading aliens.

Also, as later commentators have remarked, *UFO* boasted 'one of television's shapeliest regiment of women, dressed to kill in tight-fitting catsuits', not to mention their boutique-style mauve wigs.[20] The commander of the Moonbase is a female, Lieutenant Gay Ellis (Gabrielle Drake). If, on one level, the series depicts a future world of gender equality where women work alongside men in positions of authority, it is nevertheless frequently the commander's physical attributes that the show chooses to foreground: for example, the very first episode, 'Identified' (1st tx. ATV Midlands, 16 September 1970), presents a short 'striptease montage' sequence of her changing into a silver miniskirt at the Moonbase (accompanied by a very knowing, innuendo-laden organ theme on the soundtrack), openly watched by a male colleague. Hence while this is a depicted future of greater freedom and equality between the sexes, it is also a veritable sexual playground. Its world of gadgets, super-vehicles and pneumatic, available women in the workplace, commanded over by identity-inviting male heroes such as Ed Straker, is ultimately a late-1960s' male liberatory fantasy.

Perhaps *UFO*'s most explicit – and controversial – nod towards the new freedoms afforded by the social and cultural changes of the late 1960s came in its final episode, 'The Long Sleep', which was in fact never transmitted in the series' original transmission run during 1970–71. This was because the episode contained specific references to hallucinogenic drug use, which proved too much for the ITV of the period; the episode was pulled from the initial series run, only to be premiered finally in March 1973 in a late-night slot.[21] The episode emphasised the difficulties during this time of attempting to make a popular British TV science fiction series with more adult themes on the commercial ITV channel. The desire to produce a science fiction series that would also have appeal to adults through the use of knowing sexual innuendo and reflection of contemporary mores had, in the case of this particular episode, the effect of simply exiling *UFO* to a graveyard slot far away from the important youth audience. Among ITV schedulers and regulators of the period, science fiction TV was still something regarded as mainly for kids, and hence 'adult' themes in this genre were especially difficult to handle. *UFO* ran for only one series and never got a prime-time network launch, with many ITV regional companies either burying it in a late-night-viewing slot or scheduling it where they felt science fiction TV belonged most comfortably – in children's viewing slots, such as teatime or Saturday morning.[22]

Popular generic drama of the period would thus always have difficulties explicitly mediating the full extent of the proclaimed freedoms of the new counterculture to a mass audience. One area of programming that was permitted to do so with more licence, however, was the single television play, particularly at the BBC. In the 1960s and 1970s, the single TV play functioned as a kind of 'cutting edge' for British television, extending the limits of what could be said on screen socially, sexually and politically, and, even more, what could be *shown*.[23] It provided a 'free space' for challenge and innovation in the schedules, often from new writing and directing talent that was allowed to experiment and find its voice. Each week, with BBC TV play slots such as *The Wednesday Play* (1964–70) and *Play for Today* (1970–84), viewers knew, when they sat down to watch, that for the next 75 minutes they might well have their tastes and preconceptions challenged. Particularly at the BBC, television managers and schedulers tacitly encouraged this. In contrast to widespread institutional attitudes of the time to popular series and serial programming, which were often regarded as 'anonymous mass-produced fodder', the single play was seen to a far greater extent as 'art'. Thus it was more immune (though not wholly) to the twin television pressures of ratings imperatives and censorship since to interfere with a play would be to challenge the right to artistic freedom of expression of the TV playwright.

Due to these various factors, the single play could engage more directly with the social and cultural battles of the period, including the push for greater freedom and permissiveness advocated by proponents of the new counterculture, against those who were implacably opposed. In an early play, one of these new TV playwrights, Dennis Potter, dramatised how much this was a battle that was taking place right inside the home itself and in front of the television screen, as suburban families found themselves confronted for the first time with the 'fruits' of the new permissiveness relayed via their TV set. In *Angels Are So Few* (1st tx. BBC 1, 5 November 1970), Potter portrays a suburban husband and wife who suddenly find themselves watching a BBC TV documentary – a parody of the style of socially voyeuristic 'fly on the wall' documentaries of the period that often featured in BBC 2's *Man Alive* series (1965–82) – in which cameras are recording the filming of an orgy for a blue movie. Asked in an interview why she is taking part, one of the female participants boldly iterates the spirit of the new Aquarian counterculture: 'I – um – have found a sense of personal freedom and self confidence… You finally discover that [sex] is something to enjoy, a harmless thing, a beautiful thing.' The suburban husband, watching at home, is outraged: 'That is a straightforward incitement to perversion and immorality. The BBC have lost all sense of responsibility and decorum.' His wife simply watches on, fascinated.[24]

For those TV playwrights like Potter who were ambiguous about and conflicted by the advent of the new counterculture, these changes had happened with bewildering speed: 'The way things are going, in a few years time, actresses will be required to copulate on the stage', he would remark in an interview a few years later.[25] But it was a science fiction writer, Nigel Kneale, utilising the greater freedoms afforded to him by the single play format, who would explore these ideas more fully and extrapolate from them a startling conclusion in his 1968 television play *The Year of the Sex Olympics*.

First broadcast in colour on 29 July 1968 in the *Theatre 625* slot, as part of early colour transmissions on BBC 2, *The Year of the Sex Olympics* looks forward to a future that a teasing subtitle at the very start of the play announces is 'Sooner than you think…'[26] Society is divided into two distinct classes – 'high-drives' and 'low-drives'. The 'high-drive' class has a range of freedoms which the 'low-drives' are denied due to a serious overpopulation problem. As with George Orwell's famous novel *Nineteen Eighty-Four* (1949), the masses must be constantly watched and controlled by an elite few with access to special privileges and knowledge which the majority are forbidden, and, like Orwell's notion of the 'telescreen' in *Nineteen Eighty-Four* that watched citizens' every move, key to this surveillance is television.

In Orwell's novel, the personal intimacy of sex, however, was a means for refuseniks of the Big Brother society to escape temporarily its utter dehumanisation. In Kneale's play, by stark contrast, sex becomes the ultimate means of social control. A key speech in *The Year of the Sex Olympics* crystallises this theme as TV executive Ugo Priest (played by Leonard Rossiter) recalls for young producer Nat Mender (Tony Vogel) a time when there used to be such concepts as 'censorship' and 'pornography'. Then came the breakthrough: those in control found that if they simply screened everything on TV with no censorship and screened it 'king-style', the audience would basically make do with that – the second-hand sexual experience in place of the real thing. The breakthrough, he says, was therefore to 'fight fire with fire. Sex with sex' until 'they doused it in the end' and there were no more tensions in the world: no more wars; no more overpopulation issues. Everything, instead, had come under complete 'apathy control'. In this way, the mantra that all the pacified characters chant as a kind of article of faith in *The Year of the Sex Olympics* is 'Watch. Not do.'[27]

Given the period in which the play was written – the era of peace and free love in which sexual liberation, it was believed, was going to help usher in the much-vaunted Age of Aquarius – this was a startling proposition to make on Kneale's part. Far from the sexual revolution producing the desired utopia as the counterculture promised, Kneale was suggesting it could actually bring about its precise opposite: a nightmare society of stifling control and conformity where the sheer ubiquity of sexual imagery of all kinds would render citizens completely apathetic, desensitised, not to mention turned off the real thing; thus nullifying any revolutionary challenge to the established order which greater explicitness in sexual representation might once have posed.

The play fleetingly depicts the 'sex Olympics' of its title, in which sex has been reduced to the ultimate spectator sport for the vicarious society as nubile couples compete in ever more elaborate positions for their fifteen minutes of fame on TV, while slick commentators translate their every move for a watching audience that is shown in the play to be equally as inactive, trapped and repressed as the suburban couple who viewed the orgy in Dennis Potter's *Angels Are So Few*. Thus Kneale's strikingly paradoxical insight was that the greater explicitness of representations that the 1960s had ushered in (which, of course, would only proliferate in subsequent decades) might in the end come to serve the interests of those who wished to control and curtail our sexual behaviour; 'Watch. Not do' succeeding where the censor had failed. As the writer himself put it in a 1998 interview:

> It was a comment on television and the idea of the passive audience. At that time, the population explosion was a very hot topic and it was also the time when *Hair* was on and people were saying 'let's put porn on stage'. So I put these ideas together and took them to their logical conclusion.[28]

While the children of Aquarius were singing on stage of the promised future of 'golden living dreams of visions' which the imminent collapse of censorship would help bring about, Kneale was looking forward and postulating a very different kind of conclusion. His play was also a satire on television and the direction he believed it could go. His world of 'high-drives' – television cognoscenti pumping out bland visual palliatives to legions of 'low-drives' – is a savage auto-critique of 1960s' TV, with its elite cadre of television professionals free to indulge in the fruits of liberation of the new 'permissive society', whilst the watching masses, like the couple from Dennis Potter's similarly minded play, remain trapped and repressed, looking in from outside. This reading is reinforced by Kneale's own comments to *The Times* in an interview at the time the play was being filmed, when he talked of the small, untypical, active 'in-group' who ran the TV service in his futuristic society and made the programmes: 'They're the ones who have the real fun as indeed I suppose is true of television today.'[29]

Yet while it may have distinct 1960s' echoes, of all the imagined visions of the future Age of Aquarius which this chapter has examined, only *The Year of the Sex Olympics* still seems to have resonance for our own time. As we have seen, popular British science fiction series such as the Century 21 productions *Joe 90* and *UFO*, as well as Thames TV's *The Tomorrow People*, mediated in their different ways the utopian hopes and dreams of a new Aquarian order of enlightenment and rationality led by the young. Yet these are now looked back upon fondly with nostalgia precisely because their visions of the future have become so dated; they tell us much about the culture and attitudes of the late 1960s and early 1970s which produced them.

The Year of the Sex Olympics is different. At the time it was transmitted, many TV reviewers did not know quite what to make of it, finding, in particular, the second half of the play somewhat troubling and implausible.[30] In this, a young and idealistic 'high-drive' accidentally falls to his death during a live TV broadcast. Far from being horrified, however, the audience loves it. Soon the TV controllers, realising that saturation point has been reached with sexual images, hit upon a new idea to keep the viewers watching and so neutralise social tensions: a family of 'high-drives' is cast away on a desert island where the various members have to eke out a raw survival for the audience's entertainment, all the time being watched 24 hours a day by hidden TV cameras. In this way, with what he calls in his play the 'Live-Life Show', Kneale predicts the world of reality TV shows such as *Big Brother* (Endemol for Channel Four, 2000–), *Castaway 2000* (BBC TV, 2000) and *Survivor* (CBS, 2000–; ITV, 2001) thirty years before they actually happened. Shifting distinctly from sex to sadism in its second half, the play ends in an orgy of violence as the family discovers it shares its new home with a psychotic inhabitant and murder starts to take place on the island, all of this lapped up in a frenzy of voyeuristic excitement by the 'low-drive' audience watching at home.

The Year of the Sex Olympics may have been greeted with some puzzlement in its own time but it thus leaps startlingly forward to our own: to today's world of media saturation; 'reality TV', as well as graphic and explicit sexual images deployed casually for commercial purposes in a media climate where previously strict regulations on content are rapidly being relaxed in the name of greater freedom and competition. In Kneale's play, the TV controller Ugo Priest also compares past with present. In the past, he says, the 'censor stopped things for going too far'. Now 'we stop 'em for not going far enough'.[31] The question that Kneale posed by the play and that, unlike those other more dated visions of the future we have examined, arguably still has applicability for our own time is, if everything becomes permissible and can be shown, at what point do you stop and where do you draw the line? If everything can be filmed and shown, what is the value of what you do film? In a world of no limits, will the result quickly be apathy if there is nothing any more to get excited about, nothing precious or illicit to fight for in the teeth of the censor? On one level, as a reaction to the changes and challenges of the 1960s which these other sf TV dramas were also reflecting upon in their various ways, Kneale's play can be read from the vantage point of its own time as quite a conservative commentary on a period of tremendous and positive upheaval that was being spearheaded by the young; of a society and culture, it might be argued, that was simply stepping out from the long shadow cast by Victorianism and Victorian values.[32] But, on another level, when viewed from the vantage point of today's TV culture of the twenty-first century, with its cornucopia of commercial satellite channels, its general 'sex sells' ethos and its frequent accusations of 'dumbing down', the title 'Sooner than you think…', which opens *The Year of the Sex Olympics*, starts to take on a different and more troubling resonance.

NOTES

An earlier version of the material in this essay on *The Year of the Sex Olympics* appeared in a review by the author of the 2003 BFI DVD release of the play, published in *Film International* 4 (2003), pp. 44–7.

1. 'Lyrics from *Hair*', www.janfox.com/sixties_live_lyrics.htm (accessed 24 September 2004).
2. For further details on the historical powers of the Lord Chamberlain to license plays, see, for example, Vincent J. Liesenfield, *The Licensing Act of 1737* (Madison: University of Wisconsin Press, 1984).
3. 'Musical *Hair* opens as censors withdraw', www.news.bbc.co.uk/onthisday/hi/dates/stories/september/27/newsid_3107000/3107815.stm (accessed 24 September 2004). There were limits, however, to the new freedom – strong language and obscenity were still potentially liable to criminal prosecution.
4. As evidence of this heady spirit, see, for example, Charles Marowitz, '*Hair* at the Shaftesbury', *Plays and Players*, November 1968: 'Every so often, a show comes along which consolidates some part of the *zeitgeist* and whose significance is less in what it is than the time in which it arrives and in the face of such a show, drama criticism suddenly appears like a gross impertinence because one can no sooner review the present than attempt to evaluate the latitude and longitude of one's native city. *Hair* is such a show.'
5. 'Age of Aquarius', www.paranormality.com/age_of_aquarius.shtml (accessed 24 September 2004).
6. In his address to the Democratic Party Convention on 15 July 1960, accepting their nomination of him for the presidency of the United States, John F. Kennedy promised the American people a 'New Frontier': 'We stand at the edge of a New Frontier – the frontier of unfulfilled hopes and dreams. It will deal with unsolved problems of peace and war, unconquered pockets of ignorance and prejudice, unanswered questions of poverty and surplus.' Following his election that year as one of the youngest presidents of the United States, Kennedy went on to make a speech at Rice University, Houston, Texas, on 12 September 1962 in which he pledged America would put a man on the moon by the end of the decade: 'We choose to go to the moon in this decade and do the other things, not because they are easy but because they are hard…', he said. Thus a direct equation was made in the public mind between the youth and vigour projected by the Kennedy administration and the new 'science fiction'-type world of the space race (as indicated

by the Kennedy-like Captain James T. Kirk's proclamation of 'Space. The Final Frontier' at the start of every episode of *Star Trek*, NBC, 1966–69). On 21 July 1969 American astronaut Neil Armstrong, became the first man to walk on the moon.

7. At the Labour Party conference in October 1963, the then Leader of the Opposition, Harold Wilson, made a significant speech in which he promised that in the 1960s 'the Britain that will be forged in the white heat of the scientific and technological revolution will have no place for restrictive practices and outdated measures on either side of industry'. The notion of a Britain 'burning with the white heat of technology' became Wilson's electoral mantra and he was elected Labour prime minister a year later in the October 1964 general election.

8. Examples of this scrutiny would include documentaries such as *We Are the Lambeth Boys* (dir. Karel Reisz, UK, 1959), examining young people growing up in London in the late 1950s; newspaper articles such as Group 60's 'Focus on Youth' series of articles which ran in the *Daily Herald* throughout 1960; and books such as Richard Hoggart's *The Uses of Literacy* (Harmondsworth: Penguin, 1957), which famously examined the plight of the working-class 'scholarship boy', who, because of the greater opportunities for educational advancement to grammar school and beyond now afforded by the welfare state, often felt himself educated out of his class and estranged from his cultural background.

9. *Tomorrow's World* (1965–2002) was BBC TV's most popular factual science programme of the period. In its early years in the 1960s, it tended to present the latest developments in science and technology in a largely uncritical 'gee-whiz' kind of way.

10. It is a measure of how much the passing of time can change perceptions as well as perspectives that when *Joe 90* was repeated on British television in the 1990s, Joe, with his light hair, bland puppet's expression and NHS-style 'electrode' spectacles, was widely remarked at the time to bear a striking resemblance to then British Prime Minister John Major, who had taken office in 1990.

11. 'The Doors of Perception' (from a verse by William Blake) was an essay written by Aldous Huxley recording and reflecting upon his experiences of taking the hallucinogenic drug mescaline. It would prove an influential text for the counterculture in the late 1960s, including Jim Morrison's rock group The Doors, which took its name from the phrase. See Aldous Huxley, *The Doors of Perception* (London: Chatto & Windus, 1954).

12. The London Underground as a place to combat the threat of alien invasion is a common British science fiction trope clearly evoking the British spirit of the Blitz in World War II. It recurs in British sf cinema, as well as television. For analysis of it in cinema, see numerous essays in I.Q. Hunter (ed.), *British Science Fiction Cinema* (London: Routledge, 1999).

13. *The Champions* (ITC, 1968–69) was an action adventure TV show in which the *homo superiors* were international agents who had acquired their special powers from a lost Tibetan tribe. For extended analysis of *The Champions*, see James Chapman, *Saints and Avengers: British Adventure Series of the 1960s* (London: I.B. Tauris, 2002), pp. 171–88.

14. Christopher Evans (ed.), *Mind at Bay* (London: Panther, 1969), and *Mind in Chains* (London: Panther, 1970). The enhancement of brain potential through the power of computers echoes *Joe 90*. The Evans and Wilson short story, 'The Dreams of the Computer' was first published in *New Worlds* magazine, May 1969.

15. See, for example, 'The Ziggy Stardust Companion', www.5years.com/triv.htm (accessed 29 September 2004).

16. 'Oh You Pretty Things', written and performed by David Bowie, *Hunky Dory*, EMI 1971 (remastered 1999), CMI 5218890.

17. This and all other quoted dialogue between Stephen and Carol taken from episode 1, 'The Slaves of Jedikiah', *The Tomorrow People*, Series 1 (1st tx. ITV, 30 April 1973). DVD release PAR 61129, Revelation Films/Fremantle Media, 2002.

18. Jon Lewis and Penny Stempel, *Cult TV: The Essential Critical Guide* (London: Pavilion, 1993), p. 169.

19. 'War of the Empires', *The Tomorrow People* (1st tx. ITV, 29 January–19 February 1979). The original series ended there but its rerun success on the Nickelodeon cable channel in the 1980s led to a 1990s' revival co-funded by Thames TV and Nickelodeon (1992–95). This starred *Neighbours* (Grundy, 1986–) actor Kristian Schmid. But inevitably the possibility of young people being able to change their world seemed less potent a prospect in the 1990s compared to the era of the early 1970s and the series did not have the same impact as its predecessor.

20. Roger Fulton, '*UFO*', *The Encyclopedia of TV Science Fiction* (London: Boxtree/Independent Television Books, 1997), p. 584.

21. 'The Long Sleep', *UFO* (1st tx. ITV, 15 March 1973). The episode showed a young couple high on LSD: the man jumps off a farmhouse roof, killing himself.

22. By 'prime-time network launch' it is meant that the series was not networked across all the ITV regions in a peak viewing slot as determined by the ITV network committee which controlled programme scheduling in this period. Gerry Anderson's production company later went on to attempt another live action sf TV series, *Space: 1999*, which ran on ITV in the mid-1970s for two seasons (1975–77) with equally mixed results.

23. For further discussion of the notion of the single play as television's 'cutting edge', see John Caughie, 'Progressive Television and Documentary Drama', in Tony Bennett, Susan Boyd-Bowman, Colin Mercer and Janet Woollacott (eds), *Popular Television and Film* (London: British Film Institute, 1981), p. 355.

24. Dennis Potter, *Angels Are So Few*, BBC Camera Script, April 1970, pp. 26–7. BBC Written Archives, Project No. 2140/3500.

25. Dennis Potter, 'What the Devil Are They Playing At?', interview by James Murray, *Daily Express*, 29 March 1976.

26. *The Year of the Sex Olympics*, BBC TV 1968, writer Nigel Kneale; dir. Michael Elliott, 1st tx BBC 2, *Theatre 625*, 29 July 1968. The play was repeated on BBC 1 in *The Wednesday Play* slot on 11 March 1970. *The Year of the Sex Olympics* was originally filmed in colour, its sets and costumes a vivid dayglo; however the recording was long thought to have been junked by the BBC (the tape recorded over to make way for other programmes) until a black-and-white telecine print was discovered many years later. This was the version restored and released by the British Film Institute on DVD and video in 2003 (BFIVD 552).

27. Nigel Kneale, published play script, *3 TV Plays: The Road; The Year of the Sex Olympics; The Stone Tape* (London: Fantasy Ferret, 1976), p. 101.

28. Nigel Kneale, 'Quatermass and the Pen', interview by Kim Newman and Julian Petley, *Video Watchdog* 47 (September/October 1998).

29. Nigel Kneale, 'The Year of the Sex Olympics', interview, Diary, *The Times*, 25 May 1968, p. 8.

30. See, for example, Henry Raynor, 'A Break with Custom', *The Times*, 30 July 1968, p. 11: 'A family provides a new programme for the dissatisfied: it goes out live under the eyes of the camera, in an almost uninhabited island and it meets horror and tragedy. It is here experience tells us that Mr. Kneale lost his way...'

31. Kneale, *3 TV Plays*, p. 101.

32. For justification of this reading, see Kneale's later *The Quatermass Conclusion* (Euston Films for Thames, 1979), where it is the old, in the form of Quatermass and other ageing scientists, who have to save the hippy young (or 'Planet People') from themselves, after the latter have been led astray by 'New Age' alien-worshipping philosophies which have left them and the Earth open to 'harvesting' by hostile alien forces. See James Chapman's essay in this volume, '*Quatermass* and the Origins of British Television sf', for further discussion of this.

6

The man who made *Thunderbirds*: an interview with Gerry Anderson

NICHOLAS J. CULL

In the foyer of the British Council offices, just off Trafalgar Square in London, a video screen carries images of 'Britishness' to distract visitors who have come to discuss student exchange projects, English-language teaching or overseas lecture tours. There are street signs and red pillar boxes; cream teas and factory chimneys; beefeaters and punks; and a curiously shaped model aircraft with a rounded snout, stumpy wings and double tailfins linked by a bar. Lettering on the side reads 'Thunderbird 2'. It is just one symptom of the degree to which the television programmes created by Gerry Anderson have become part of the fabric of British life.

Gerry Anderson was born in north London in 1929. He left school at 14 with the ambition of being an architect. On finding himself allergic to the plaster used to create models, he soon redirected his ambition to the film industry. He joined the colonial film unit of the Ministry of Information, where he trained as an editor. He then moved to Gainsborough Pictures, where his early jobs included re-editing the studio's 1945 hit *The Wicked Lady* to make it suitable for release for a prudish American market. After working his way up through the British studios, in 1957 Anderson formed his own production company called A.P. Films to make TV commercials. Its output included a puppet show for Associated Rediffusion called *The Adventures of Twizzle* (A.P. Films for Associated Rediffusion, 1957–58) and he followed it up with *The Adventures of Torchy the Battery Boy* (A.P.

THE MAN WHO MADE THUNDERBIRDS Gerry Anderson, early 1980s.

Films for Associated Rediffusion, 1958–59). A.P. Films resolved to develop a puppet show of its own and came up with a programme called *Four Feather Falls* (A.P. Films for Granada, 1959–60), a fantasy western about a cowboy with a talking horse and a magic feather. Anderson also made a live action crime drama at this time: *Crossroads to Crime* (A.P. Films/Anglo Amalgamated, 1960). The success of *Four Feather Falls* was followed by further puppet shows with science fiction content, commissioned by the British entertainment mogul to whose fortune Gerry Anderson's would become inextricably linked: Lew Grade of ATV (Associated Television).

Anderson's first series for Grade was *Supercar* (ATV/ITC, 1960–62). Next came *Fireball XL5* (ATV/ITC, 1962), the adventures of the crew of a rocket ship exploring outer space. At this point the team switched to colour and created *Stingray* (ATV/ITC, 1963), an adventure set around a futuristic submarine. As Anderson's programmes succeeded in the financially vital American market, Grade's confidence in

Anderson as a programme maker grew, and in 1964 he commissioned a new series to play in a full hour slot on television: this series was *Thunderbirds* (ITC, 1965–66). *Thunderbirds* told the story of a secret rescue organisation with fabulous machines called International Rescue, run by a retired astronaut and his five sons, from a secret Pacific island. *Thunderbirds* was so successful that Anderson made two full-length feature films *Thunderbirds Are Go* (Century 21/United Artists, 1966) and *Thunderbird 6* (Century 21/United Artists, 1967). Unfortunately Grade failed to sell the TV programme to the US and commissioned an entirely new project from Anderson for 1967.

Throughout the 1960s, Anderson's teams refined the puppet process, which they called 'super marionation', with the puppets becoming ever more lifelike. The 1967 show *Captain Scarlet and the Mysterons* (ITC, 1967–68), in which a secret organisation with secret agents with coloured coded names defended Earth from invisible aliens, used puppets with natural proportions. The next year brought *Joe 90* (ITC, 1968), a show featuring the adventures of a boy secret agent whose father had invented a machine that gave him the brain patterns of skilled adults, and 1969 saw *The Secret Service* (ITC), a series about a vicar who doubled as a secret agent and who was voiced by comedian 'Professor' Stanley Unwin, famous for speaking in gobbledygook – a trait which did not go down well with Lew Grade. The show failed to receive proper distribution.

In 1968, Anderson wrote and produced a live action adult science fiction film called *Doppelgänger* (aka *Journey to the Far Side of the Sun*) (dir. Robert Parrish, Century 21/Universal) about a space mission to a mysterious planet discovered on the far side of the sun. This disturbing film opened the way for Anderson's jump into live action film-making for television. 1969–70 brought *UFO* (ITC), a complex and frequently dark science fiction drama about a secret organisation defending the Earth from aliens who are coming to harvest humans for spare part surgery. As with all Anderson's work, fantastic futuristic machines abounded, but yet again the series failed to capture American ratings and Grade cancelled a second series. After an interlude working on a contemporary thriller series called *The Protectors* (ITC, 1972–74), Anderson created *Space: 1999* (ITC). This show, starring Martin Landau and Barbara Bain, which ran from 1975 to 1977, followed the adventures of the crew of a moon base, after an atomic accident has ripped the moon out of orbit and sent it hurtling into space. Excellent special effects and imaginative writing created a television series that, like *UFO*, remains a cult classic.

The later 1970s brought personal and financial difficulties for Anderson. He divorced from his wife Sylvia, who had collaborated on the various programmes, and he sold the rights to most of his work for just £20,000. But Anderson weathered the storms and went on to create a steady stream of well-received programmes, including *Terrahawks* (Anderson/Burr, LWT, 1983–84), *Space Precinct* (Gerry Anderson Productions/Mentorn Films, 1994–95) and *Lavender Castle* (Gerry Anderson Productions/Cosgrove Hall, 1996–98). Yet, despite the ingenuity and quality of these programmes, they have been overshadowed by the continuing public devotion to the classic 1960s' shows and particularly *Thunderbirds*. Repeat screenings of *Thunderbirds* on Carlton television sparked the famed *Thunderbirds* Christmas of 1992 when fistfights broke out in British toyshops over *Thunderbirds* toys. In 2001, Anderson received an MBE for his programme-making. 2004 saw a Universal Pictures/Working Title live action film of *Thunderbirds* (US/UK, dir. Jonathan Frakes), but Anderson had no input and received no credit as creator. Though he was offered a substantial sum of money for his endorsement of production designs, Anderson felt that he could not in honesty give his approval to designs that fell so far short of the original. Anderson remains active. His latest project (2005) is a return to classic territory: a new computer-animated series of *Captain Scarlet*.[1]

NICHOLAS J. CULL   Am I correct in assuming that you didn't intend to work with puppets? How did you come to be so closely identified with them?

GERRY ANDERSON   Well, of course, the first thing is what you have just said is an understatement. Briefly, I had formed my own film company and I had great ideas. I wanted to make big feature films – and six months after starting the company we had no work at all. Then we were about to shut shop and a women came in who wrote children's stories and asked if we would be prepared to make a television series called *The Adventures of Twizzle*. We only had one answer, which was yes, because we were broke – and then she said the immortal words 'it's to be made using puppets' and I nearly vomited on the floor.

The idea of all these glamorous female stars and the excitement of the big studio vaporised instantly – but as I say, we needed the money so we made that show. I was so ashamed of what I was doing I was determined to make the puppet film look as close to a live action picture as possible because I thought the broadcasters would say 'Well why is this guy making puppet films – he should be making big pictures.' But, guess what, they said 'Aren't these puppet films good – let's give him some more.' That's how it started.

NC You became closely identified with films of a science fiction theme. How did your personal ideas of what the future would, or should, be like influence the images you put on the screen?

GA First of all, just briefly, I never intended to go into science fiction. What happened was I made a series called *Supercar* – this was because the puppets couldn't walk and couldn't do anything remotely believable, and so we put them in a car. The car can zoom around all over the place and give the show a lot of movement. When the show was transmitted, people would always say 'Oh I see you are in science fiction now, Gerry', and I thought 'Am I?' But yes, now I can deal with your question because obviously I became steeped in science fiction very quickly.

I have always been interested in aircraft but I have never trained as a pilot, regrettably. My interest was heightened when I went into the RAF, not to fight the Battle of Britain, I hasten to add, but when I was conscripted. Also, when the first rockets were being launched, I became desperately interested in that and, of course, I looked forward to the landing on the moon.

If I can just give you a quick example of what triggers ideas. I came home from the studio one night and I was watching television news and they had a man with a flying helmet and a flying suit standing on a square-welded metal frame, in the centre of which was a jet engine pointing downwards. This frame was tethered to the ground by very heavy chains and the jet engine started and it rose up into the air all of three feet, and of course it couldn't go any further because of the chains. The engine was wound down and the thing came down none too gently and landed – well, that excited me enormously because, obviously, it was the promise of a vertical takeoff.

So, the next morning, I went into the studio and said 'Quick, quick, quick – design a vertical-takeoff aircraft' – which they did. I was busy writing scripts where we could use vertical takeoff, and so our vertical-takeoff aircraft were a long way ahead of the real thing, which came much later. That's an example and there are many cases when I enlarged what was happening at the time.

I remember that I went to Canada and we went into a revolving restaurant and had a meal. So my idea immediately was, 'What will they do in the future if they can revolve one floor now? Maybe in the future they can revolve the whole building and everybody will get this panoramic view.' These are the sorts of things that triggered my imagination and I have always been a great believer that science fiction entertainment makes a great contribution to the progress that we make in all sorts of spheres because I think that the desire of people is to do something or other that is not possible. If that desire is strong enough, scientists and engineers get to work to bring it to reality – so I think it's the trigger for many of today's aircraft and innovations that I believe make our lives more interesting.

NC One of the most positive things that we see in *Thunderbirds* and *Stingray* and *Captain Scarlet* is the idea of a world government.

GA I had all sorts of fancy ideas about the future. You know, we had the United Nations and I imagined that the world would come together and there would be a world government and, with all the modern materials that were available, everybody would dress superbly; everything would be neat and tidy. But my 18-year-old son has shattered that illusion, I can tell you! I was wrong. It hasn't turned out that way at all. By the way, if I can explain something and I get a lot about being in the business for sixty years. I am not as old as I look – the reason is I made my first production when I was five years old. Not many people realise that.

NC One of the great themes of your work and one of the delights watching it is the way in which appearances are deceptive. In your world, rockets take off from under swimming pools; high-tech pursuit vehicles are hidden in barns; little boys can be secret agents and secret bases can be located under film studios. Where did that come from, because it's sort of your trademark?

GA Well, there's probably a different answer to each of those points you have raised. First of all, let's just deal with *UFO*, where we had an underground base in a film studio. This was a commercial decision because science fiction films, even today, all too often for my money, show the artist in the foreground and they are lit, of course, and you get a certain amount of props around them suggesting 'future' and the rest of the screen is black. I really couldn't stand that. I felt that you should be able to see the science fiction set. Well, of course, science fiction sets are very expensive to build. A small example: if you had a set that was square, like this room, that's fairly economical. If you have a circular room, it immediately becomes ten times more expensive because of the curves and double curves. So I wanted to have in *UFO* science fiction sets that we could see and, of course, I quickly realised we simply couldn't afford to do that for a television series. So I came up with the idea of building a super-science-fiction set which was the headquarters. We would be able to use this throughout the series and we would, in the stories, say that this was located under a film studio. The boss would come into his office in the morning and the whole office would go down like an elevator into the science sector alone, and this meant that we were able to shoot all round the studio and get all the production value of the studio at no extra expense.

NC I am really interested in the way nothing is quite what it seems.

GA Well, really, this was just my idea. Originally, these shows were designed to be shown to children but we never wrote down to children. We wouldn't do it today but I always felt that, as a child, I had a particularly active imagination. Anything that was hidden and anything that was secret immediately attracted me, and then again, there was the commercial side, which is unavoidable when you're making a television series. It meant that, for example, a science fiction car could emerge from a haystack from an underground hiding place and then we, the producers, were justified in showing it drive along country lanes.

A lot of it had to do with the practicalities of trying to make a good television series – not cheaply, because all my shows have been very expensive, but good science fiction programmes that were affordable with the budgets that we had.

NC Who were your movie heroes growing up and who influenced your style of filming?

GA I don't honestly think anyone influenced my style. What I can tell you is I made a picture that none of you would have ever heard of – it was called *They Who Dare* (UK, 1953), a story about the SAS and it starred Dirk Bogarde, but more importantly it was directed by Lewis Milestone.[2] Now Lewis Milestone, in terms of cinematic history, is one of the most important figures of all time. He directed *All Quiet on the Western Front* (USA, 1930), the original one, which was, and has become to those who are interested in cinema history, a cinema classic. He said to me: 'Gerry, let me give you a little bit of advice. Don't ever, ever try and second-guess your audience. You do, regardless, exactly what you want to do and what appeals to you and if the audience like that, you're very lucky and you will become very famous, but if you try and guess what the audience wants, you're gonna fail.' And that was the key to my approach to filming.

NC What gave you the inspiration for *Thunderbirds*?

GA Well, we had a specialised studio at the time for making puppet films and we were in continuous production without a break for about twelve years. What would happen is I would be finishing one production, in this case it was *Stingray*, and my boss Lew Grade, who was a lovely man, would ring me and say 'Gerry could you pop in tomorrow morning?' – he always gave me a half-past seven appointment, don't ask me why. He said, 'I wanna hear what you're going to make next', so I went in there and there he was. He had a silver coffee tray with two lovely cups and he poured a coffee. We both lit a big Havana cigar and he said 'Okay, tell me what the show is.' Now today, people can't believe this story. I had no script. I had no drawings. I had no budget. I had nothing. But I told him about a German mine disaster which happened a few weeks before and miners were trapped underground. They were trapped underground for two weeks and everybody in the country was following this story – you know, they drilled a pilot hole; they drilled a bigger hole in order to bring them out – and I said to him: 'The whole country's been captivated by this rescue. I'd like to do a rescue story.'

Now I had given it some thought and I said the story would be called *International Rescue* and they'd all have super-duper machines. I said: 'The only thing, before I go any further, Lew, is you've backed everything I've done but I'm not sure you want to back this one' – because I knew it was going to be hellishly expensive. He leapt out of his seat and he came round the desk. He grabbed me by the scruff of the neck; he dragged me into the centre of the office and he said 'You see that light up there. Gerry, if you want to make a television series about that light bulb, I'll back it.'

Well, you can imagine, that gave me tremendous confidence. So I told him what I had invented about the story so far and we talked for, I suppose, twenty minutes and he said 'go ahead'. Now, in today's money, allowing for inflation, he had made a commitment of 15 million dollars – you try doing that today. Trying to get five dollars today is a job.

NC You've talked about the expense of making these series and one of the consequences of this expense is that you needed to make sales overseas and particularly in the American market. How did the desire to reach the American market affect what you were doing in the content of your programmes?

GA OK. Well, let me just give everyone a little bit of background here. It's the same story today but it was worse at the time. American audiences allegedly did not want to watch British programmes. We were told that, for example, people in the South couldn't understand the English accent. We were told that the pace of our shows was too slow for the American audience and I suspect that there was a certain amount of protectionism going on – you know, they didn't want foreign products to come in. They were very happy to sell products to our country but there was a great deal of resistance to any British shows.

And so, there was one producer, whom I remember very well, who tried to overcome this problem by making a British police show about the new Scotland Yard and he imported an American lead. This lead was a very tired, faded American star who was no longer popular and the series was written for the American market. Consequently, you had an American cop running around London with his pretty English girl cop, who kind of made the coffee and all that sort of thing.

People over here thought it was an insult and people over in America thought it was boring. I didn't do that. I thought, the shows that I'm making are about futuristic aircraft; they were about futuristic submarines; they were about all sorts of high-tech stuff. All the stuff we were writing about was taking place in America – so we made the show as an American show. I cannot tell you the lengths we went to – we even went to the length of getting hold of American paper and typing our scripts on American paper. We also used all-American spellings. We sent out our key people to New York for a week to pick up the latest expressions, to look at the buildings, to look at the cars and we then went on to produce a show of which I am not the least bit ashamed, because what we did really was to break into the American market in a way no other British producer had been able to do. And when you consider that 50 per cent of the entire world's take comes from America, you can see how important it was financially, and that approach enabled us to make more and more shows across the years because, obviously, if you take someone's money, make a show and then you lose it, they're not going to give you any more.

NC   Which show did the best in the United States?

GA   I would say that *Supercar* was the first one. The American company which was going to distribute *Supercar* was on the verge of bankruptcy, and when we arrived with *Supercar* they were very excited. They came back about four weeks later and the whole place was electric. People were writing sales contracts; it had a huge response in the States and then, of course, *Stingray* was big. *Thunderbirds* is a sad story, really.

America has three major networks, which at the time were the most important TV stations in the States, and if a British show got on to one network, it was just like a miracle. Lew Grade took *Thunderbirds* to America and he showed it to NBC and they said 'We will take it.' He showed it to CBS, the other network. They said 'We will take it' and ABC said 'Pass'. He took a plane back to England and when he got back to Heathrow, he was tannoyed and it was ABC who said they'd had a very quick meeting and they would take it. Now all three American networks wanted the show. You couldn't have a better success than that, but unfortunately – and I don't say this in a critical way because Lew was a great guy – he got so excited, he shot the price up absolutely sky high and one of the American networks backed out; then, of course, the other two thought 'what's wrong, what's wrong' and they backed out and consequently the show didn't get a showing in America, but it should have done.

I went along to see him and I had no plans for a new series because *Thunderbirds* was so successful. I just assumed we would go on, but he said: 'Look Gerry, you know *Thunderbirds* is still on the air. Quite honestly, it would be easier for me to sell a new show as opposed to renewing' and I was heartbroken, but I didn't argue with him because he had been so wonderful to me. I couldn't bring myself to say 'Sorry I'm going to fight that one', so we didn't make any more.

NC I want to shift a little bit now towards the content of the programme. The 1960s was a time of tremendous upheaval. How did the politics of that time shape your programmes, thinking in particular of the way you seemed to avoid the clichés of 1960s' villains – we don't have Germans and we don't have Russian villains. Was this deliberate? Were you trying to move beyond the Cold War?

GA It is and it was then absolutely deliberate. It made me quite ill to watch British programmes where the villains were Russians and to see *James Bond* and the arch villain being Russian.

I knew by then that my programmes were not only being seen by maybe a hundred countries around the world but they were also being repeated over and over again and I sort of took a guesstimate and thought: 'Well, hundreds of millions of children are watching these programmes and I don't want to contribute to a global conflict between two superpowers!'

NC One of the things that we notice in *Captain Scarlet* and in *UFO* and *Space: 1999* is that you have an unusually ethnically diverse cast, and, talking to British people with different racial backgrounds, quite often people would say to me that their first experience of seeing someone who looked like them on television was watching *Captain Scarlet* or watching *UFO* and feeling represented on the screen for the first time. That was a deliberate choice too – to have a racially diverse future?

GA Absolutely. I don't want to sound pompous or anything but I think people who make television programmes have a responsibility, particularly when children are watching avidly and you know their minds can be affected almost irreversibly as they grow up. We were very conscious of introducing different ethnic backgrounds.

NC As a child you suffered racism, didn't you?

GA Yes. We're going to get into a contentious area here. I came from a mixed marriage – my father was Jewish and my mother was Christian and my home and upbringing were like World War III. Today, I have absolutely no time for any religion. If people want to follow a religion, we live in a free country, thank God. Personally, I don't want to touch it because when I look around the world, I find the amount of trouble which is caused over religion – I have abdicated totally.

NC I want to talk a bit more about the live action programmes and what it was like finally to shift from working with puppets through to live actors? How did you and your team find the transition?

GA Well, at first it was like a dream come true. Moving into a major film studio, being able to walk onto a big film stage with big sets, masses of lights, a huge unit of international stars – it was like a dream come true. But, little by little, I began to realise that both types of film-making had problems. I guess all forms of film-making

MORE THAN JUST PUPPETS Gerry Anderson also produced live action series such as *Space: 1999*.

are exciting and all forms of film-making are worrying. The joy is when the film is completed, and if the audience claps, that's worth everything. The trouble is, that only lasts ten minutes, then it's back to all the struggle again.

NC Was there a way in which people couldn't really accept you as a creator of live action programmes?

GA I think film critics generally are the lowest form of life – I'm sure there are exceptions; I'm gonna think very hard to see if I can think of one. But when I moved into live action, it was all too easy for the critics. I think the critics are generally more anxious that people enjoy what they are writing than they should pay attention to their view of the picture and how they liked it and try and fore-cast whether the audience would like it. So we had such wonderful appraisals – I'm sure they sat up all night to think of them: 'Gerry no longer pulls the strings.' Well done! 'Gerry's actors are wooden.' I was a great target for them.

NC Was there a point when you realised that your programmes had moved beyond being important in your own time and had become part of British culture. Something that transcends the period in which they were created?

GA This is something I can be very, very clear about. When I first started making films, the puppet films, a small fan club started called 'Fanderson'. This has grown over the years and is now a very big fan club known all over the world. But the first thing that happened to me was kiddies of seven to eight would say 'Can I have your autograph?' or 'Can I have your picture?' Some years later, a film crew would interview me and I would be paralysed with fear. I prefer looking through the camera rather than standing in front of one. Then a cameraman would come over and say 'Can I have your autograph?' and so would the rest of the crew. I used to think: 'I wish they had done that before the interview. It would have made it so much easier for me.'

More years went by and it's ideal to illustrate this with a story. I was coming home on a Virgin Atlantic flight. The stewardess came up to me and said the captain would like to see me. 747 – the captain wants to see ME! Wow! I went up on to the flight deck and it was on autopilot and he turned round, we shook hands and so did the other guys and then he said he used to be a member of the *Stingray* club. I wanted to get off the aircraft! When I arrived some weeks ago, not that long ago actually, I received a letter from an MP who invited me and my wife to the House of Commons. He said he was unashamedly an Anderson fan.

NC If you could have your career over again, what would you change?

GA Everything. That may be a slightly unfair answer I gave just now because the answer to that question has been modified over the years. Had you have asked me in the 1960s, I would have given you that answer and I would have said that I would have liked to have been a powerful producer in Hollywood to make all kinds of wonderful movies and I didn't want to be involved with puppets at all. But then, as the years rolled by and these films gained respect-ability, I became a little kinder towards my product, but I suppose the answer is: I would have liked to have had the career of Steven Spielberg, to name but one.

NC What are you proudest of and what would you like to be remembered for?

GA I, in all honesty, don't watch my programmes because I don't enjoy them. All I see on the screen are mistakes and why can't I do it again. And so I don't really get any enjoyment out of watching my old shows. But there are some Hollywood actors who have a movie theatre in the basement and they sit there every evening and watch their old picture films – that's not me. I think the enjoyment I get, although I try to conceal my reactions, is when people are pleased to meet me and say how much they enjoy the programmes. Then you say how would I like to be remembered? Well, I'm not too fussed about that, I guess. I would like to be remembered by my family whom I hope would be proud of me and would have enough money to live comfortably and that would be my legacy.

NOTES

This interview took place at the University of Leicester on 19 July 2003 as part of the XXth International Association for Media History conference: 'The History of the Future: Visions from the Past'. The interview was transcribed by Joe Parkes.

1. This potted biography of Gerry Anderson is drawn from Simon Archer and Marcus Hearn, *What Made Thunderbirds Go! The Authorised Biography of Gerry Anderson* (London: BBC Books, 2002) and a pre-interview discussion with Anderson. For further details on Anderson's life and career, see also the website of 'Fanderson – The Official Gerry Ander-son Appreciation Society', www.fanderson.org.uk/fanderson.html.

2. Anderson worked as the sound editor on the film.

7

Everyday life in the post-catastrophe future: Terry Nation's *Survivors*

ANDY SAWYER

[T]he barriers between us and epidemics are not so strong as is commonly supposed. Not only is it increasingly difficult to control the vectors of disease, but it is more than probable that urban populations are being insidiously weakened by overall pollution levels, even when they are not high enough to be incriminated in any one illness. At the same time international mobility speeds the spread of disease. With this background, and at a time of widespread public demoralisation, the collapse of vital social services such as power and sanitation could easily provoke a series of epidemics – and we cannot say with confidence that we would be able to cope with them.

Edward Goldsmith et. al., *A Blueprint for Survival* (1972)[1]

The government strongly advised Britons yesterday not to travel to Hong Kong and Guangdong province, southern China, as the mystery bug that has so far killed 78 people and infected 2,223 continued to spread panic through south-east Asia.

Guardian, 3 April 2003[2]

The 1970s' television drama *Survivors*, broadcast in 38 episodes over three series between 16 April 1975 and 8 June 1977, seemed, until recently, curiously absent from the nostalgia market. While videos and DVDs of numerous other 1970s' television programmes crowded the shelves, the DVD release of the first two series seemed late in coming.[3] The programme has its enthusiastic fandom but, compared to others with which the name of its creator Terry Nation has been linked, it seems to have faded from public consciousness. Perhaps its subject, the fate of the scattered remnants of the British population following a worldwide plague, was too sombre. Indeed, in some ways, although a commercial television entertainment rather than docudrama or propaganda, *Survivors* is closer to the bleak and angry engagement of Peter Watkins's *The War Game* (made in 1965 but banned by the BBC until 1985) or Mick Jackson's *Threads*, written by Barry Hines (BBC 2, 1984), which offered direct dramatisations of the post-nuclear landscape. Its closest science fiction analogue, in terms of its exploration of viewers' anxieties, is John Wyndham's *The Day of the Triffids*, although this was not adapted by the BBC until 1981 and any direct reflection must come, therefore, from images cast by the novel (1951); the radio dramatisations (BBC Light Programme, 1957; BBC Radio 4, 1968, 1973) and the film directed by Steve Sekeley (1963); or, indeed, the general context of 'disaster' science fiction.[4]

It is perhaps significant that *Survivors* was broadcast almost parallel with the popular comedy series *The Good Life*, which depicted dropping out from society to develop self-sufficiency as a matter of lifestyle choice. Association with this, as much as its lack of fan-friendly 'hooks', may account for the relative neglect of what is an interest-ing, occasionally well-written, and at times thoughtful exploration of the sense of social and political dislocation of the 1970s, during which much of the modern 'green' or 'environmentalist' vocabulary was being formed. In this discussion, I intend to present, first, a summary of the context within which this television programme appeared, and, second, a more extended consideration of how the plotlines and characters of *Survivors* dramatise some of the positions and arguments within its representation of survivalist anxieties.

Survivors could be placed within a number of contexts. The two most relevant are those political movements which stressed the pos-sibility of social cataclysm followed by a less sophisticated culture dependent on self-sufficiency and community, and the literary tra-dition of secular apocalypse that includes Mary Shelley's *The Last Man* (1826) and M.P. Sheil's *The Purple Cloud* (1901). The former is a feature of millenarian movements throughout history,[5] but in the British context might be traced from the Peasant's Revolt through the Diggers, Levellers and Ranters of the Civil War, then through the socialists of the nineteenth century to the 'Back to the Land' movement springing from Jesse Collings's *Land Reform* (1906) and the social ferment of the 1960s.[6] The latter, once separated from overtly religious writing, becomes a feature of various strands of British and American science fiction, including Jack London's *The Scarlet Plague* (1912); 'J.J. Connington' (i.e. A.W. Stewart)'s *Nordenholt's Million* (1923); Sydney Fowler Wright's *Deluge* (1928); George R. Stewart's *Earth Abides* (1949); John Christopher's *The Death of Grass* (1956); Brian Aldiss's *Greybeard* (1964); and, viewing disaster differently, J.G. Ballard's early sf, *The Drowned World* (1962) and *Drought* (first published in 1964 as *The Burning World*). In many of these fictions, a plague (after the model of Shelley's novel), an ecological catastrophe, a natural disaster or, increasingly after 1945, an atomic war, leaves a small group of survivors ready to rebuild the old or to strike off after the new.[7] Each owes a debt to the popular image of the 'last man' in Romantic writing and poetry, a projection of the solitary individual into a series of landscapes reflecting personal and social isolation and loss.[8] In presenting a debate between different aspects of this isolation, *Survivors* recreated this Romanticism for television audiences of the 1970s – even to the point of using a quotation from Wordsworth to underline the moral stance of an episode (discussed later in this chapter).

Anna Bramwell remarks how such 'predictions of apocalypse were a significant milestone in the development of environmentalism in the 1960s.'[9] Although Rachel Carson's *Silent Spring* (1962) is sometimes seen as a suitable beginning for the environmental concerns which were to occupy much of the following decades, it is important to recognise that protests about human effects on the natural environment were already overt. They appeared in British popular sf for the young in the BBC radio serial *Journey into Space* (1953–55) and in American satires such as Frederik Pohl and C.M. Kornbluth's *The Space Merchants* (1953; first serialised in *Galaxy* as 'Gravy Planet', 1952), in which conservationists appear as the subversive 'Consies'. Occasionally, of course, the two strands – of political ecology/counterculture and science fiction or sf-like disaster or utopian stories – fuse, as they did with William Morris's *News from Nowhere* (1890) (itself reacting to Edward Bellamy's *Looking Backward* of 1888), or Ernest Callenbach's *Ecotopia* (1975). More often, they worked in counterpoint or opposition, often ignorant of one another. However, by the early 1970s, it seemed inevitable that the two would achieve a unified, popular expression, so extensive were the articulations of environmental anxieties. Popular science fiction was a natural forum for this debate.

While not necessarily inspired by fictional models, unemployment agitation was frequently accompanied by 'back-to-the-land' movements, as happened in 1906 when there were seizures of land in Manchester, Salford, Bradford and Plaistow, East London. The retreat of disaffected youth to rural communes in the 1960s and nomadic rave and protest/traveller lifestyles in the 1980s/90s was often accompanied by the rhetoric of self-sufficiency in various forms.[10] However, the dialogue between alternative politics and 'lifestyle' underground press during the 1960s and 1970s was frequently one of mutual abuse. Nigel Fountain quotes John Hopkins ('Hoppy'), one of the faces of the London underground, as saying 'There was no contact with the straight left. They hated us.'[11] Activist and writer David Widgery is reported as saying 'there was quite a lot of opposition within the underground against whatever flower power was.'[12] Fountain's book ends at the point where magazines such as the mid-1970s' *Undercurrents*, which tried, however vaguely, to synthesise the two wings of the 'alternative', began to operate. It is tempting to consider *Survivors* as part of this synthesis, but only in the sense that while it shares some of the rhetoric of 'self-sufficiency' described below, this rhetoric is set within a slightly different context. Both the left and the 'alternative' were concerned to change behaviour before the inevitable ecological and political catastrophe happened. In *Survivors*, random characters, most without an ecological or political agenda, are left to pick up the pieces.

A key outlet for the ideals of the environmentally 'concerned' alternative was *The Ecologist* magazine, established in 1970 by Edward Goldsmith. Goldsmith's *Blueprint for Survival*, appearing in the January 1972 issue, was published later that year in book form. That same year saw the publication of *Only One Earth*, a report, commissioned by the UN secretary-general, of the United Nations Conference on the Human Environment, and of *The Limits to Growth*, another report commissioned by the Club of Rome, an 'invisible college' of scientists, industrialists and civil servants, on 'The Predicament of Mankind', which forecast within the following century 'a rather sudden and controllable decline in both population and industrial capacity.'[13] The following year John and Sally Seymour's *Self-Sufficiency* and E.F. Schumacher's *Small is Beautiful* both argued, from different perspectives, that such alarmist futures could to some extent be averted by means of appropriate action on the personal and social scales. That year also witnessed the founding of the Centre for Alternative Technology in Machynlleth, Wales, and yet another radio broadcast of *The Day of the Triffids*, a condensation of Giles Cooper's second (1968) adaptation. Such political speculation and debate must also be set against the context of the attempts of the 1970 Conservative government to reverse the gains of the Wilson Labour administration; the debate within the Labour and extra-Labour left concerning the reasons for that administration's fall; a sense of apocalyptic unease throughout the political spectrum caused by events such as the IRA mainland bombing campaign, as well as the 1973 'oil crisis' and the 1974 miners' strike, which led to a three-day working week, power cuts and rumours of military coups and private armies.[14] There may well be echoes of the general Middle England distrust of union activists, especially Northern ones, in the character of Arthur Wormley (played by George Baker), the sinister trade-union president of *Survivors'* second episode, 'Genesis' (1st tx. BBC 1, 23 April 1975), in which the question of the 'survival' of pre-catastrophe social structures is raised.

The initial seed of *Survivors*, then, must lie in the fact that it appeared at a time when serious concern about environmental issues was feeding into popular culture. Already, the TV series *Doomwatch*, created by Kit Pedler and Gerry Davis, had run for three series (38 episodes, including one unbroadcast, beginning 9 February 1970 and ending 14 August 1972), bringing ecological awareness into the living room. *Doomwatch*, which concerned a task force involved with the misuse of science, had partly spun out of the creators' work on *Doctor Who* in the 1960s and played upon a sense of uncertainty and pessimism about the future. There were also, however, arguments that society could avoid or rebuild itself after the apocalypse; that a more frugal, self-sufficient lifestyle was possible and even desirable.

'Green' politics, then, infused much of the context within which *Survivors* was viewed. The Ecology Party (from 1986 the Green Party) was formed in 1973 and, although much of the political activity was

SURVIVORS Victim of the fall of 'a tremendous industry'.

based around issue-based pressure-groups or organisations such as Friends of the Earth or the Soil Association, or the general feeling that action along a line spreading from recycling household waste to joining a rural commune was in some way a good thing, such ideas were circulating widely. Terry Nation ascribes the genesis of *Survivors* partly to his awareness of his own lack of survival skills when living in the country: 'I didn't know how to preserve food. I didn't know how to make anything and I suddenly realized that I and my whole generation were virtual victims of a tremendous industry.'[15] Nation's epiphany was not unlike that of the fictional Tom Good (Richard Briers) in *The Good Life*.

Running for four series from April 1975 to May 1977 (with a 1977 Christmas Special and a Royal Command Performance in June 1978), *The Good Life* is an oft-repeated sitcom which echoed this new 'green' movement. Clearly inspired more by the message of individual self-sufficiency promoted by the Seymours (whose message is today available in a coffee-table edition from Dorling Kindersley) than by apocalyptic fiction, Tom persuades his wife Barbara (Felicity Kendall) to join him in dropping out of the rat race in order to live, so far as one can in suburbia, off the land. Meanwhile their friends and neighbours, Jerry and his snobbish and acquisitive wife Margot (Paul Eddington and Penelope Keith), look upon their antics with amusement and exasperation, mixed, at least on Jerry's part, with a touch of envy. Such contrasts and the character-acting of the cast brought out by John Esmonde and Bob Larbey's script, make for sterling comedy but it is often hard to discern the heart of the programme. Is this self-sufficiency in action or defusing the threat to suburbia by turning it into a gentle comedy? Is Tom Good an idealistic buffoon or a role model?

Survivors, broadcast almost simultaneously with *The Good Life*, could be seen as its 'serious' twin, and this was one of the obvious facts about it which was noted at the time and in subsequent commentary: 'At times, this can seem like nothing more than a serious version of *The Good Life*. In fact, where *Survivors* falls flattest is in attempts to make day-to-day life in the post-catastrophe future seem anything more than a media-mythology of life in a trendy middle class commune.' Ultimately, '*Survivors* lapsed into ... becoming a carbolic soap opera of neo-country folk.'[16] However, it used the 'soap' format to inter-rogate – even if weakly – some of the fundamental questions of post-catastrophe life and articulate the implications (often avoided) of the emerging 'green' politics regarding the kind of society that would have to emerge in order to ensure survival. Terry Nation, the programme's creator, was the celebrated originator of *Doctor Who*'s Daleks, which were first seen, significantly, on a world devastated by nuclear war. Neil Alsop notes how Nation developed the initial concept and wrote the first three (and four further) episodes of the first series, with fellow writer Jack Ronder steering subsequent storylines away from the ultimate goal (Abby's search for her son) and the antagonist (Wormley's proto-dictatorship), towards the more pastoral, issue-based survivalism indicated above.[17] Early episodes in Series Two (31 March–23 June 1976) focused on the need to record and acquire skills, with much emphasis on the invaluable knowledge of medical student Ruth (Celia Gregory).

Producer Terence Dudley, who had written for and produced *Doomwatch*, clearly shared a concern for the issues arising from this scenario, but the collective nature of the enterprise, involving concept creator, producer and several major writers (one of whom, Ian McCulloch, was also one of the main actors), resulted in tensions. Nation's 1976 novelisation, which presents the central characters as wanderers moving towards a conclusion not dealt with in the series, may represent his original plan. A subsequent *Survivors* novel, John Eyers's *Genesis of a Hero* (1979), steps altogether outside of the canonical storyline to become an effectively bitter future-history of the warlordism that follows social breakdown. In a 1992 *TV Zone* interview, Terry Nation was reported as being antagonistic to the producer, who 'didn't understand what I was trying to do ... I was tremendously disappointed by the way the show went.'[18] Nation departed and later developed his best-known sf series, *Blake's 7* (1978–81), a dark and ambiguous space-opera, to which some of his ideas about military autocracies were transferred.

The collaborative nature of *Survivors* obviously precludes ascribing particular influences to individual creators. Nevertheless, it is quite clear to see the 'collective' nature of science fiction working its way through the series. If there is an *Urtext*, it must be *The Day of the Triffids* (1951), which was not produced and broadcast by BBC Television until September–October 1981, although the Light Programme radio dramatisation in October–November 1957 was enormously influential. As has been suggested above, 'catastrophe sf' from various sources has a range of possible precursors: influences less specific than the general context against which the concept or composition of *Survivors* developed. Nevertheless, *Triffids* begins with a somewhat similar catastrophe (not a disease but a sudden blindness, which may have been an accidental or deliberate triggering of a satellite weapons system) and proceeds to dramatise the practical and ethical questions of post-catastrophe survival. The swiftly spreading plague in *Survivors* happens by accident, although it is less clear how and why the disease existed in the first place (perhaps an attempt to develop a biological weapon). Nation's 1976 novel merely has the plague beginning with the sudden illness of a passenger on board an international flight.

Beyond their similar dramatic starting points, *Triffids* and *Survivors* share further affinities. If *The Good Life* suggests an amused condescension towards dropping out of the bourgeois rat race, there is a similar tension in the 'cosy catastrophe', a term invented by Brian Aldiss to describe middle-class fictions like Wyndham's, in which 'the hero should have a pretty good time (a girl, free suites at the Savoy, automobiles for the taking) while everyone else is dying off'.[19] In such fiction, there is clearly an adolescent fantasy of taking without responsibility, but most science fiction examples are much more anxious than the description suggests. This anxiety, of course, comes from a number of sources. An obvious one, in stories published during the 1950s, is the terror instilled after Hiroshima and Nagasaki. However, the basic story, in which a man (usually) is left alone after society has mysteriously disappeared, can be used in a number of ways. Shelley and Shiel use the device to suggest existential terror. Alfred Bester's short story 'They Don't Make Life Like They Used To' (1963) possesses hauntingly psychotic overtones. Judith Merril, introducing the story in *The Best of Science Fiction 9*, remarks on what she sees as the central theme of the 'survivor story', which is dealing with 'the alienated: with "normal people" in a world suddenly turned alien.'[20] Bester's tale, though, with its non sequiturs, displacement activity and deliberate inattention to what is actually *happening* – '"There goes another skyscraper," Linda said. "What were we talking about?"' – would suggest how impossible it is to *be* normal in such a trans-formed world.[21]

Part of this alienation, at least in the fiction Aldiss identifies, boils down to the simple fear of sharing resources with the working class. *The Good Life* can be seen as part of this sensibility; the Goods and the Ledbetters next door are equally middle class. Tom Good has dropped out through choice. Wyndham, although himself middle class, opened the debate in *Triffids* with the important figure of the declassé Coker. A working-class intellectual, who, disgusted by what he sees as the selfishness of the sighted towards the blind, he aims, at first, to establish a kind of benevolent dictatorship which *forces* the sighted few to direct the scavenging operations of the blinded many. He later comes to realise that the rules have been rewritten. Nevertheless, class is important through the novel. Masen, the narrator, comes from a comfortable suburban background, though opting for a less predictable and traditional career. The nature of the commune which he later joins is apolitical as only the English middle class can be: 'It'd take too long to go into constitutional questions now'[22] is the reply to a question posed about the forming of its governing council.

Survivors is equally middle class, as it opens with Abby (Carolyn Seymour) in her isolated, protected environment. All the main actors in the first two episodes, bar the comic-threatening Welshman Tom Price (Talfryn Thomas) and the sinister Wormley, have nice, neat, educated voices. We notice how Jenny (Lucy Fleming) is threatened by youths with working-class accents as she flees London on foot. Part of this, of course, is to establish a sense of cosiness for the audience. To return to our touchstone of *The Good Life*, such a sitcom would be far less amusing if it were about a struggle to achieve autonomy waged by someone from an unprivileged background.

In *Survivors*, a sense of wish-fulfilment security is also flagged by the difficulty some of the characters have in understanding that the world has changed utterly. Throughout the first scenes, the pandemic is referred to as 'flu' although the symptoms are closer to those of bubonic plague. Abby's conversation with the local stationmaster suggests more a country in the grip of temporary industrial turmoil (like a strike) than imminent collapse. Her husband David (Peter Bowles) is angry because he has had to take a lengthy and roundabout journey home, not fearful because of what might happen. Some of this, of course, could be traditional English stiff-upper-lip reserve, but it is the sense of avoidance which matters, a sense we see in more comic vein in the half-mad Price's insistence that 'The Yanks' will help – a hope expressed in *The Day of the Triffids* that 'they' will clear the mess up.[23] Price insists again in 'Genesis' that 'The Yanks'll fix us up.' But it is clear that there will be no 'they', no 'Yanks', and soon Bronson (Peter Copley), a teacher at the school where Abby's son Peter had been sent, is telling how terrible the time of the survivors will be. 'All the old crafts and skills must be learned', he says, echoing Coker in *The Day of the Triffids*.[24]

Survivalism is necessary. But what kind of society will survive? 'Crafts and skills' suggests a return to a social structure of peasants and artisans. In later episodes, the nagging question is the politics of such structures. Who makes the decisions and on whose behalf will those decisions be made? Tom Good is not particularly interested in converting, or working with, others. Self-sufficiency is a personal goal, as it was for John Seymour, one which emphasises the local, the parochial.[25] While Wyndham, as a novelist, structures much of his tale upon questions of how a post-catastrophe *society* (as opposed to a chance collective of individuals) can survive, and a propagandist discourse like the later *Threads* combats governmental wish-fulfilment by suggesting, starkly, that the alternative to anarchy and extinction can only be primitive feudalism, *Survivors* is bound to the techniques of TV soap opera in the sense that it hints at possibilities and raises issues of social or (usually) personal morality in the middle of story lines. Each character has different motives for continued survival: Abby to find her son; Jenny to get out of London; Tom Price to scavenge; and Ann (Myra Frances) to use her scavenged resources in order to regain her position as a social parasite. The exception is Greg (Ian McCulloch), who is initially uncertain, with no clear goal, although he later becomes a strong leader.

Nation clearly intended his series to discuss questions of wealth and leadership. The initial negative figures are those of vested interest. The fur-coated Anne is privileged – 'Daddy had sent the servants away' – and greedy, with her plans to acquire objects and use them to pay off serfs whose labour she will live on in a manner reflecting her previous status. Arthur Wormley is a trade-union man with flat Northern vowels. The surviving people, he argues, will want someone to lead them and he will be that man. Both represent power, but the power of the pre-plague world, which has little relevance to the new environment. Abby lectures Wormley in the same way as the teacher lectured her: 'The aim is to become more and more self-reliant.'[26] Wormley, though, does not seem to distinguish between self-reliance and power-hunger. His ruthlessness is shown by the way he executes a raider, assuming the 'right' of the last vestiges of nationalism, and Nation's novel makes his hypocrisy clear: 'He faltered over some of the words as though his uncertainty added sincerity … what alarmed her was that his conviction hid his motives even from himself.'[27] The character of the populist, ruthless leader appears again as Manny (Sydney Tafler) in Series Two's two-parter 'Lights of London', whose role model is identified when the hard-bitten nurse Nessie (Lennox Milne) tells him to 'stop the Napoleon act'.[28]

For the survivors, Abby is the initial leader figure. It is she who has the strongest personal motives for survival (the search for her son) but she also has, thanks to Mr Bronson's early warnings, most successfully internalised the qualities necessary for survival. Both her quest, resulting at the end of Episode Two ('Genesis') in finding a place to stay but resumed at several points during the series, and Jenny's trek from London recall the off-stage journey to Shirning Farm made by Josella Playton in *The Day of the Triffids*. Abby's leadership adds a strong feminist element to the series. However, the early shots establishing her privileged position, playing tennis against an automatic server and being waited on by her housekeeper, undercut some of the later achievement, and as a character she lacks the irony established by the equally privileged Josella, who supports herself by writing a lurid bestseller.

Although Alsop calls Abby a 'symbolic socio-sexual appendage to [her husband's] financial success',[29] she is more accurately someone who has achieved this position by right, safely 'cocooned in a middle-class existence' while her husband braves the collapsing society to struggle home to her. While this satirises the conventional image of harassed commuter returning to a scotch and a cooked meal while wife stays secluded in suburbia, the Grants are more than this. Their home is not suburbia but village stockbroker belt. They are owner–manager class and Abby will remain owner–manager. Her motivating force, set up in the telephone conversation with her son Peter in the first few minutes of the opening episode of *Survivors*, is never quite explicitly articulated in the TV series although it is brilliantly suggested at the end of Nation's novel. Her quest is simply to find her son, but is this maternal feeling or simply guilt at having sent him to boarding school and realised too late the danger of the plague? We witness her exchange with Peter, which ends with a quiver in her voice as she says, 'All right darling … take care of yourself', and as she dabs sweat away from her face after she replaces the receiver, it looks suspiciously as though she is wiping away tears.[30] Later, in bed with her husband, she wonders about bringing Peter home from school. There are a number of reasons why she *should* embark upon a search for Peter but guilt may well be among the most important.[31]

On quitting her home, she sets fire to it. However, this does not seem to be a symbolic destruction of the old way of life, for her reaction to Wormley and his plans for 'order' is ambivalent. At first she takes readily to a return to a familiar environment, accepting a vodka, requesting a hot bath, and politely exclaiming 'This is nice' when she sees the working kitchen.[32] She even seems prepared to accept Wormley's protection for the 'self-reliant' community she is going to found. However, her growing antipathy seems based not upon a humanistic feeling that Wormley's expropriations and executions are 'wrong' but because someone with a different accent has taken over the properties of folk with accents like her. (She is, after all, planning to take over a convenient farm which would have belonged to someone else. What if other people had designs on the same location?) This hesitation is not because she may be wrong in concluding that warlordism is morally indefensible, but because the nature of the characters in dramatic performance shows a different conversation taking place than appears in the script. If Wormley had been a suave Oxbridge type and we had been shown the transfer of power from the 'legitimate' authorities, and the executed raider had been an uncouth working-class thug, would our reaction be the same? Perhaps, but the story would have been, in a genuine way, more subversive, and it is this uncertain tone in the series which undermines subsequent scenes of confrontational morality. A similar question of leadership is raised in Series One's 'Garland's War'[33] in which audience sympathy – and Abby's – appears to veer towards the glamorous Garland (Richard Heffer), who, as 'rightful owner' of an estate and an aristocratic adventurer trained in leadership, is more 'suitable' for the role than the pragmatic and ruthless Knox (Peter Jeffrey).

Abby's class seems to carry more weight than her gender, and the way she lectures Wormley, using more or less the same words we have recently heard Bronson use to her, suggests not so much a person who is fully aware of the implications of her situation than one who is parroting the opinions of others. She is less a 'survivor' and more the kind of person who would discuss at a dinner party only those books reviewed in that weekend's broadsheet literary supplement. At this point in the story, she has still not quite thought through the implications of her position. Nation's examination here of the moral position is taken up later by fellow writer Jack Ronder in Series Two's 'Lights of London', a more melodramatic scenario which blurs the interesting choice medical student Ruth feels she has to make: to return to her small group or stay as doctor for the London group of 500. (We are told – true or not, the point is that Ruth believes it

– that a human population of fewer than 500 is unviable in terms of species survival.) Is Manny a 'failed' leader because his charm hides a ruthless and treacherous nature or because he is so clearly procrastinating in his plan to lead the 500 out of London? This is a valid question, but while, in plot terms, the story ends with Manny's downfall and benefits for both groups, Ruth's dilemma has been taken from her by the resolution. In following the conflict between 'good' and 'bad', she no longer has to choose between 'good' and 'better', or 'least bad', options because of Ronder's development of the story line. The situation has been defused.

By the end of the series, we are shown the need for a king as figurehead. Perhaps, with the choice of (the dead) Greg, who has throughout displayed reluctance when called upon to play a leadership role, we have a dramatisation of the old saw that the best leader is someone who has no wish to be such. It is certainly unwise, however, to suggest overt ideological motives on anyone's part when considering an artefact so prone to compromise as a television series. *Survivors*, according to Alsop and other commentators, seems to have undergone at least one major rift concerning the direction its creator and subsequent writers felt the storyline should take. *Doomwatch*, likewise, moved in directions Pedler and Davis were not responsible for, and the ending of Nation's later project *Blake's 7*, in which the entire cast is eliminated, caused much fan discussion about its motives.[34] Nevertheless, it is because of this complex of sometimes opposing tensions between the creator's vision, audience expectations, the broadcasting company's ideas of what audiences want, and the sheer logistics of a long-running TV series that such programmes are naked locations of cultural debate.

The stunted nature of the discussion of ethics in *Survivors* is partly due to the lack of the currently fashionable story arc, a device used – as in contemporary US sf and fantasy TV series like *Babylon 5* (Rattlesnake Productions for Warners, 1993–9) or *Buffy, the Vampire Slayer* (Warners/UPN, 1997–2003) – to create a novelistic effect or, more specifically, the sense of a mosaic of linked short stories; what is often called a 'fixup'.[35] 'Arc' TV fiction brings closure to the story; not necessarily a *final* closure, but the tying up and consolidating of a particular story line so that any possible sequel will have to move on from what has gone before. Although Roger

Fulton points out that each series of *Survivors* focuses on a specific theme,[36] and Neil Alsop notes that producer Terence Dudley was 'the single cohesive force behind all thirty-eight episodes',[37] there are too many 'singleton' episodes featuring 'this week's moral problem' to consider the 'arc' as the primary narrative structure, even though the coming and going of major characters makes it important to view the series in order.

Consequently, in *Survivors* the debate is not as fully formed as it is in *The Day of the Triffids*, where the moral issues – the responsibility of the sighted for the blind and the questions of polygamy as a method of increasing the sighted population – are central and a number of possible social scenarios (military; Coker's 'forced ethical' structure; theocracy) are experimented with in the text before an apolitical communal model is adopted. As a novelist, Wyndham can allow his characters to express their doubts and speculations in conversation, particularly between Bill Masen and Josella, or Bill and Coker, although many of the most powerful scenes in the novel appear as mini-dramas. These include, for instance, Bill's dilemma when, on the verge of quitting the group of blinded for whom he has taken responsibility and returning to his search for Josella, he is offered the sexual services of a teenage virgin;[38] and the earlier scene when he intervenes (in vain) to rescue a blind woman taken up by a blind gang led by a sighted man before realising 'that if there was to be any survival, anyone adopted by this gang would stand a far better chance than she would on her own'.[39]

Nevertheless, the structure of the television programme allows for such discussion of ethical questions at episode length. For example, in Series Two's 'Face of the Tiger' (written by Don Shaw; 1st tx. BBC 1, 28 April 1976), Alistair (John Line), a gentle expert in herbal lore, is initially welcomed into the group, although this increases pressure on dwelling space. However, before the plague, Alistair was a child murderer. This is one of a number of episodes which explore the post-catastrophe alienation effect, and its combination of moral dilemmas and cosiness makes it one of the most interesting *Survivors* episodes. As well as the questions of resources and duties, we are reminded of the apparent random nature of survival. Are identities post-catastrophe the same as those pre-catastrophe? In other words, should we apply the same moral strictures when circumstances have changed? Ultimately, Alistair is 'cured' and the group, apart from John Abineri's bigoted Hubert (who speaks with a rural accent, smells, and lives in ramshackle accommodation – so we know better than to believe him) are prepared to accept him.

The contrast between Alistair, who, after a year spent in meditative solitude, is at one with himself, and the bickering, harassed individuals who have come together largely by chance, is well handled, with him quizzically observing several minor arguments. But, because of Hubert's malice, one of the community's children is encouraged to fear him and, in a scene notable for remarkably wooden acting, runs away and cannot be found. Here we have the same problem that we are faced with in the series' consideration of 'leader' figures like Wormley, Garland or Manny, and it is solved by the same means: evasion of the real issue. Alistair is now 'good'. But what if he was not and the community needed his skills? Conversely, if he *is* guilty of another murder and is a threat, what can the community do? Hubert, naturally, talks about shooting him. Greg, without consulting with co-leader Charles (Denis Lill), decides that all they can do is banish Alistair. The community is not structured to deal with serious crime: they 'haven't got any policemen'. And thus responsibilities of living together are evaded. The 'Alistair' thread, in fact, offers interesting human contradictions in facing moral dilemmas. Ruth agrees to accept Alistair because he has come to 'know himself', is safe, and a community must take a moral position: 'We're civilised by choice.' But later, when Greg mentions Hubert's solution to the question of sanctions, she is first horrified ('You're not shooting anyone, Greg!') and then, once Greg announces his more merciful decision, wracked with doubts ('What if you're wrong?'). The irony is that Alistair has himself decided to leave, horrified by the community's constant bickering. The plague had freed him from his inability to control his antagonism to others but he is still not a social being: merely one who has come to terms with being asocial. 'I thought we'd *all* be changed', he says. 'I came out of a nightmare into reality', but mundane squabbles over 'petty things like soap' have not departed.[40] The first law of self-reliance is to know oneself: this the community has not achieved.

When the missing child is found safe, Alistair departs for a hermit's life. His final message to the community is from Wordsworth:

...Tis nature's law
That none, the meanest of created things,
Of forms created the most vile and brute,
The dullest or most noxious, should exist
Divorced from good...[41]

It is a message that they first take to refer to the workshy, malicious Hubert (whom Ruth has just insisted 'must go') but then, uncomfortably, they realise that it perhaps highlights their own complacency in the face of how far they have fallen short of these ideals. Their inability to deal convincingly with the problem of the discovery that someone in their midst was, in the 'former life' before the plague, guilty of a crime which should bar him from a community is only a symptom of their inability to deal with the day-to-day conflicts that arise in their here-and-now. The episode is riddled with sentimentality (the Wordsworth quotation is repeated in the closing scene in case we missed it the first time), and its domestic focus, after the wider exposure of 'Lights of London', brings us back to the soap-opera elements of the series. Nevertheless in terms of the question underlying the whole series – the political-with-a-small-'p' debate about the values a recovering society should hold most dear – it is an important discussion.

The wider Political (with a large 'P') debate, however, is shown in the series' final three episodes. Much of it is woven from the threads showing the construction of a web of communities by Greg and Agnes (Anna Pitt) and the journey northwards by Charles, Jenny and Hubert with the engineer Alec Campbell (William Dysart), to restore electrical power via a Scottish hydro-electric power station. 'The Last Laugh' (1st tx. BBC 1, 25 May 1977) has Greg encountering a symbolic group of four horsemen who are emissaries of another petty warlord, the Captain (Roy Marsden). Stabbed and left for dead, Greg is taken in by a once-thriving community where smallpox (actually another of the mysterious plagues, like the 'London Sickness', which might be a mutated variant of the original one), has killed everyone except two men and Dr Adams (Clifton Jones), who is dying. The infection spreads to Greg, who pretends to be converted to the Captain's cause in order to lead the latter's men away from his own community at Sloton Spencer, thus sacrificing himself as a kind of biological warfare weapon.

In the next episode, 'Long Live the King' (1st tx. BBC 1, 1 June 1977), it is confirmed that Greg brought the disease to the Captain's group, although the Captain himself survived. The main strand, however, shows us the efficient Agnes in military uniform, working from a base in Yorkshire and linking people and communities in Greg's name to form a real government. Money is being issued, with petrol as the backing collateral. This leads to a number of conflicts about how far this is re-creating negative aspects of the old society, notably in respect of Robert Gillespie's Sam (whose role becomes clearer in the next two episodes), when he tells Jenny, 'You were one of the haves', and between Agnes and Charles. Agnes here speaks like any other of the series' warlords, threatening to blow up alternative sources of petrol in order to safeguard the monopoly she claims to have and asking, in words not too different from Wormley's in the first episode: 'How can you have a country without law and order and people to enforce it?' 'All we want', says Charles, 'is a loose confederation of communities.' Agnes replies: 'And who is going to keep the peace?'[42]

The only real difference – and it may be the significant one – is that a constitutional council is being formed. Nevertheless, we may remember that the 'fascist' Manny in 'Lights of London' was elected by his community and that Agnes is prepared to lie and use force to achieve her goal. Greg, though dead, is the man known to most of the settled communities as a link between them. He is a convenient figurehead and an interestingly British king. The money is issued in his name, as is the call for national unity. As a dead man, he embodies par excellence the constitutional monarchy in which monarchy is a symbol of the realm – and in whose name the realm's people can safely be deceived. The final scene shows the Union Jack, with Greg's initials embroidered in the centre, waving in the breeze, as Jenny utters the classic phrase of royalist continuity from which the title is taken: 'The king is dead, long live the king.' We know that the decencies will survive because Charles has come round to the use of Greg as figurehead. But the counter-argument – why have anything resembling a monarchy at all? – has not really been addressed.

This penultimate episode can be read as a sardonic recapitulation of the 'hero-dying-for-his-people' myth and an exploration of the fictional nature of monarchy. However, as a fiction exploring the nature of post-catastrophe society, it celebrates conservatism rather than change. With a climax of stunning cosiness, it reassures its audience that however sweeping the coming social changes, the cut-glass accents and the Flag will still be there: a bastion against upstarts and working people.

Importantly, 'Long Live the King' is not the final episode of *Survivors*. Although Neil Alsop calls 'Power' (1st tx. BBC 1, 8 June 1977) 'anti-climactic in the extreme',[43] it is hard not to see it as a comment, in the form of an ironic coda, to the issues raised in 'Long Live the King'. Although the structure of the political arguments raised shows itself to be firmly in the *Survivors* mould of A saying 'I'm against it', B saying 'I'm for it,' and A saying 'Oh, all right then', there is some fascinating background which suggests that the Little Britain implied by the penultimate episode is more unstable than it appears to be and that it is certainly possible to read against its apparent cosiness. The clue is in the ambiguity of the title. Alec and Sam have reached the power station ready to turn on the generators and Charles, Jenny and Hubert are on their way by train to meet them. They contact the immaculately tweedy and well-spoken McAlister (Iain Cuthbertson), who tells them he is the local laird. The Highlands, with a surviving population of 150,000, is now the most densely populated part of the former United Kingdom and McAlister is suspicious of the idea of using a Scottish power station to kick-start the economy of a distant England.

Meanwhile, more fundamental questions are being raised. Alec echoes the contemporary discussions about power and its generation that were being raised by champions of 'appropriate' (or 'alternative') technology. Electricity generated from water is renewable, non-polluting, and 'the only kind of energy we should ever use'. Sam, however, turns out to question the whole project. Switching on the power will lead to the bad old days of factory workers and wage-slaves: 'People have learned to be self-sufficient – give them electricity … and they depend for their livelihood on something they have no control over.'[44] Electricity, he says, should come from local sources such as water mills and windmills – the argument often put forward by radical self-sufficiency propagandists such as John Seymour.

As Sam tries to sabotage the project, the episode offers an interesting exploration of national interests and identities. A Welshman

(Charles) defends the English right to electricity generated in Scotland. More fundamentally, the episode highlights the whole idea of the nation-state in the context dramatised by *Survivors*: is there any way in which concepts like England, Wales, Scotland or the 'United Kingdom' are meaningful in the post-catastrophe future? The way out that is offered is reminiscent of the technocratic mind-set that links British literary sf of the H.G. Wells mode to American equivalents such as that by Hugo Gernsback and John W. Campbell. Who will control the power station? Alec cuts into the argument by saying that he will control it and choose his own assistants, responsible to neither England nor Scotland. As a Scot who worked, pre-plague, in England, he has ties to both communities, but more importantly he is, perhaps, to be the founder of a new caste of technocratic experts. Greg, we might be reminded here, was an engineer. The future in the hands of scientists and technologists rather than politicians is an old science fiction dream. It is too late in the timeline of the programme for any suggestions about how this society might look, but the Wellsian 'dictatorship of experts' is implied in Alec's argument.

However, there is a coda to the coda. The final scene shows the housekeeper in the large candlelit dining room of McAlister's stately home coming towards us in an evening dress of thin folds of turquoise fabric and jewels, which, together in the soft light cast by the candles she holds, give a sexually charged allure to the scene. She turns off the electric lights and sits opposite McAlister. They exchange smiles and raise glasses in a toast. What can we take from this scene? That their relationship as introduced earlier in the episode was fake? (McAlister had said that his wife had died and loaned Jenny some of her clothing.) Or that the future is to be feudal, whatever the middle-class liberals might say? There is a strong hint in this episode that the entire English 'story' has been sidelined: that the future of civilisation lies in the roots of societies which had naturally been more self-reliant, where a greater degree of isolation led to comparatively fewer deaths. But this self-reliance and self-sufficiency is not that of the ecological 'thinkers' nor of the dreamers of hippy communes, nor even of the new structures which can arise from the chance collision of survivors, but that of societies where everyone knows their place. King Greg Preston is an artificial construct. Laird McAlister is either a genuine survivor of a much older regime, or a very astute and successful warlord indeed. Either way, we seem not to be offered much hope for the future of post-industrial society.

NOTES

1. Edward Goldsmith et al., *A Blueprint for Survival*, Penguin Special (Harmondsworth: Penguin, 1972), p. 27.
2. *Guardian*, 3 April 2003, p. 13.
3. *Survivors: The Complete First Series* (London: BBC Worldwide, 2003) and *The Complete Second Series* (London: BBC Worldwide 2004). Most of the research for this chapter was done using personal copies of taped television broadcasts.
4. I am indebted for the information on dates of Wyndham-related material to Phil Stephensen-Payne's *John Wyndham: Creator of the Cosy Catastrophe*, Galactic Central Bibliographies for the Avid Reader, Vol. 16, 3rd rev. edn (Leeds: Galactic Central Publications, 2001).
5. See Norman Cohn's *The Pursuit of the Millennium* (Oxford: Oxford University Press, 1970) for instances of such movements in Western Europe.
6. Anna Bramwell's *Ecology in the 20th Century: A History* (New Haven: Yale University Press, 1989) and *The Fading of the Greens* (New Haven: Yale University Press, 1994) establish a much more defined and analytical context for these ideas. See, however, Piers H.G. Stephens, 'Blood, Not Soil: Anna Bramwell and the Myth of Hitler's Green Party', *Organization & Environment* 14/2 (June 2001), pp. 173–87, for another view of Bramwell's stance towards the history of the Green movement.
7. The best known of these fictions is almost certainly John Wyndham's *The Day of the Triffids* (1951). More recent 'collapse' scenarios include Christopher Priest's *Fugue for a Darkening Island* (London: Faber & Faber, 1972), Doris Lessing's *Memoirs of a Survivor* (London: Octagon, 1974), and Maggie Gee's *The Ice People* (London: Richard Cohen Books, 1998).
8. See Mary Shelley's *The Last Man* (1826), ed. Anne McWhir (Ontario: Broadview Press, 1996), for other works on this theme.
9. Bramwell, *The Fading of the Greens* p. 54. Bramwell's more extensive work, *Ecology in the 20th Century*, notes in passing several instances of the science fiction or utopian novels with which ecological ideas since the nineteenth century were linked (e.g. pp. 66, 87, 94) although not television or the underground press.
10. See, for instance, George McKay, *Senseless Acts of Beauty* (London: Verso, 1996), ch. 5, for descriptions of and statements by Dongas and others involved in anti-road protest movements.
11. Nigel Fountain, *Underground: The London Alternative Press 1966–74* (London: Routledge, 1988), p. 35.

12. Ibid., p. 56.

13. Donella Meadows et. al., *The Limits to Growth: A Report for the Club of Rome's Project on the Predicament of Mankind 1972* (London: Pan, 1974), p. 23.

14. See Bernard Porter, *Plots and Paranoia: A History of Political Espionage in Britain 1790–1988* (London: Unwin Hyman, 1989), pp. 197–227; and David Leigh, *The Wilson Plot* (London: Heinemann, 1988), pp. 220–26.

15. Joe Nazarro, 'Terry Nation's *Survivors*', *TV Zone* 31 (1992), p. 28.

16. Neil Alsop, 'A Horseman Riding By', http://timescreen.virtualave.net. suv1art.htm (accessed 2 April 2004), originally published in *Time Screen* 10 (Winter 1987). See Andy Sawyer, 'The Catastrophe Show', *O'Ryan* 4 (July 1976), pp. 12–14.

17. See Neil Alsop, 'Birth of a Nation', http://timescreen.virtualave.net. suv2art.htm (accessed 2 April 2004), originally published in *Time Screen* 13 (Spring 1989).

18. Nazarro, 'Terry Nation's *Survivors*', p. 30.

19. Brian Aldiss with David Wingrove, *Trillion Year Spree: The History of Science Fiction* (London: Gollancz, 1986), p. 254.

20. Alfred Bester, 'They Don't Make Life Like They Used To', in Judith Merril (ed.), *The Best of Science Fiction 9* (London: Mayflower, 1967), p. 59.

21. Ibid., p. 82.

22. John Wyndham, *The Day of the Triffids* (Harmondsworth: Penguin, 1954), p. 258.

23. Ibid., pp. 101, 130, 194.

24. Ibid., pp. 203–4.

25. 'For an overcrowded country like England to now allow floods of immigrants in, is madness…. If a global culture is really emerging I want no part of it, and I hope it does not succeed. A world in which such a culture prevailed would be for me quite intolerable', John Seymour tells an interviewer on www.thirdway.org/files/articles/intseymo.html (accessed 2 April 2004).

26. 'Genesis' (1st tx. BBC 1, 23 April 1975).

27. Terry Nation, *Survivors* (London: Weidenfeld and Nicolson, 1976), pp. 72–3.

28. 'Lights of London (Part 2)' (1st tx. BBC 1, 21 April 1976).

29. Alsop, 'A Horseman Riding By'.

30. 'The Fourth Horseman' (1st tx. BBC 1, 16 April 1975).

31. Guilt is also a theme of Series 1, Episode 5, 'Gone to the Angels' (1st tx. BBC 1, 14 May 1975), in which Abby realises too late that she has carried the plague to a religious community so far protected by its isolation.

32. 'Genesis'.

33. 'Garland's War' (1st tx. BBC 1 21 May 1975).

34. See the *Blake's 7* FAQ site, www.uran.net/sci_fi/blake7/b7_faq.html. (accessed 2 April 2004) for various theories about how this apparent slaughter might have been resolved had there been a further series.

35. See John Clute and Peter Nicholls (eds), *Encyclopaedia of Science Fiction* (London: Orbit, 1993), p. 432.

36. Roger Fulton, *The Encyclopaedia of TV Science Fiction* (London: Boxtree/ Independent Television Books, 1997), p. 516.

37. Alsop, 'Birth of a Nation'.

38. Wyndham, *The Day of the Triffids*, pp. 146–8.

39. Ibid., p. 59.

40. 'Face of the Tiger' (1st tx. BBC 1 28 April 1976).

41. William Wordsworth, 'The Old Cumberland Beggar', in *William Wordsworth*, ed. Stephen Gill (Oxford: Oxford University Press, 1941), p. 51.

42. 'Long Live the King' (1st tx. BBC 1, 1 June 1977).

43. Alsop, 'Birth of a Nation'.

44. 'Power' (1st tx. BBC 1, 8 June 1977).

8

TV docudrama and the nuclear subject: *The War Game, The Day After* and *Threads*

DAVID SEED

The combination of documentary and drama in a hybrid genre specially designed for television dates from 1930s' documentaries as well
as reconstructions for TV purposes, but the engagement of that genre
with the subject of nuclear war has been rare and controversial.[1] Apart
from the fears of the distress such dramatisations might cause in
the audience, the nuclear subject brought into question the issue of
national survival and with it the very possibility of quasi-documentary
reportage within a situation of ultimate crisis. The number of novels
published on the nuclear threat in the USA vastly outnumbered those
published in Britain.[2] However, these American novels were widely
distributed in Britain and so it is likely that British imaginations of
nuclear war were partly shaped by American versions of such crises.
This chapter will concentrate on the British TV films *The War Game*
(BBC TV, 1965) and *Threads* (BBC TV, 1984), but a briefer discussion
of the US TV film *The Day After* (ABC, 1983) will also be used to
compare methods and to contrast the national symbolism of *The
Day After* with the documentary methods of the British films. As
early as 1951, the American novelist Philip Wylie was planning a
film to be called *The Bomb* which would educate the public about the
effects of nuclear attack. That year, in an article drafted as 'Terror
– and the Terror Weapons', he reflected: 'It would seem advisable
now to acquaint all city populations, by film, TV, and 'live shows' in
public parks and stadia, with every imaginable look of atomic bomb

casualties from nudity through the most grisly burns to evisceration, decapitation, and the like'.[3] Not surprisingly, he was unable to secure backing for such a film and turned instead to projecting an account of nuclear attack through the medium of fiction in *Tomorrow!* (1954) which combined future reportage with a dramatisation of the experience of key families in a Midwestern city.

THE WAR GAME

In Britain, Peter Watkins commenced work on his TV documentary *The War Game* in 1965, originally planning to 'start with a long build-up of an international crisis', but in the event opened his narrative with an already existing state of emergency.[4] The main opening shot follows a police motorcycle courier taking orders to a town centre while a radio newsreader announces a Chinese invasion of South Vietnam and a blockade of Berlin by Soviet forces 'in sympathy'. The film pays no attention to the origins of these crises – that is no part of its purpose – but it does recount an inevitability to escalation. Faced with massive military action in Germany, the US president has 'no alternative' but to launch a tactical nuclear weapon, and the same is true of the Soviet premier for different reasons. Early shots of the civil defence machine moving into action in Britain are intercut with sequences in Berlin showing rioting on the East–West border. Watkins uses shaky hand-held camera footage here to suggest immediate authenticity and keeps all shots in close focus on crowd scenes. The resultant impression of confusion forms an integral part of the film's polemic, an effect further developed in *Threads* (1984): both films apply the premise that the first casualty in the outbreak of nuclear war, or the events immediately triggering such a war, would be clarity of information. Indeed Watkins foregrounds the lack of information about nuclear radiation in vox-pop-style interviews, which are spliced in with shots of the Berlin crisis and house requisitioning by the domestic authorities. These interviews were designed to display public ignorance of matters like radioactive carbon and strontium and formed part of Watkins's method of giving the lie to statements of government policy.

The status of the voice-over in this film is a complex mixture of irony and information. Derek Paget has noted that *The War Game* uses the '*authoritative* (as against the *character*) voice-over and ... the "purely" informational insert (of statistics, maps, graphs, etc.)' and he helpfully alerts us to the different formal means Watkins uses to question the notion of authority throughout the film.[5] The opening sequence presents statistics – or, rather, one chilling statistic: that Britain has the highest number of nuclear targets relative to land area in the world. This is stated over an outline map of the country showing their locations. Then, once fallout areas are displayed, virtually the whole of England comes under erasure. Through these graphics, Watkins sums up in the abstract what the film then proceeds to render in human terms. There is a further unobtrusive irony introduced here into the film's location. Kent is one of the areas shown to be relatively safe from fallout, but that is exactly the area where the film was shot.[6] The alert viewer might pick up this disparity and as a result question the authoritative statements made during the film. One of the most obvious problems of a 'future documentary' on nuclear war is that, with the exceptions of Hiroshima and Nagasaki (which were bombings of a non-nuclear power with what now seem small devices), there are no clear facts available, only better- or worse-informed predictions. Watkins scrupulously avoided any political alignment in his film, which attempted to give the lie to bland government statements about nuclear attack, but nevertheless when his film was completed he was repeatedly attacked for supporting the Campaign for Nuclear Disarmament.[7]

Watkins sets up a dialogue with official sources of information, which reaches its most ironic points when interviews are excerpted. Watkins has explained the effect on his own website as follows: 'Interwoven among scenes of "reality" were stylised interviews with a series of "establishment" figures – an Anglican Bishop, a nuclear strategist, etc.... In this film I was interested in breaking the illusion of media-produced "reality".'[8] One of the ways Watkins did this was to break the frame of the film constantly so that we continually have to reposition ourselves in relation to the material being shown. For Derek Paget, such strategies have always been present in the genre of docudrama, which, since the 1950s,

> has routinely broken the boundaries of documentary's historic claim to be directly evidential. The narrative concerns of drama

THE HUMAN FACE OF NUCLEAR WAR   Peter Watkins's *The War Game*.

have caused the Fact to be constantly re-positioned relative to its permanently pro-filmic status. Captioning simultaneously marks a distance from the factual (documentary) and prevents a sinking of facts into the empathetic (drama).[9]

The ruptures Watkins uses are more varied than captioning, and include the staged interviews he himself describes as repeating actual public statements. Here the camera angle is fixed, the interviewees are composed and – in grotesque contrast to the nuclear victims – clean and smartly dressed. In short, these scenes follow a different decorum, shown to be not merely anachronistic but increasingly offensive as the film proceeds. The risk he runs is of discrediting all expert statements in a visual contrast where 'immediate' reportage characterised by jerky and confused footage is invested with authenticity while general and abstract descriptions become discredited as at best ignorant and at worst part of a concerted attempt to lull the public while the arms race goes ahead.

In the film, Watkins skilfully avoids this dilemma by making the nuclear attack and its consequences into the true protagonist of the film. Unlike *Threads*, which focuses on two Sheffield families, *The*

War Game traces out a process over which the emergency services have virtually no control. Second, Watkins does not allow us to yield to the spectacle he is evoking in many scenes. For instance, the main external scene dramatising the effects of a nuclear blast shows firemen battling to cope with a fire raging in a high building (actually shot in a disused barracks). At first the scene recalls news footage of the London Blitz but then Watkins destabilises the camera angle and shows figures falling to the ground or struggling against a fierce wind. The commentator at this point situates the scene within a historical sequence from Dresden through Tokyo to Hiroshima and explains the nature of a firestorm. Over a shot of fallen firemen the commentator explains that 'these men are dying both of heat stroke and of gas'. Indeed, it is a grim theme of the whole film that nuclear attack is not a singular event but one which can bring death from a whole range of causes.

The pacing of such sequences has been enthusiastically described by John Corner:

> The passage from frantic preparation for possible attack through to the strike itself and the phases of physical, psychic and social deterioration which follow, is depicted in a brilliantly edited mix of newsreel, verité and interview sequences. Continuity is provided by keeping the main focus on one locality.[10]

For Corner, it is the particularity of the future reportage that gives *The War Game* its impact because it positions the viewer as witness.

This effect is also achieved with the figures within the film. A major strategy Watkins uses to avoid the viewer identifying with specific protagonists is a traditional one in documentary: to represent virtually every human figure as a witness. Even when they do not speak, traumatised or wounded characters look directly into the camera. Their mute gaze becomes part of a collective act of testimony where the camera follows the movements of a concerned investigator. Watkins shows the workers in the emergency services to be equally vulnerable to trauma. Thus shots of appalling burns and other casualties – which may have caused the reports of audience faintings when the film was finally shown in cinemas – are followed by statements from an exhausted nurse; scenes of food riots are followed by a senior police officer describing how his men are succumbing to stress. Watkins establishes this principle of testimony through the explicit early interview scenes and develops it through the repeated directing of the victims' gaze to the camera as if they are appealing to the viewer for help. By the end of the film, the viewer has been drawn into scenes charged with the most harrowing extremes of suffering. Graphic close-ups of casualties might be expected in this context. Less predictable are shots of armed policemen – still a rare sight in the mid-1960s – engaged in mercy killings, soldiers burning piles of dead bodies or looters being shot. In the last two instances, Watkins thematises official secrecy when the implied investigator is waved away from the scenes, but these gestures give way to a greater need for the officials to explain (and so justify) their actions.

As many commentators have pointed out, representations of nuclear attack have an apocalyptic dimension varying according to the degree of hope held out for the continuation of human life. In such narratives, children symbolically embody the future. If they die, as happens in novels like the American writer Helen Clarkson's *The Last Day* (1959), so do hopes for a future generation.[11] Watkins makes this point not by deaths, but by showing a group of assembled children who mumble that they do not want to be anything when they grow up. This despair within the documentary fiction, Watkins has explained, was intended to have an external shock impact: 'At the end of the film everything is in chaos. People can't cope. They face a hopeless future. Because of this people may see that something has to be done about it now.'[12] The minimal release of his film, however, prevented this general purpose from being realised in the 1960s. Furthermore, Watkins's explanation raises a paradox about his documentary method which relates specifically to the nuclear subject.

In Philip Wylie's novel *Tomorrow!*, a newspaper editor is used as a witness to the bombing of a city in the American Midwest, especially to the nuclear flash:

> It was a Light of such intensity that Coley could see nothing except its lightness and its expanding dimensions. It swelled over the sky above and burst down toward him. He felt, at the same time, a strange physical sensation – just a brief start of a sensation – as if gravity had vanished and he, too, were a rushing thing, and a prickling through his body, and a heat.[13]

Wylie wants to convey the appalling force of the nuclear blast but can only do so in a contradictory way. No sooner has this notional act of witness been recorded, than the editor is vaporised along with the other citizens near ground zero. Once he has disappeared, the visual vantage point becomes an impossibility. Similarly, if Watkins's Britain has no future, his documentary has a purely notional audience. Traditional documentaries have investigated social problems always with the implied possibility of improvement or rectification, but when taken to its pessimistic conclusion, the nuclear subject can only address an audience formally distinguished from the very figures with which the film is seeking identification.

Since 1965, Watkins has repeatedly stated that he wanted to 'break down the uneasy silence [of] the authorities about nuclear war'.[14] Hence the crucial importance in *The War Game* of eloquent witness. The viewer's concern is directly solicited by overt address, where we are positioned as interviewers, and by the mute gaze of casualties. We shall never know how this would have worked on a mid-1960s' television audience because the film was banned, apparently because of a desire to avoid a confrontation between the governors and the director-general of the BBC, to avoid government embarrassment, and out of a general concern in some quarters about its possibly disturbing impact on audiences.[15]

Unsurprisingly, then, the subject remained largely unaddressed in British television until the 1980s, which saw a startling revival of concern over nuclear war both in British domestic policy and in film production. Steve Fox has recorded how British civil defence had lapsed after 1968 and from 1980 onwards was being laboriously renewed.[16] By the middle of that decade, in 1984, the year that *Threads* was first transmitted, sub-regional headquarters were being renewed and re-equipped. The 1980s saw the debate over Ronald Reagan's Strategic Defence Initiative (SDI) – popularly known as his 'Star Wars' plan – and in his survey of nuclear war films, Mick Broderick lists 33 as being released during the decade, twice the number to come out in the 1960s.[17] It is a reflection of this resurgence of concern that in 1982 the most viable plan emerged for Peter Watkins to remake *The War Game*, although the plan was abandoned before shooting could start.[18] During 1984 and 1985, BBC TV ran a series of programmes on nuclear war which included a dramatisation of

Robert O'Brien's 1974 post-holocaust novel *Z for Zachariah* (1st tx. BBC 1, 28 February 1984) and the eventual transmission of *The War Game* on BBC 2 on 31 July 1985.

THE DAY AFTER

In the USA, an important contribution to the emerging tradition of nuclear docudrama was made by *The Day After*, which was shown on ABC TV on 20 November 1983 and then shown in Britain the following month by ITV. The guiding force behind this production was Brandon Stoddard, the president of ABC Motion Pictures, who had seen *The War Game*.[19] Here, Berlin is again used as a flashpoint for a confrontation between East and West, the action being set against opening shots of the Kansas countryside. This location was crucially different from either *The War Game* or, as we shall see, *Threads*. *The War Game* is set in Kent towns and *Threads* in a northern industrial city, both of which were targeted in the German bombing raids of World War II. *The Day After* is set in the agricultural heartland of America. Early shots establish an idealised rural pattern of life through images of a school, a housewife hanging out washing, and cultivated farmlands. But embedded within this land lie the nuclear 'silos'. Indeed the linkage within this term between farming and nuclear weaponry implicitly makes the same point that *Threads* would make a year later: that there is no refuge from nuclear attack. *The Day After* focuses on an individual family and also shows the first nuclear strikes on NATO bases, avoiding a tight documentary focus on a specific locale. As the crisis mounts, characters argue over its nature. One exclaims that it is a replay of the 1962 Berlin confrontation; another (a surgeon) dismisses any analogy with Hiroshima, insisting 'We're not talking about Hiroshima any more. Hiroshima was peanuts.' Once the strike occurs, it challenges characters' capacity to make sense of the event. The protagonist Dr Russell Oakes (played by Jason Robards), whose name suggests rural rootedness and stability, struggles to articulate seeing the blast from a distance. Echoing the words of the Manhattan Project scientists at the first atomic test, he states: 'It was like the sun exploding. It was like… I don't know why I'm here.'[20] His failure to complete the analogy reflects a general resistance in the film to coherent summary or resolution.

Every nuclear narrative, whether film or prose, engages with the question of whether there will be a surviving remnant and whether that remnant will be able to re-form society. In a detailed scene-by-scene analysis of *The Day After*, Peter Jeffrey and Michael O'Toole propose that, in Derrida's sense, the film is an 'exploding' work because it refuses such resolutions: '*The Day After* argues that atomic holocaust will be apocalyptic and that society will not be able to reconstitute itself, because the individuals – if they survive – will have no capacity to reintegrate or reidentify.'[21] The city hospital shown in the film is remorselessly swamped by the sheer number of casualties. The family huddled in their basement gradually collapses; one of the first signs of this comes when the daughter runs outside into dust-covered wasteland, later to fall victim to radiation sickness. Religion is shown to be totally inadequate in its attempt to rationalise destruction through nationalism; at an improvised service the preacher gives thanks to God 'for destroying the destroyers of the earth'. Similarly, the US president announces over the radio that 'America has survived this terrible tribulation. There has been no surrender, no retreat from the principles of liberty and democracy for which the free world looks towards us for leadership.'[22] The film ironically situates this declaration over shots of nuclear shelters, totally divorcing word from image so that the claim of a triumphalist narrative collapses into empty referents. The words claim a continuing collective in the nation but the film's images show a fragmented, traumatised population. As Jeffery and O'Toole point out, 'medicine, commerce, farming, religion, the military machine itself – all lose their hegemonic structures and integrating role.'[23]

If the house is taken as a metonym of the nation, Dr Oakes's attempts to locate his home in the ruins of Kansas City at least raise the possibility of reconstituting his own family base, but his attempts fail. When he finds his 'house', a ruin indistinguishable from all the other ruins surrounding it, and finds refugees camping there, he makes a futile attempt to reclaim ownership: 'Get out of my house', he shouts at the fugitives, ignoring the fact that the destruction of the city has even erased distinctions between inside and outside. The ending of the film is saved from the visual cliché of the rising panning shot across the ruins by the soundtrack of a radio voice calling, 'Hello, is anybody there?' This open message problematises survival in that it goes unanswered, but at the same time the question articulates the solicitation of the film itself of some kind of response from its audience.

In the USA and in Britain, the reactions to *The Day After* were very mixed. Peter Watkins found a problem in its methods: 'The film is using theatrical TV film form and thus poses the question as to how we are supposed to differentiate between this film (and its subject) and all the countless other films using the same structural and psychological methods of presentation – such as *Dallas*, *Winds of War*, and *Kojak*.'[24] In her invaluable commentary on the production and reception of *The Day After*, Susan Boyd-Bowman argues that it is an 'incoherent film referencing [too] many different cinema and television genres' resulting from the 'contradictory strains on its production'.[25]

THREADS

The Day After takes a rural community and extends its fate to that of the whole nation. Director Mick Jackson and writer Barry Hines's *Threads* (first broadcast on BBC 2 on 23 September 1984 and subsequently repeated in 1985) is constructed around an image representing any city. This central notion, identified in its title, is explained in the pre-credits sequence: 'In an urban society, everything connects. Each person's needs are fed by the skills of many others. Our lives are woven together in a fabric. But the connections that make society strong also make it vulnerable.'[26] The very first shot of the film is a slow pan along the thread of a spider's web. Once the whole web is shown, it is displayed against the background of a panorama of Sheffield. The superimposed images invite a reading of one as a metaphor of the other and draw the viewer's attention to the city's network of streets and rail connections. This peaceful scene is suddenly disturbed by the roar of a military aircraft passing over the viewer's vantage point, which is close to that of a young couple sitting in a parked car on the moors overlooking the city. When they start speaking, their first word is 'Peaceful'. Hines and Jackson skilfully give us an overview already informed by the figure of the web, which connotes primarily connectedness and fragility throughout the film. The opening sequence invites a special reading of every detail in the film as a synecdoche, as part of a system which locks into other systems. For instance, Sheffield is the main centre of steel production in Britain. Among the countless metal products depending on this industry are military hardware (the plane), domestic transportation (the car) and even the electronics of the media – first the car radio, then the television. A further system is introduced in the casual conversation between Ruth (Karen Meagher) and Jimmy (Reece Dinsdale): the seasonal cycle of nature. Passing remarks on the pure air and the new plants of spring conclude with a long shot of their car parked near the edge of a precipice, imagistically suggesting the precarious balance between the different systems of life (soon to be augmented by Ruth's pregnancy) and production. The destruction of this balance is imminent.

Once the nuclear attack takes place, the true significance of the film's title becomes graphically evident. The very first image of damage is of power cables rupturing, set against a caption stating 'Massive damage to communications across Britain and North West Europe'. This represents the first of many threads breaking, an image anticipated by the closing of road links to Berlin as the international crisis mounts.[27] From that point on, more and more ruptures occur – to groups, individual bodies, city and nation. Hines and Jackson dramatically rupture the film itself at the point of a detonation over Sheffield. Mrs Kemp (Rita May) has been looking for her young son Michael (Nicholas Lane). She finds his body in the rubble and is just about to scream when the screen goes white and sound stops. A rapid montage of images then evokes the nature of the destruction through a series of synecdoches: water gushing from a pipe (loss of water); a burning milk float (the destruction of another life-giving liquid); a figure crawling through the ruins (collapse of the postural distinction between humans and animals; an anticipation of the scavengers); a burning toy (fate of children); a burning bus among other vehicles, symbolising the destruction of transport, and so on.[28] From the attack onwards, the film's use of montage – of discontinuous images and shots – raises an implicit question: can these fragments ever come back together?

Unlike *The War Game*, *Threads* builds its narrative around the experiences of a young couple – Jimmy Kemp and Ruth Beckett – whose relationship takes on an urgency near the beginning of the film when Ruth discovers she is pregnant. The conventionality of this plot-line makes it all the easier for the viewer to identify with the two families' fortunes without losing sight of the larger factual issues. Through these characters, Hines and Jackson demonstrate that a characteristic of the experience of the mass media lies in their discontinuity with the immediate concrete details of the viewers' experience. This disparity between international political events and private experience had already emerged through such works as Ray Bradbury's *Fahrenheit 451* (1953), where suburban characters have no meaningful connection with the events going on, as it were, over their heads. In *Threads*, many of the early sequences show a television news programme playing without characters paying much attention to it. Initially, the news in these scenes forms part of the background noise characters take for granted; it is only as the international crisis mounts that reports begin to impact on their consciousness. Hines and Jackson draw the viewer's attention to this by alternating the frame of the film so that at one point we are positioned as an audience in front of a filmed TV newscast, while in another we see TV broadcasts within situations where words or images are blocked by the action within those scenes. In other words, from the very beginning Hines and Jackson thematise characters' responsiveness (or lack of response) to the media. At this early stage of the film, Hines and Jackson throw in many ironic examples of casual references in dialogue to death ('well, it's not the end of the world'; 'over my dead body', and so on) in order to dramatise characters' oblivious-ness towards the dangers facing them. When Jimmy and a friend are arguing over whether the crisis is developing in the Middle or Far East, Jimmy retorts: 'So what? It's far enough, isn't it?'[29] But the whole point about nuclear confrontation is the collapse of distance. *Threads*, too, draws on the analogy with Afghanistan to trace out a growing crisis in Iran, which becomes the site of a confrontation between Soviet and American forces. Gradually events move from remote news reportage to domestic witness (seeing the movement of lorry convoys, the stocking up of schools with blankets, and so on) and, finally, participation.

In *The War Game*, we saw that key interview sequences dramatised public ignorance of nuclear war. *Threads* shifts this emphasis on to the capacity of the civil defence organisation to cope with nuclear attack. Immediately before the nuclear blasts occur, the soundtrack includes a number of public information announcements designated 'Protect and Survive', after the Home Office booklet of that title which was published in 1980. This pamphlet contained advice about constructing and equipping a fallout refuge, probably modelled on US civil defence publications of the 1950s which had become anachronisms even by the end of that decade. The advice still being broadcast in *Threads* advising citizens to stay at home is obviously intended to prevent mass panic, but in effect is condemning to certain death those living in cities like Sheffield. Section 2 of *Protect and Survive* declares: 'Your own local authority will best be able to help you in war', but the film contradicts this advice in showing the ultimate failure of the city's emergency services to cope, and of various domestic measures.[30]

Each of the two families in *Threads* constructs a shelter of sorts: the Kemps improvise a lean-to in the recommended fashion using doors; the Becketts take refuge in their cellar. Neither place helps them survive, partly because of the trauma of the attack (which reduces the Kemps to despair) and partly because of the inadequacy of their food supplies. But it is the fate of the city control bunker that carries a special symbolism in the film because if this fails, so does the system. The bunker itself is shown to be vulnerable to blast damage; in fact one of the first deaths occurs here. The shots showing figures picking their way through the darkness of the control room by torchlight sum up the plight of all the survivors. The death of the superintendent and the impending death of his fellow workers finally demonstrate the failure of the bunker to function, something foreshadowed when the bunker loses radio contact with the outside world after only a few broken messages.

Inevitably, the prime aim of government civil defence information is to reassure by projecting images of local and national order in a condition of emergency. Kevin Hall has made the darker suggestion that advice on family self-help was given because no outside help would be offered to the fatally contaminated or injured in the central blast areas.[31] One purpose realised in *Threads* was to question the bland general assertions of official statements by juxtaposing these statements with dramatisations of the most likely actuality of nuclear attack, as happens in *The War Game*. Outside the 'newsreel' footage and dramatised sequences, the *Protect and Survive* information is presented in the early sections of the film so that its already questionable authority lapses completely. Its place in the film has already been taken over by a series of captions which perform the twin functions of dating scenes and contextualising the post-blast sequences. Thus a shot of rats scurrying through ruins is captioned 'Likely Epidemics: Cholera, Dysentery, Typhoid'.[32] The dating captions come up on the screen like teletype, encoding the action as a form of news and measuring scenes against the day of attack.

Threads, here, follows a convention used in other nuclear narratives. Philip Wylie's *Tomorrow!* follows a countdown sequence up to and after 'X-day', the day of attack which erases ('x-es') normal life. In Eugene L. Burdick and Harvey Wheeler's *Fail-Safe* (1962), the narrative segments are timed precisely to convey a mounting crisis where even seconds count.[33] *Threads* dates the scenes before the attack with simple chronology, appropriately since no one knew when the attack would take place. Because the factual captions resemble these dating tags visually, they take on the authority of time itself and form part of an anonymous voice perceived by the viewer in a similar way to characters' responses to media within the film: 'What did *it* say on the telly?' a character asks at one point (emphasis added).[34] Inevitably, *Threads* counterpoints the different personal voices of those who will not survive against the anonymous statements of an informed voice-over and of the captions, which are based on a premise of survival. On the one hand, it would damage realism to suggest that the characters could live through a nuclear war; on the other hand, the anonymous statements perform a function similar to that of epitaphs. Or, to express the hybridity of the film differently, the dramatised sections evoke a problematic, minimal survival after nuclear war, while the captions and voice-over remind the viewer that these episodes form part of a hypothetical, predicted narrative which the film is designed to deter. Paradoxically for a documentary, if the film fails in its predicted descriptions, it has succeeded.

Threads uses its captions to negotiate a potential problem in nuclear narratives: how to reconcile a dramatisation of destruction without sacrificing the viewer's understanding of the process taking place. When preparing for the film, Hines attended an official survivors' centre in Easingwold, Yorkshire, and there became restive over the sheer orderliness of the exercises being rehearsed.[35] Thus one of the most impressive aspects of *Threads* is its evocation of confusion

DAZED AND CONFUSED   Two doomed survivors in Barry Hines and Mick Jackson's *Threads*.

without the viewer ever becoming confused. *The War Game* also dramatises confusion, but keeps the action limited to a specific area of Britain. *Threads*, by contrast, shows Sheffield to be a centre in a network of communications which break and also a place vulnerable to strikes elsewhere. Thus a detonation over Crewe produces massive fallout, which is blown over Sheffield. Gradually the scale of the film's reference expands, through shots of dramatic red clouds changing to grey, to give visual expression to the notion of nuclear winter. These images extend the iconic symbolism of the mushroom cloud – conspicuously absent from *The War Game* – which by the 1980s had become a familiar emblem of feared consequences. Throughout the 1980s, scientists such as Carl Sagan (who was acknowledged in the end credits of *Threads* as an adviser) argued that the one factor neglected in calculating the effects of nuclear weapons was the cumulative effects of the massive fires that would be caused. The smoke generated by these fires, the argument went, would lower the temperature over landmasses so drastically that a widespread period of frost would result.[36] Hines and Jackson time the nuclear attack to take place in summer and show that the immediate result would be a deadly radioactive dust reducing the countryside to a wasteland and then a radical drop in temperature to a winter-in-summer. The last scenes of the film therefore lose their specificity of time as well as place to suggest a process of destruction extending into the whole climate of the region.

Many nuclear narratives show society reverting to a pre-industrial state. A new medievalism comes to characterise the post-war societies described by the American novelists Edgar Pangborn, Walter M. Miller and Russell Hoban.[37] In the latter's *Riddley Walker* (1980), language itself has become a casualty by mutating into a primitive form of English. The novel narrates the attempt by the eponymous Riddley to make his way across the devastated county of Kent to Cambry, the location of Canterbury. Riddley embodies a narrative role of taking enigmas (riddles) for a walk; in other words his motion across the post-nuclear landscape is inseparable from his attempts to understand his situation. Just as the landscape contains buried traces of a lost technology, so his language too contains terms like 'blips' from a lost era of computerised military hardware. Early in the novel he loses his father, just as Jane (Victoria O'Keefe) loses her mother Ruth in *Threads*. And Hines and Jackson signal a cultural reversion similar to that described in Hoban's novel through the caption: 'U.K. numbers [of population] may decline to mediaeval levels.' A further similarity emerges in the scavenging of survivors among the ruins for metal, again common to *Riddley Walker*.

Although Hines and Jackson date this reversion as only thirteen years after the attack, in a sense the dating of such scenes does not matter because the implied cultural gap between character and viewer is so big. The effect is of a radical estrangement from twentieth-century technology taking place within a single generation of characters (Hoban shows it happening after several generations). This estrangement shows itself in the younger characters' speech, which has to be glossed in the script. Thus when Jane is found with a rabbit (in Elizabethan English, a 'coney'), they tell her:

GAZ   Seed'n. N'coney. [I saw it. It's a rabbit].

SPIKE   Giss'n. Come on. Giss'n. [Give it to us].[38]

Hines and Jackson have to keep the language simple enough to be understood by a viewer, whereas Hoban can play on puns and a complex sequence of resemblances in his words. And although Riddley Walker seems to use what could be called a 'primitive' form of English, in fact such a label would be a misnomer because he demonstrates a complex subjectivity in his narration. Hines and Jackson's young characters, by contrast, show a limited range of expression and a lack of emotion, as if their generation has become calloused by the national trauma. Their alienation from technology is enacted in a scene where children sit watching an old school video playing about the relation of words to image. Their 'dumb-looking faces' suggest at once a lack of response and a silence, which suggests in turn a virtual loss of words.

When *Threads* was first shown in September 1984, Russell Hoban wrote an appreciative review which praised its austere vision of cultural collapse by arguing that it needed a special kind of viewing and response: 'This is not a film to be reviewed as a film; its art is that it cancels all aesthetic distance between our unthinking and the unthinkable: here is the death of our life and the birth of a new life for our children, a life of rats and maggots, of slow death by radiation sickness and plagues and starvation and quick death by violence.' Hoban found the film so powerful that it made him speculate about the nature of human motivation, particularly about whether there was 'some nameless thing looking out through our eyeholes and this nameless thing must make everything possible happen'.[39]

It is debatable whether *Threads* justifies this general inference, figured here as an embodiment of the death wish. Stanley Kubrick's *Dr Strangelove* (1963) had earlier popularised this self-destructive impulse through an absurdist view of the Western military–industrial complex as being fed by compensatory sexual fantasies. A number of subsequent commentators on nuclear weaponry have pointed out the phallic symbolism of the super-weapons and the sublimated sexuality in their promotion by male tacticians.[40] *Threads* is, of course, committed to a realist vision where black comedy has no place, but it engages with the issue of gender to construct important functions for its female characters. Indeed, it is a female public speaker in Sheffield who asserts a position authenticated by the film and also in passing makes an allusion to *The War Game*: 'This time they are playing with, at best, the destruction of life as we know it and, at worst, total annihilation. You cannot win a nuclear war!'[41] Her Cassandra warning, however, goes unheard in the general noise of the crowd.

It is women again who enact the connection between Hines and Jackson's title image and the promotion of life in the sense of knitting clothes for Ruth's baby and picking the threads apart of old clothes in order to make new ones long after the nuclear strike. Ruth survives, unlike Jimmy. Her daughter Jane is the last figure to appear in the film, which closes with a scene that could carry hope. Jane gives birth in an improvised hospital and is given her baby wrapped in a bloodstained cloth. At the point where we expect her to clutch the baby to her body, she opens the cloth in horror and pushes the baby away from her with her mouth open as if she is about to scream. Is the baby still-born? Deformed? We never know because the film stops dead at that point. As Kevin Hall points out, *Threads* is unusual in its 'absence of people who really do think they can prepare for and survive a nuclear war.'[42] Jane's last experience marks the beginning of a new generation but it contains no forward-looking connotations at all. The ending is effective because it is impossible to conceive of a narrative resolution to the sequence Hines and Jackson have traced out. Jane is thus the last in a whole series of horrified witnesses to the nuclear holocaust that *Threads* attempts to prevent through projected realisation.

NOTES

1. John Corner, *The Art of Record: A Critical Introduction to Documentary* (Manchester: Manchester University Press, 1996), p. 31.
2. The standard listing of nuclear war fiction is Paul Brians's *Nuclear Holocausts: Atomic War in Fiction, 1895–1984* (Kent OH and London: Kent State University Press, 1987).
3. Philip Wylie, 'Terror – and the Terror Weapons', Wylie MSS, Princeton University, p. 21.
4. Peter Watkins, *Observer*, 24 January 1965, quoted in James M. Welsh, 'The Modern Apocalypse: *The War Game*', *Journal of Popular Film and Television* 11/1 (1983), p. 28.
5. Derek Paget, 'Tales of Cultural Tourism', in Alan Rosenthal (ed.), *Why Docudrama? Fact-Fiction on Film and TV* (Carbondale: Southern Illinois University Press, 1999), p. 59.
6. The film was shot in Tonbridge, Gravesend, Chatham and Dover. Its credits acknowledge the participation of the residents of Chatham

particularly, just as *Threads* was to acknowledge the help of the residents of Sheffield.

7. Peter Watkins, '*The War Game*', at www.peterwatkins.lt/a_antra.htm/ (accessed 30 March 2004).

8. Ibid.

9. Derek Paget, 'Disclaimers, Denials and Direct Address: Captioning in Docudrama', in John Izod and Richard Kilborn (eds), *From Grierson to the Docu-Soap: Breaking the Boundaries* (Luton: University of Luton Press, 2000), p. 201.

10. Corner, *The Art of Record*, p. 40.

11. From many potential examples, Poul Anderson and F.N. Waldrop's 1947 story 'Tomorrow's Children' (collected in Anderson's *Twilight World*, 1961) addresses the theme most explicitly.

12. Peter Watkins, www.peterwatkins.lt/a_antra.htm/ (accessed 30 March 2004).

13. Philip Wylie, *Tomorrow!* (New York: Rinehart, 1954), p. 268.

14. Peter Watkins, *Newcastle Journal*, 30 November 1965, quoted in Welsh, 'The Modern Apocalypse', p. 27.

15. Michael Tracey, 'Censored: *The War Game* Story', in Crispin Aubrey (ed.), *Nukespeak: The Media and the Bomb* (London: Comedia, 1982), pp. 38–54; and *A Variety of Lives: A Biography of Sir Hugh Greene* (London: Chatto & Windus, 1984).

16. Steve Fox, 'Beyond *War Plan UK*: Civil Defence in the 1980s', at www.subbrit.org.uk/rsg/features/beyond/ (accessed 30 March 2004).

17. Mick Broderick, 'Surviving Armageddon: Beyond the Imagination of Disaster', *Science-Fiction Studies* 20 (1993), p. 365.

18. Welsh, 'The Modern Apocalypse', pp. 40–41. The project collapsed when Central TV pulled out of the funding.

19. Susan Boyd-Bowman, '*The Day After*: Representations of the Nuclear Holocaust', *Screen* 25/4–5 (July-October 1984), p. 74. I am grateful to John Corner for bringing this article to my attention and for discussing many of the issues raised in this chapter.

20. Soundtrack, *The Day After* (1st tx. ABC, 20 November 1983).

21. Peter Jeffery and Michael O'Toole, 'Disintegrating Narrative: An Analysis of the Television Film *The Day After*', in Paul Chilton (ed.), *Language and the Nuclear Arms Debate: Nukespeak Today* (London and Dover NH: Frances Pinter, 1985), p. 167.

22. Soundtrack, *The Day After*.

23. Jeffery and O'Toole, 'Disintegrating Narrative', p. 181.

24. Peter Watkins, quoted in Boyd-Bowman, '*The Day After*', p. 83.

25. Boyd-Bowman, '*The Day After*', p. 85.

26. Michael Mangan (ed.), *Threads and Other Sheffield Plays* (Sheffield: Sheffield Academic Press, 1990), p. 159. The text of *Threads* given here is that of a shooting script with each scene numbered.

27. *Threads*, p. 199.

28. *Threads*, p. 203. Writer Hines makes milk into a significant motif in

the film. Its delivery is one of the signs of social routine, but more importantly it comes to signify life itself. A public information broadcast on how to deal with corpses occurs over close-ups of bottles of milk; when Sheffield is bombed, one of the signs is a bottle of milk exploding; and when Ruth wanders the streets, one of the figures she sees is a woman nursing a dead child.

29. *Threads*, p. 176.
30. *Protect and Survive* is quoted in the public information broadcasts in the film. It can be found, along with other nuclear civil defence pamphlets, at www.cybetrn.demon.co.uk/atomic/ (accessed 30 March 2004).
31. Kevin Hall, 'Thoughts on *Threads*', at www.chandrella.org/documents/nuclear/threads_thoughts.shtml/ (accessed 30 March 2004).
32. *Threads*, p. 220. The film incorporates the latest scientific calculations in these captions; forecasts like those contained in the 1983 publication from the Royal Swedish Academy of Sciences, *Nuclear War: The Aftermath*.
33. Wylie, *Tomorrow!*; Eugene Burdick and Harvey Wheeler, *Fail-Safe* (New York: McGraw-Hill, 1962). An adaptation of the latter by Sidney Lumet was released in 1964 and starred Henry Fonda in the lead role.
34. *Threads*, p. 196.
35. Patrick Bean, '*Threads* by Barry Hines', at www.btinternet.com/~pdbean/threads.html (accessed 30 March 2004).
36. For accounts of the nuclear winter, see Carl Sagan and Tom Wilkie, 'After the Bomb: Winter of Our Destruction', *Listener*, 27 September 1984, pp. 4–6. Sagan collaborated with Richard Turco (also named as an advisor to *Threads*) in a detailed study, *A Path Where No Man Thought: Nuclear Winter and the End of the Arms Race* (London: Century, 1991). One last adviser on *Threads* to note was Robert Jay Lifton, author of *Death In Life: The Survivors of Hiroshima* (London: Weidenfeld & Nicolson, 1968).
37. Edgar Pangborn, *Davy* (1964), and *The Judgement of Eve* (1966); Walter M. Miller, Jr., *A Canticle for Leibowitz* (1959). Paul Brians's commentary on this fiction is invaluable; see *Nuclear Holocausts*.
38. *Threads*, p. 233.
39. Russell Hoban, 'A Personal View of *Threads*: It Cancels All Distance between Our Unthinking and the Unthinkable', *Listener*, 27 September 1984, pp. 3–4.
40. See, for example, Ira Chernus, *Dr Strangegod: On the Symbolic Meaning of Nuclear Weapons* (South Carolina: University of South Carolina Press, 1986).
41. *Threads*, p. 180. As the speaker's words are drowned out, she is predicting the very situation of destruction and pollution the film is about to show.
42. Hall, 'Thoughts on *Threads*'.

9

Resist the host:
Blake's 7 – a very British future

UNA McCORMACK

In January 1978, audiences in the UK were able to watch for the first time the adventures of a small group of rebels struggling against overwhelming odds to overthrow the forces of an evil galactic empire. *Star Wars* (*Episode IV: A New Hope*) had finally reached British cinemas. Meanwhile, on Monday evenings on BBC 1, a very different story of another revolution was being transmitted. *Blake's 7* had reached British televisions. Cheaply executed, *Blake's 7* often showed too clearly British television's roots in the theatrical tradition. Nonetheless, it combined cynical and dry scripts with a pervading sense of pessimism and realpolitik, not least in the memorable final episode, 'Blake' (1st tx. BBC 1, 21 December 1981), where the eponymous hero (played by Gareth Thomas) is shot dead by his former crewmate Avon (Paul Darrow), who believes himself betrayed, and the rest of the crew are subsequently killed in a shoot-out. While the rebels of *Star Wars* fight and win, the rebels of *Blake's 7* doubt their motives, commit questionable acts, end badly – and all before the 9 o'clock watershed.

In this chaper, I place *Blake's 7* in the context of British anti-utopia, indicating its debt to the literary tradition as typified by H.G. Wells, George Orwell and Aldous Huxley. The series' debt to this tradition lies not only in its representation of totalitarianism, which borrows particularly from Orwell, but also in the themes it addresses in the course of various episodes. These include: the nature and extent of the total surveillance society; the conflict between private and public loyalties; and, in particular, a deep pessimism about both the scope for individual resistance within totalitarian regimes and the possibility of social progress. I go on to locate *Blake's 7* within the context of television drama series production and argue that its particular contribution (as both anti-utopia and television series) is its attempt to present such an uncompromising vision of the future on prime-time, mainstream television. The programme's failures come from the tension that exists in presenting such a vision whilst working within the production and narrative constraints of episodic television series drama. Its success and its influence lie in precisely how it breaks from these constraints.

Nightmare futures were settings that the show's creator, Terry Nation, had already explored in the war-destroyed world of his *Doctor Who* story 'The Mutants' aka 'The Daleks' (BBC TV, 1963) and the post-plague scenario of *Survivors* (BBC TV, 1975–77). Images of totalitarian societies also appear in Nation's other scripts for *Doctor Who*, particularly the Nazi-styled Kaled Elite in 'Genesis of the Daleks' (BBC TV, 1975).[1] The script editor of *Blake's 7*, Chris Boucher, whose increased influence upon the show in its second season marked the programme's distinct turn towards the politically ambiguous, has described his inspirations as being more general than the late 1970s' British situation in which the programme was being broadcast, citing diverse inspirations such as South American revolutionaries for the characterization of Blake[2] and the defences made by soldiers responsible for the My Lai massacre for the justifications made by the Federation officer Travis (Brian Croucher) in his trial for the mass murder of civilians.[3] In this way, *Blake's 7* reflects a general disillusionment with a society gone wrong and a deep scepticism about the options available to those who wish to change the world around them.

Throughout the programme's run, the apparatus of totalitarianism is plainly at work and the debts to the literary tradition are clear. On Earth, as it is seen in the first episode, 'The Way Back' (1st tx. BBC 1, 2 January 1978), the Administration operates a total surveillance society. Apart from a few ostracised 'Outsiders', the bulk of the population is enclosed within domed cities such as described in Wells's novel *When the Sleeper Wakes* (1899) and adopted by Yevgeny Zamyatin for the Green Wall which separates the Taylorist society from the wild remnants of humanity kept outside in *We* (1924).[4] Inside the domes, surveillance cameras monitor the corridors, similar to the 24-hour television screens in Orwell's *Nineteen Eighty-Four* (1949), and detailed computer records seem to be kept on all citizens. In *A Modern Utopia* (1905), Wells sees his 'World Index of Population' as a positive use of technological advances (current debates in the UK about a national identity card indicate that not all citizens consider such close scrutiny of individuals by government part of an ideal society), but the ultimate fallibility of technology is a recurring theme of anti-utopian responses to Wells. In *Blake's 7*, technology is treated ambivalently. In Season Four's 'Power' (1st tx. BBC 1, 5 October 1981), the technologically dependent Seska are ultimately overcome by brute force; their leader Pella is physically overcome and disempowered by Avon. In 'Redemption', the opening episode of Season Two (1st tx. BBC 1, 9 January 1979), the creator of the advanced technology of the rebels' alien spaceship *Liberator*, upon which Blake and the crew are dependent, turns out to be a computer complex enslaving the population of three planets (the complex is called the 'System', which, on this occasion at least, Blake does manage to beat).[5]

The population in 'The Way Back' is also apparently manipulated by propaganda machines – reminiscent of the audio broadcasts that interrupt everyday life in *Nineteen Eighty-Four*, or the 'Bubble Machines' that dispense propaganda in *When the Sleeper Wakes* – and, in an allusion to Huxley's *Brave New World* (1932), is kept pacified by the use of drugs.[6] A network of informers is also at work in the city: Blake's lawyer, who has discovered irregularities in the evidence against Blake, is betrayed by the minor civil servant monitoring the central computer records. The conflict between public and private loyalties and the betrayal of lovers, friends and relatives, which occurs repeatedly in anti-utopian literature, is also dramatized throughout *Blake's 7*. Winston Smith is eventually driven to betray his love for Julia in *Nineteen Eighty-Four*, while his neighbour Parsons's daughter denounces her father to the authorities. In Arthur Koestler's *Darkness at Noon* (1940), Rubashov sacrifices his lover Arlova; in *We*, anticipating Orwell, the protagonist is brainwashed and ultimately betrays his lover to torture and execution. In *Blake's 7*, Avon learns that his girlfriend, Anna Grant (Lorna Heilbron) is also the Federation agent Bartolomew ('Rumours of Death', 1st tx. BBC 1, 25 February 1980); Veron (Yolande Palfrey) sacrifices Blake to secure the freedom of her mother, the rebel leader Kasabi (Jane Sherwin), in 'Pressure Point' (1st tx. BBC 1, 6 February 1979); and Blake's uncle is forced to choose between his nephew and his daughter ('Hostage' 1st tx. BBC 1, 27 February 1979). Blake himself eventually faces a choice between his own desire to destroy the Federation and maintaining its security in the face of an unanticipated external threat ('Star One', 1st tx. BBC 1, 3 April 1979). Private loyalties are thus inextricably bound up in the political.

'The Way Back' follows Blake as he is contacted by the resistance and persuaded to attend a meeting outside the domed city. The episode shows the various means by which rebellious elements on Earth are either controlled or suppressed: a spy has infiltrated the movement and the attendees are massacred. Blake, who has learned that he was once a leader in the resistance movement, is arrested and placed under interrogation, begins to experience flashbacks to his previous arrest and subsequent brainwashing. Such torture and mind-control are recurring elements in various episodes: through violence in Season One's 'Time Squad' (1st tx. BBC 1, 23 January 1978) and Season Three's 'Rumours of Death'; so-called aversion therapy in Season Four's 'Animals' (1st tx. BBC 1, 26 October 1981) and the administration of drugs in 'The Way Back', in which Blake's psychological torture leads to 'tranquillized dreams' that recall the 'psychic surgery' of *When the Sleeper Wakes* and the cure for the imagination found in *We*. False charges of paedophilia are brought against Blake to discredit him; he is tried, convicted and exiled to a penal planet. (This again draws from the British anti-utopian tradition: Wells had suggested that hardened criminals should be exiled to islands in *A Modern Utopia*, something Huxley satirized in *Brave New World* with the exile of Helmholtz the poet to the Falkland Islands.) Blake's escape from imprisonment and his capture of the *Liberator* shift the focus of the action beyond Earth and its domed cities, into a galaxy where the Federation engages in military expansion and aggression, undermining independent states on its borders through covert activities (Season One's 'Bounty', 1st tx. BBC 1, 13 March 1978; and Season Three's 'Death-Watch' 1st tx. BBC 1, 24 March 1980); biological warfare ('Children of Auron', also in Season Three, 1st tx. BBC 1, 19 February 1980), and neo-imperialism – for example in Season Two's 'Horizon' (1st tx. BBC 1, 30 January 1979), in which the puppet leader

Ro's (Darien Angadi) loyalty to his Federation mentor the Kommissar (William Squire) is tested by making him watch the interrogation of his lover Selma (Souad Faress). Conquered worlds are kept subdued by the threat of annihilation (Season Two's 'Countdown', 1st tx. BBC 1, 6 March 1979) or by a programme administering pacification drugs (in Season Four's 'Traitor' and 'Warlord', 1st tx. BBC 1, 12 October and 14 December 1981, respectively).

Krishan Kumar, in *Utopia and Anti-Utopia* (1987), attributes the rise of the anti-utopia in the post-war period to the 'general tenor of world events, and the apparent direction of world history.... But there was a special pathos and poignancy in the fate of two particular societies, the American and the Russian, for America and the Soviet Union are the two great utopian experiments of modern times.'[7] *Brave New World* critiques the USA for excessive consumerism, as does Ursula Le Guin's depiction of the planet Urras in *The Dispossessed* (1974). After Hiroshima, the Cuban missile crisis and the expansion of American activity in Southeast Asia, US military power seemed capable of bringing the world to destruction rather than making it 'safe for democracy', themes addressed by Le Guin in her novella *The Word for World is Forest* (1976). Similarly, disillusionment with the Soviet experiment in utopia is shown powerfully in *Darkness at Noon* and found expression in Orwell's *Animal Farm* (1945) as well as in *Nineteen Eighty-Four*. Soviet imperialism was proven by the suppression of popular uprisings in Hungary in 1956 and Czechoslovakia in 1968 and the invasion of Afghanistan in 1979.

As well as a general critique of such imperialism, *Blake's 7* inherits the twentieth-century anti-utopia's preoccupation with the false promise of progress. Throughout the series' run, we are repeatedly shown societies in decline. Whether suffering cultural, social or biological decay, most of the civilisations visited by the crew of the *Liberator* are failing, rather than progressing. The most common reason for this is war – for example, in the first season the episodes 'Duel' (1st tx. BBC 1, 20 February 1978), where war has extinguished one society entirely, and 'Deliverance' (1st tx. BBC 1, 20 March 1978), where nuclear war has caused a planetary civilisation to revert to barbarism, as in Huxley's *Ape and Essence* (1948) and Russell Hoban's *Riddley Walker* (1980). In publicity material for *Blake's 7*, the Federation itself is described as emerging out of a nuclear war,[8] a context deriving, perhaps ironically, from the Wellsian notion that a utopian society could only emerge after some form of catastrophic break with the past (*The Shape of Things to Come* [1933] provides an appropriate illustration, for example). There is also a recurring sense of the inevitability of decline. In Season Three's 'Terminal' (1st tx. BBC 1, 31 October 1980), the planet visited by Avon and the crew is inhabited by ape-like creatures, which, it transpires, are not ancestors of humanity but a scientific extrapolation of its destiny: the evolutionary end-point of humanity is one of regression to a primitive rather than an advanced state. In Season Three's 'The City at the Edge of the World' (1st tx. BBC 1, 11 February 1980), the civilisation on the planet Keezarn has collapsed for no other reason than having reached a peak, and so it has subsequently lapsed into a prolonged and apparently inexorable decline. This stands in stark contrast to the semi-divine images of advanced humanity that appear in, for example, the concluding episode of *Babylon 5*'s fourth season, 'The Deconstruction of Falling Stars' (1st tx. Warners' Prime Time Entertainment Network, 27 October 1997), or the evolved humans of *Star Trek*'s United Federation of Planets.

Yet while the programme's debt to the anti-utopian tradition is clear, its relevance is specific and contemporary. *Blake's 7*'s period of transmission (1978–81) coincides precisely with the end of the troubled Wilson/Callaghan Labour government, continuing economic decline, the rise of mass unemployment and social unrest and the political shift towards Thatcherism. Importantly, though, the programme is responding to more than Britain's post-war decline. Its specific subject matter is the armed struggle for freedom against an imperial regime, and one does not need to stray far from the British context to see the show's relevance. From the late 1960s and onwards throughout the 1970s, there had been an upsurge in the Troubles in Northern Ireland and increased IRA activity on the British mainland. *Blake's 7* scrutinises the response of government to terrorism and considers in what kind of society armed resistance becomes a logical activity. Travis's defence in Season Two's 'Trial' (1st tx. BBC 1, 13 February 1979) that he was a 'product of his training' and 'an instrument of the service' may have arisen, according to Chris Boucher, from the aftershocks of the Vietnam War, but it had a greater pertinence much closer to home. During the Saville Inquiry into the Bloody Sunday massacre (30 January 1972), one soldier made an argument very close to that used by Travis: 'The attributes and mentality of a battalion like 1 Para and the way in which it operated were known. The responsibility for its actions lies with those who selected and directed an outfit like that.'[9] A television programme that charted the rise, fall and brutal extinction of a resistance movement made for powerful, if uneasy, viewing between 1978 and 1981.

However, while we are left in no doubt of the Federation's totalitarianism, *Blake's 7* also examines the limits and the ethics of armed resistance, and is ambivalent towards those who choose to fight and the methods that they use. The society on board Blake's ship, the *Liberator*, is far from being ideal. The crew consists not of the committed resistance fighters seen in 'The Way Back' but of convicted criminals who have seized the opportunity offered by Blake to escape imprisonment. As a result, the danger often comes from within. Avon attempts to bribe Jenna (Sally Knyvette) to leave Blake behind in Season One's 'Cygnus Alpha' (1st tx. BBC 1, 16 January 1978); Blake mistrusts Avon throughout, suspecting he will abandon the crew in 'Horizon' and apparently doubting that Avon will ally the *Liberator* alongside the Federation to stave off an alien invasion in the final episode of Season Two, 'Star One'. Cally (Jan Chappell), the only other member of the resistance besides Blake, puts the crew repeatedly at risk as a result of having psychic abilities that leave her vulnerable to outside control. Blake's closest allies endanger him, let him down, challenge his authority and show more interest in money and their own personal safety than in risking their lives in the name of Blake's cause. In the final episode, 'Blake', Avon sums up himself and his crew as 'thieves, killers, mercenaries, psychopaths'. And in Season Two's 'Shadow' (1st tx. BBC 1, 16 January 1979), both Blake and his crew alike show an unromantic perception of themselves as a resistance movement:

> VILA   Where are all the good guys?
> BLAKE   You could be looking at them.
> AVON   What a very depressing thought.

At various points, crew members challenge the ethics of Blake's fight and even its very purpose. In 'Shadow', Blake attempts to enlist the assistance of an organized crime syndicate, the Terra Nostra, to provide an infrastructure for his rebellion. Gan (David Jackson) queries whether making such alliances is morally justifiable, since the Terra Nostra controls the production and supply of Shadow, an illegal and powerfully addictive drug and 'everything dirty, degrading, and cruel on just about every colonised world'. In 'Star One', Blake's mission to destroy Star One, the central computer system that provides the control and coordination for the Federation, is questioned even by Cally. And while the status of the main cast as 'heroes' is debatable, *Blake's 7* also puts a human face to their enemy. It is true that Federation troopers are frequently anonymous and implacable, wearing black leather uniforms and gas-mask helmets with visors; we see them massacre unarmed civilians ('The Way Back'), a resistance group ('Project Avalon', 1st tx. BBC 1, 27 February 1978) and assault Blake as they arrest him ('The Way Back'). However, throughout the series, troopers are shown taking off their masks or being completely without them. These are not simply faceless enemies, it is suggested, but individuals situated within a specific social context. In the third-season episode 'Rumours of Death', the banter of the insubordinate NCO Forres (David Haig) and his world-weary superior Major Grenlee (Donald Douglas) establishes them as individuals with their own histories; they are killed towards the end of the episode by resistance fighters disguised – even helmeted – as Federation troopers.

This repeated blurring of the line between the heroes and the villains, the human and the inhuman, between the side of 'good' and the side of 'evil', recurs throughout *Blake's 7*, as does the theme of the moral cost faced by those who wish to fight oppression. At the end of 'Shadow', it is revealed that the Federation runs the Terra Nostra (it is its shadow), exposing how even the criminal elements of Federation society are bound within its structures. The symbolism is invoked again in Season Two's 'Pressure Point' when Blake's attempt to locate and destroy Central Control results in his capture of an empty room. This shadow of Control has been established as a false focus towards which attempts to destroy the Federation are continually directed, just as O'Brien attempts to recruit Winston Smith to a false rebellion in *Nineteen Eighty-Four*. Once again, there is no scope for resistance outside of the boundaries of society.

The abortive attempt to seize Control also results in the death of Gan, and the following episode, 'Trial', deals in part with Blake's resulting re-examination of his motives. It also continues contrasts

RESISTING THE HOST   Six of the original *Blake's 7*.

made between Blake and Travis which had been established in the first season (for example, in the morality play 'Duel', where the antagonism between the two men is enacted in direct and literal terms). Congruent with the more ambiguous turn in the show, parallels, however, are now drawn between them. 'Trial' deals with questions at the heart of *Blake's 7*: the relationship of the individual to society and the extent to which one's actions are embedded in a broader social context from which it is difficult, if not impossible, to break free. The episode contains parallel plot strands which focus on Blake and Travis. The first concerns Blake's retreat to an apparently uninhabited planet where he encounters an alien, Zil (Claire Lewis), who tells him: 'Resist the host, or your oneness will be absorbed.' It transpires that the planet is itself a living entity and that Zil is a parasite creature that the planet absorbs back into itself when the numbers become too great. Zil protects Blake, believing him to be newly hatched, but is ultimately absorbed; Blake (not unaware of the allegorical nature of his situation) determines to continue resisting the host and takes to the high ground and returns to the *Liberator*.

The parallel plot in 'Trial' follows Travis's trial for a massacre of civilians, the outcome of which is being manipulated by his superior Servalan (Jacqueline Pearce) to cover her failure to capture Blake. Travis therefore finds himself in a similar position to Blake in 'The Way Back'. Travis's defence is unsuccessful and he is condemned to death. Blake, his commitment to the cause now renewed, launches an attack on the space station where Travis is being tried and Travis breaks out in the mêlée. Travis threatens Servalan into giving him a ship to escape the station and Servalan does – on condition that he continues to pursue Blake. At the climax of the episode, therefore, Blake's act of resistance has freed Travis; Travis is now, like Blake, an outlaw – but his actions, like the Terra Nostra in 'Shadow', have been harnessed to the aims of the Federation. 'Trial' is therefore a deeply pessimistic view of the extent of the individual's freedom to act.

The final episode of the second season, 'Star One', draws these themes together. Having located Star One, the *Liberator* crew set out to destroy it – but not without first an explicit consideration of the ethics of terrorism. In *Nineteen Eighty-Four*, Winston and Julia assure O'Brien of their willingness to commit a list of crimes in the name of destroying the Party, including murder, acts of sabotage and injuring children. In *Blake's 7*, the chaos ensuing from the destruction of Star One will result in the deaths of millions of ordinary Federation citizens. Cally, the only other guerrilla fighter in the crew, expresses her extreme reservations, but Blake insists that they must continue in order to prove that he was right – a single-mindedness towards his purpose reminiscent of Travis's pursuit of Blake, which leaves Cally uncertain of his motives:

CALLY   Are we fanatics?

BLAKE   Does it matter?

CALLY   Many, many people will die without Star One.

BLAKE   I know.

CALLY   Are you sure that what we're going to do is justified?

BLAKE   It has to be. Don't you see, Cally? If we stop now then all we have done is senseless killing and destruction. Without

> purpose, without reason. We have to win. It's the only way I can be sure that I was right.
>
> CALLY   That *you* were right?

Here, Blake seems to have set aside his humanity in the name of his own ideology. However, at Star One itself, the base has been infiltrated by aliens from the Andromeda galaxy with the intention of invading Federation space. They have been assisted in this by Travis. The intersection of the narrative trajectories of Blake and Travis is made when Travis commits the 'final act' that will destroy the Federation (by switching off part of the minefield protecting Federation space from the alien invasion fleet) and Blake elects to place the *Liberator* alongside the Federation fleets to fight off the invasion. Ultimately, then, Blake sets aside his own ideological beliefs: he foregoes the opportunity to destroy the Federation when the cost is the destruction of the whole of humanity.

Blake's 7 has no character story arcs such as appear in more recent shows like *Babylon 5* (Rattlesnake Productions for Warners, 1993–99) and *Star Trek: Deep Space Nine* (NBC, 1993–99). Nevertheless, a discernible trajectory is present in Blake's story across the course of the series as he makes the transition from passionate idealist to thwarted cynic. This transition reflects the distinction made by Krishan Kumar between what he calls the 'anti-utopian temperament' and the drive that lay behind the creation of such anti-utopias as *Brave New World* and *Nineteen Eighty-Four*. The anti-utopian temperament, Kumar argues, is a pragmatic critique of utopia derived (in the post-Enlightenment period, at least) from a Burkean conservatism and it comes, he suggests, 'from a fundamental pessimism, or at least scepticism, about the capacities of human beings and the possibility of attaining more than a moderate degree of happiness in human society'.[10] He differentiates this from the utopian leanings of writers such as Huxley and Orwell, who, as he points out, had little in common with defenders of hierarchy, property and religion, and who believed in equality and reason. Kumar goes so far as to argue that

> The anti-utopia is largely the creation of men for whom it represented the dark obverse of their own profound and passionate utopian temperament. Their anti-utopias are born of a sense of frustrated and thwarted utopianism.... The intimate connection

of utopia and anti-utopia here most clearly reveals itself as the anguished cry of a single divided self.[11]

Where Blake begins as a thwarted utopian eager for political revolution, he dies pessimistic and sceptical. 'At least you're still alive,' Jenna tells Blake in 'Space Fall', the second episode (1st tx. BBC 1, 9 January 1978). 'Not until free men can think and speak', Blake responds. 'Not until power is back in the hands of the honest man.' This is a different man from the one about whom the Federation agent Arlen (Sasha Mitchell) can say (in the final episode, 'Blake'), 'Your friend Blake said he couldn't tell anymore who was Federation and who wasn't. He was right. He couldn't.'

After 'Star One', Blake is no longer the focus of the show (Gareth Thomas having left) and the spotlight moves more to the character of Avon, with episodes focusing on his betrayal by his girlfriend ('Rumours of Death') and his intermittent attempts to find Blake ('Volcano', 1st tx. BBC 1, 21 January 1980; 'Terminal'; 'Blake') in order to relieve Avon of the ambivalent responsibility of the *Liberator* and its crew. Avon, too, at one point chases a chimera of freedom, a false lead on Blake's whereabouts set up by Servalan ('Terminal').

When the audience does see Blake again, in the final episode, the most striking immediate change is in his physical appearance: he now has a scar over one eye, inviting comparison to Travis's eye-patch (and presumably signifying a loss of vision). The other most obvious change is Blake's cynicism and world-weariness. He presents himself to Arlen as a bounty hunter and tells her he can no longer tell who his enemies are; this 'bounty hunter routine' is later revealed as a cover and Blake recruits Arlen to his nascent resistance movement. The arrival of Avon and the crew brings the situation to a crisis: when Blake and Avon come face to face, Avon believes that Blake is a bounty hunter and has sold him out. This revelation comes to Avon in the light of what he has learnt about his girlfriend Anna Grant. The (seemingly inevitable) conclusion to the individual decline of these men resulting from their environment is the death of Blake at the hands of Avon, who believes (falsely) that Blake has betrayed him. Arlen is revealed to be a Federation officer; Federation troopers overrun the base and the crew are shot dead in the ensuing firefight. The final image of the programme is that of

Avon standing alone, surrounded by faceless troopers, raising a gun to kill in the only option left available to him other than immediate extinction. All the major themes of *Blake's 7* – moral ambiguity and degradation; the limited possibilities for individual action; the extent to which in fighting your enemy you must become your enemy – are drawn together in a dramatic finale which is profoundly sceptical of the possibility of freedom. Avon's final act of resistance is one that will lead to his annihilation. As in *Nineteen Eighty-Four*, it seems we must learn to love Big Brother or die.

Blake's 7 can find little space for resistance, whether individual or in the progressive movements of the 1960s and 1970s such as feminism. 'Power', in Season Four, for example, is concerned with a battle between two tribes organized along gender lines: the Hommiks are a male-dominated society that has abandoned technology. They are waging (and winning) a war against the technically sophisticated and entirely female Seska. The Hommiks entrap Seska and operate to remove the devices which enable their psycho-kinetic abilities, thus absorbing the women into Hommik society. The attribution of psychic powers to women is common in the many feminist novels that were revitalising utopian literature during this period, including Sally Miller Gearhart's *The Wanderground* (1979) and Marge Piercy's *Woman on the Edge of Time* (1976). The intervention of Avon and the crew in the Hommik–Seska war brings about the final destruction of Seska civilisation. A case has been made that 'Power' urges for greater recognition of the subtlety of the ties that bind men and women together.[12] However, the series' pessimistic stance on the possibility of social transformation, coupled with disturbing images of captured and brutalised women, give 'Power' unpleasantly misogynistic overtones. The attempt by the Seska to determine their own future is destroyed by brute force, given the legitimacy of inevitability which is attributed to all forces of moral and social decline throughout the narrative of *Blake's 7*. In its treatment of feminism, *Blake's 7*, as an exemplar of the anti-utopian tradition and in response to the feminist revival of the utopia from the 1970s onwards, comes very close to the pessimism about the capacity for human beings and human society to achieve happiness that Kumar sees as reactionary.

Yet it is this pessimistic vision – from a mainstream series rather than a serial drama – that is *Blake's 7*'s claim to originality. At the time *Blake's 7* was being produced, the BBC distinguished between drama series – that is, popular episodic drama productions such as *Blake's 7* – and drama serials, for example flagship 'mini-series' programming. Understood within this production context, *Blake's 7* can more clearly be seen as occupying a unique position in the history of British television drama. It is the BBC's last attempt, to date, at producing a mainstream, politically oriented science fiction series, and it is the last to be transmitted in a primetime slot on BBC 1. From the late 1970s and throughout the 1980s, speculations of what the future might hold became the province of minority slots or channels, or were considered suitable for treatment only within flagship, serial drama form. For example, *Star Cops* (BBC TV, 1987), created by Chris Boucher, is a hybrid show combining elements of the series format (ensemble cast, episodic format) with those of the serial form (particularly its short duration of only nine episodes). It was transmitted in a minority slot on BBC 2 and did not progress beyond a first season. Dark visions of the future were presented in, for example, *A Very British Coup* (1988) and *Edge of Darkness* (1985); yet both of these were in serial format and transmitted first on (respectively) Channel 4 and BBC2. Dramas such as *Threads* (BBC TV, 1984) and *The Quatermass Conclusion* (Euston Films for Thames TV, 1979) certainly presented bleak futures, but again these were in flagship viewing single play and serial form respectively.

This is not to say that *Blake's 7* was consistent in its treatment of its political themes throughout its run. In its final season, in particular, a new producer with a background in light entertainment came on to the show and this sat uneasily with the gritty themes of some of the fourth-season episodes, particularly those dealing with the Federation's pacification programme in terms of its use of a new drug to suppress planetary populations before invasion. The penultimate episode, 'Warlord', shows these tensions very clearly: the story follows Avon's attempts to organise an alliance of independent planetary leaders to combat the Federation and the new drug programme. The episode opens with images of a newly suppressed population and Federation troopers shooting civilians at whim, but much of the costume design is absurd and the episode is stagy. 'Warlord' exemplifies how *Blake's 7* never wholly resolved the tension between being entertainment and drama.[13] Production notes as early as Nation's pitch for the series describe *Blake's 7* as 'kidult' – that is, suitable for adults and children alike.[14] This, in part, was because of an increasing mind-set at the BBC that science fiction was something for children and not to be taken seriously. In addition, there was reluctance, particularly after the furore led by Mary Whitehouse's National Viewers' and Listeners' Association over the *Doctor Who* story 'The Deadly Assassin' (BBC TV, 1976), to portray violence which might be seen or copied by children. There was also an unwillingness to show blood – all of which led to a lack of realism and which was in conflict with script editor Boucher's attempts to portray a darker universe. The violent (and bloody) conclusion of the series shows the impact that more realistic portrayals of violence might have had. Against these constraints, *Blake's 7* struggled to maintain serious treatment of its themes and was ultimately cancelled. Like the 'feelies' for the masses in *Brave New World*, with a few books locked away for the Controller, political science fiction drama throughout the 1980s was practically non-existent, having moved from the mainstream into minority viewing slots.

Yet the appetite for intelligent mainstream science fiction drama certainly existed. Throughout the 1990s, science fiction shows began to be imported from the USA, given credibility by their success in attracting substantial audiences to non-terrestrial channels. Much of this more recent wave of episodic and ensemble shows bears a distinct resemblance to *Blake's 7* in terms of format but, in comparison, barely touches upon the politics of their respective situations. In *Lexx* (Salter Street Films, 1998–2002), for example, a crew of renegades steal a super-spaceship and drift from planet to planet having adventures in soft porn. In *Andromeda* (Tribune Entertainment, 2000–), the premise of *Blake's 7* seems almost to be reversed, with a crew of renegades using a super-spaceship to restore an intergalactic federation of planets; and, in its later seasons, *Andromeda* attempts little more than action-adventure. In *Farscape* (Jim Henson Company, 1999–2003), the crew of renegades is made up of, among others, a man on the run being chased by a leather-clad psychopath, a 'strong man' character and an alien telepath. They flee imprisonment by a totalitarian regime, stealing a super-spaceship to make good their escape. *Farscape* avoids the tension in *Blake's 7* between drama and entertainment but this comes at the cost of explicit and serious consideration of broader political themes. Joss Whedon's short-lived *Firefly* (Fox Television, 2003) contained hints that the political context of the captain's decision to take on board fugitives from the government would have been explored in depth, but the programme was cancelled before these story arcs could be fully developed.[15] The creator of *Babylon 5* (1993–99), J. Michael Straczynski, has acknowledged a specific debt to *Blake's 7*; this is most apparent in the narrative arcs that follow the rise to power of the dictator, President Clark, on Earth and the subsequent (successful) rebellions against his regime, in particular that led by Sheridan (Bruce Boxleitner) on Babylon 5 itself. *Star Trek: Deep Space Nine* (1993–99), in its earlier seasons, shows a successful resistance against the totalitarian Cardassian occupiers on Bajor, going on to make the transition to stable government. Darker treatments of rebellion surround the story arc that follows the activities and eventual destruction of the Maquis, a group of former Federation colonists whose planets have been shifted to Cardassian control under the terms of a new treaty. The final story arc in *Star Trek: Deep Space Nine* is, in part, concerned with a series of regime changes – some peaceful, some not so peaceful. On the whole, the narrative encourages the viewer to see these as progressive moves: for example, it is strongly implied that the new leader of Ferenginar will be following a legislative programme of liberal reforms to mitigate the effects of capitalism gone rampant. The situation portrayed on Cardassia, however, is more complex. An armed rebellion against an occupying force meets with very mixed success: the rebel leader is shot dead in a firefight and while the occupiers are defeated, their response to the rebellion has left most of Cardassia in ruins. Clearly, with budgets that were not available to the production crew of *Blake's 7* and with more space to use story arcs to break from the constraints of the episodic series format, both *Babylon 5* and *Star Trek: Deep Space Nine* were in a better position to produce for mainstream television complex treatments of resistance against totalitarianism.

The narrative conservatism of long-running, episodic drama series has been well documented. Nick Freeman, in his article 'See Europe With ITC', discussing the ITC film series of the 1960s and 1970s, describes how stock footage, in maintaining fixed images of 'foreign' places and people, establishes stasis in a changing world and keeps the 'other' in its place.[16] From the writing coalface, Troy Kennedy

Martin dispenses with theorising and succinctly dismisses the purpose of police drama series as giving easy answers in order to 'super-impose over the anarchy of life a superficial order'.[17] David Buxton argues for the conservatism of long-running, episodic drama series; he attributes this to the way in which what he calls 'human nature', mass-produced television narratives tread an ideological tightrope between offering exciting entertainment on the one hand and assuaging fears of television's supposed power to undermine social cohesion on the other:

> The (good) recurring characters were not transformable and their moral determinations were immediately visible. Conflict within this static formation was necessarily catalysed by adaptable (usually bad) 'guest' characters intervening from outside.... The series had to create not only a popular form of entertainment but also a political consensus for the solutions proposed.[18]

Throughout this chapter, I have charted ways in which *Blake's 7* does not fit this description. The narrative trajectories of Blake and Travis operate, at first, in contrast; however, in the second season, parallels are drawn between the characters specifically to problematise the solutions employed by both – armed suppression and armed resistance. The decline of Blake himself shows how recurring characters are transformable and how their moral determinations can be obscured. Most conspicuously, rather than allowing the *Liberator* crew to battle through to vindicate their world-view against hostile interventions, the series shows them losing and dying. In bringing its narrative to such a definitive and dramatic conclusion, *Blake's 7* broke with the constraints of episodic series drama. And, true to its time and its tradition, its revolution does not turn out how we might wish.

NOTES

The author gratefully acknowledges the advice and input of Iain Coleman.

1. In 'The Daleks', the First Doctor and companions visit the planet Skaro, which has been largely obliterated by centuries of 'neutronic wars' between the two races that inhabit the planet, the Dals and the Thals. In 'Genesis of the Daleks', Terry Nation rewrote the origin story, transforming the Dals into the Kaleds: the Fourth Doctor arrives on Skaro at the critical point of this war when Davros, a leading Kaled scientist obsessed with absolute power, is on the verge of

creating the Daleks. A shrieking megalomaniac who is surrounded by an SS-styled 'Kaled Elite', Davros eventually dies in an underground bunker. In *Survivors*, a global pandemic wipes out 99.9 per cent of the world's population in the course of the first episode; the following three seasons, which ran between 1975 and 1977 on BBC 1, follow the attempts by the eponymous survivors to rebuild both the social and the technological infrastructure.

2. Chris Boucher, interview with the author, April 2001.
3. Chris Boucher, conversation with the author, February 2003.
4. Wells's *When the Sleeper Wakes* (1899) follows the character of Graham, a nineteenth-century man who falls asleep for two hundred years and awakes in an apparently utopian future world, only to discover that a tyrannical dictator, Ostrog, keeps most of humanity enslaved. Zamyatin's *We* (1924) is set in the twenty-sixth century, in the totalitarian society of OneState, organised on the lines of F.W. Taylor's theories of scientific management. The narratives of both books concern an uprising against the tyrannical rulers of these societies.
5. My thanks to Dana Shilling for raising this point.
6. There are passing allusions to *Brave New World* in the references throughout to how Federation society is stratified according to Alpha, Beta and Delta grades and in the *Liberator* crew's suppressant of choice, which is adrenaline and soma. However, the show undoubtedly draws most freely from *Nineteen Eighty-Four* and from Orwell's precursors Wells and Zamyatin.
7. Krishan Kumar, *Utopia and Anti-Utopia in Modern Times* (Oxford: Blackwell, 1987), p. 381.
8. Alan Stevens and Fiona Moore, *Liberation: The Unofficial and Unauthorised Guide to Blake's 7* (Tolworth: Telos Publishing, 2003), p. 20.
9. Soldier 027, written statement to Saville Inquiry. Available at: www.bloody-sunday-inquiry.org/transcripts/Archive/TS247.htm; para. 70, ll, 6–10. My thanks to Iain Coleman for raising this point.
10. Kumar, *Utopia and Anti-Utopia in Modern Times*, pp. 102–3.
11. Ibid., p. 104.
12. Stevens and Moore, *Liberation*, pp. 162–4.
13. My thanks to Iain Coleman for raising several of the points made in this section.
14. Stevens and Moore, *Liberation*, p. 12.
15. In precisely which direction it will go following the release of *Serenity* (dir. Joss Whedon, USA, 2005), a *Firefly* film, remains to be seen.
16. Nick Freeman, 'See Europe With ITC', in Deborah Cartmell, I.Q. Hunter, Heidi Kaye and Imelda Whelehan (eds), *Alien Identities: Exploring Difference in Film and Fiction* (London: Pluto Press, 1999), pp. 49–65.
17. Troy Kennedy Martin, quoted in Paul Cornell, Martin Day and Keith Topping, *The Guinness Book of Classic British Television*, 2nd edn (Enfield: Guinness Publishing, 1996), p. 209.
18. David Buxton, *From The Avengers to Miami Vice: Form and Ideology in Television Series* (Manchester: Manchester University Press, 1990), p. 24.

10

Echoes of discontent:
Conservative politics and
Sapphire and Steel

PETER WRIGHT

With the possible exception of *The Prisoner* (ITC, 1967–68), *Sapphire and Steel* (ATV, 1979–1982) remains the most perplexing British television science fiction series to date. Whilst its premise is simple – two eponymous 'time detectives' of mysterious origin act to safeguard the integrity of the temporal order – its execution produced a programme suffused with ambiguity.[1] For six untitled adventures (termed 'Assignments' in the 2002 Carlton DVD releases), it intrigued and beguiled its audience. With the exception of Assignment Five, written by Don Houghton and Anthony Read, the series was scripted by its creator, P.J. Hammond. It united Hammond's skill at writing both police procedural narratives (his former work included contributions to *Z Cars* [BBC TV, 1962–78], *The Sweeney* [Euston Films for ITV, 1975–8], *Hazell* [ITV, 1978–80] and *The Professionals* [LWT, 1977–83]) with stories dependent on fantastic conceits derived from the Gothic tradition, the Victorian ghost story and science fiction (which also informed his work on Thames Television's *Ace of Wands* [ITV, 1970–72]).[2]

Like *The Prisoner*, *Sapphire and Steel* encourages speculative and interpretive viewing, offering more opportunities for 'creative discussion and invention' than other, less equivocal, series.[3] Accordingly, this chapter offers a 'creative discussion' of the programme's response to its politically turbulent context. Since the first five assignments were written, videotaped and broadcast within a relatively short period, *Sapphire and Steel* is closely, if metaphorically, engaged with its sociopolitical milieu.[4] Although Hammond denies that there is any direct political subtext in the programme, he admits that he always keeps 'up with the daily news so I suspect that subconsciously political events may well have been woven into the stories'.[5] Arguably, the 'political events' that appear subconsciously woven into *Sapphire and Steel* show the series adopting a conservative stance, imbued elliptically with elements of Thatcherism.

Sapphire and Steel first aired on 10 July 1979, two months after the Conservative election victory of 3 May. The most significant factor in the swing against Labour was the 1978–79 'Winter of Discontent', a period of extensive strikes and antagonistic picketing following union wage claims beyond the government's 5 per cent norm. The strikes impacted deeply: there were food shortages, public transport stopped; schools, petrol stations and cemeteries were closed. The Labour government lost its credibility and many viewed the Winter of Discontent as the lowest point in Britain's long economic decline. As the perception of Labour's apparent inability to maintain civil order doubled from 18 per cent in 1975 to 36 per cent in 1978, there was a general sense of a country spiralling into chaos. Unsurprisingly, several 'commentators saw Britain's economic decline as part of a more general social, political and cultural malaise'.[6] The electorate voted for change at the first opportunity. In 1979, it was 'time for a new beginning', as the Conservative Party's manifesto phrased its bid for power.

On initial viewing, there seems little evidence that the series reflects on these events or on the philosophy of the Conservative opposition under Margaret Thatcher. The closed, claustrophobic sets so important to *Sapphire and Steel*'s Gothic atmosphere may allude to the 'introverted' perspective of Britain in its 'post-imperial phase',[7] but on the whole it seems detached from contemporary politics. Closer inspection, however, suggests that the characterisation and conflict in *Sapphire and Steel* draw peculiar parallels with Conservatism, particularly its Thatcherite revisions. Assignment One is fundamental to understanding the politics of the programme since it introduces the series' eponymous characters and major themes.

Sapphire and Steel (played, respectively, by Joanna Lumley and David McCallum) are debatably Thatcherite protagonists. Indeed, it is tempting to read Sapphire's costuming and Steel's intransigence as

MIDDLE-CLASS HEROES Sapphire and Steel (Joanna Lumley and David McCallum) have been assigned.

allusions to Thatcher's emblematic blue attire and her intractable will. Known as 'the Iron Lady' from 1976 for her frank warnings about the Soviet threat, Thatcher anticipates Steel's demeanour.[8] However trivial this may seem, the middle-class Sapphire and Steel undeniably share qualities and attitudes with the Tory leader. Thatcher's dismissal of 'consensus' politics, which had shaped British government for twenty-five years, is echoed in Steel's uncompromising, abrasive and compassionless demeanour.[9] Like Thatcher, he is rarely conciliatory; nor is he intimidated by the possibility of confrontation. More obviously, Sapphire and Steel perceive situations and resolutions in stark terms. Their power lies in their willingness to do the unthinkable, to use whatever means necessary to achieve their ends. Significantly, as Kenneth Harris observes: 'Mrs Thatcher represented an uncompromising Messianic political approach' that contrasted with 'the sceptical, inquiring mind of liberal Britain that has presided over the country's post-war economic demise.' He continues by remarking how 'her acolytes argued that only such a black and white attitude could rescue government from the powerlessness which … seemed to grip Westminster during the late 1970s.'[10] Sapphire and Steel display a comparably empowering monochrome approach.

The authoritarianism attributed to Thatcher and demonstrated by Sapphire and Steel is also a quality of fictional detectives like Conan Doyle's Sherlock Holmes, Christie's Poirot, and those found in Hammond's crime writing.[11] This is understandable given that they all champion the cause of bourgeois values. Figures like Holmes 'mediate psychic protection' to readers who may have 'faith in modern systems of scientific and rational inquiry to order an uncertain and troubling world' but who feel they 'lacked these powers themselves'.[12] Sapphire, Steel, Holmes, Poirot and Thatcher have been represented variously as protectors of bourgeois society capable of ordering 'an uncertain and troubling world.' Although it is impossible now to envision Thatcher as a guardian of the social order, the closing lines of her final broadcast before the 1979 general election elicit this ideal: 'Let us make this a country safe to work in. Let us make this a country safe to walk in. Let us make it a country safe to grow up in. Let us make it a country safe to grow old in.'[13] After the disorder of the Winter of Discontent, Thatcher's rhetoric was both appealing and reassuring (although it rang hollow following the civil unrest of the early 1980s). Nevertheless, her dogmatic restatement of 'safety' suggests how ready Britain was for a return to order, even under such an obstinate leader. It is not surprising, therefore, that Sapphire and Steel were acceptable as heroic figures for the period despite their obdurate and at times misanthropic attitude.

For Conservatives, there can be no freedom without authority. 'The first requisite of a society', stated Edmund Burke, whose *Reflections on the Revolution in France* (1790) is seen as the seminal text in conservative thought, 'is that means exist for the restraint of men's passions.'[14] Accordingly, *Sapphire and Steel*, through its appropriations from crime fiction, reflects the same attitude towards authority. Burke saw the issue of freedom as indivisible from a triangle of authority, with a mediating group between the state and the individual.[15] Into this group fall the police force, amateur detectives as well as agents like Sapphire and Steel. In the series, precisely who governs the cosmos remains unclear, although the presence of a hooded figure during the opening titles alludes to some distant authority figure. Standing between this and the human world are Sapphire, Steel and their colleagues. Within that group, there is a particular hierarchy. 'Investigators' assess temporal disruptions; 'operatives' like Sapphire and Steel rectify anomalies, although they often investigate phenomena themselves; and 'specialists' like Silver (David Collings) undertake any tasks beyond the operatives' abilities. Such hierarchies are feudal in nature. As Robert Nisbet remarks: 'There is an inexpugnable element of feudalism in the conservative theory of authority.... Authority then was manifest in a chain, one analogous to the chain of being that dominated medieval theology.'[16]

However conservative in its concept of hierarchical authority, *Sapphire and Steel* also invests in the efficacy of an individual's intelligence and perception. This contradicts the traditional conservatism of Burke, who advocated feudalism and historical structures like the family, community and church. The series' emphasis on individual ability therefore identifies it more with Thatcherism than with its antecedent conservatism. Indeed the 1979 general election 'was presented as perhaps the 'last chance' to restore the balance in society, which had been tilted in favour of the state at the expense of the individual'.[17] *Sapphire and Steel* centralises individualism through its protagonists, following the golden-age crime fiction of Agatha Christie in placing at its heart 'the pervasive individualism of bourgeois feeling and epistemology' that Stephen Knight sees as 'crucial to the whole edifice of the clue-puzzle in crime, detective and literary structure.'[18] Nevertheless, the series' subscription to individualism is unlikely to arise solely from its generic heritage. The presence of additional allusions to Thatcher suggests that the programme's championing of individualism derived as much from the contemporary political context as its literary origins.

Under Thatcher, the relationship between the individual and the state underwent a significant revision, and this transformation is mirrored in *Sapphire and Steel*. Ivor Crewe explains how 'Thatcher's objective was nothing less than a cultural revolution. The public had to be persuaded to lower its expectations of, and dependence upon, the state'.[19] Sapphire and Steel, as representatives of an indeterminate cosmic 'state', act accordingly. They keep order, permitting people to live untrammelled by anarchy but absent themselves, without interfering in the lives of those they encounter, unless a sacrifice is necessary (as in Assignment Two) or there has been a notable transgression (Assignment Three). The Jardine family in Assignment One have copies of their destroyed property restored; the dead are returned to death in Assignment Two and the family history of the Mullrines and McDees is re-established in Assignment Five. However, the non-interventionist philosophy of Thatcherism – which was broken frequently after the Conservatives' initial advertising brief to Saatchi & Saatchi of 'Freedom, Choice and Minimum Interference'[20] – is most conspicuous in Assignment Four. When the malevolent Shape is finally trapped, Steel warns Liz (Alyson Spiro) to destroy any photographs of herself and never have another one taken. He knows the Shape can use photographs to move, trap humans and hide. If it escapes, it will pursue Liz for revenge. With this warning, Sapphire and Steel depart, leaving Liz to survive by her own actions. Accordingly, Thatcher's emphasis on 'the importance of standing on one's own two feet'[21] is expressed in *Sapphire and Steel*, which embraces her ethic of self-reliance and self-sufficiency.

This philosophy represented a fundamental shift from the paternalism of traditional Tory ideology.[22] The old-fashioned Tory paternalism found in *Sapphire and Steel* is limited to Assignment One, which, as several commentators have indicated, reveals Hammond's original intention of writing *Sapphire and Steel* for children.[23] David Sheldrick, for example, notes how 'Steel is uncharacteristically conciliatory and occasionally almost fatherly towards the children' he encounters.[24] This fatherliness is not sustained throughout Assignment One and disappears in subsequent episodes, with Steel becoming increasingly dictatorial and distant.

Under Thatcher, the proposed withdrawal of state intervention formed part of what was perceived as the need for a fresh start, an end to the consensus politics that had governed Britain since 1945. The Tory manifesto promised a 'fundamental change of course', a revision of political direction that would mark a movement away from conventional conservatism whilst retaining some of its core principles. This combination of radicalism and traditionalism is dramatised through Assignment One's treatment of history.

In many cases, *Sapphire and Steel* displays a traditional conservative attitude towards history. Indeed this traditionalism provides the foundation for Sapphire and Steel's investigations. Nisbet points out that 'basic to conservative politics is its view of the role of history.'[25] History to conservatives is essentially experience, and it is the conservative faith in experience rather than abstract reasoning 'in matters of human relationships' that underpins its faith in history and historical structures.[26] In short, conservatives express confidence in deduction and the drawing of conclusions achieved by following the descent of certain phenomena through history. Sapphire and Steel are practitioners of deduction. Like their conservative ancestor Holmes, they have 'knowledge of what certain phenomena will mean' and draw 'from a set of existent theories to explain new events'.[27] In Assignment One, Sapphire, Steel and Lead (Val Pringle) all refer to a previous anomaly aboard the *Marie Celeste* and use their experiences to overcome the current threat. This emphasis on deduction identifies them as experiential operatives deriving competence from their past. The importance of one's own experience is emphasised when Rob (Steven O'Shea) asks Steel, 'Don't you know your history?' to which Steel responds dryly: 'I know mine.'[28] Here, personal history is separated from monolithic history but, as the first five Assignments demonstrate, it is only through the proficiency acquired from the former that monolithic history can be preserved.

For Burke: 'The true historical method is … the method of studying the present in such a way as to bring out *all* of what lies in the present; and that means a veritable infinity of ways of behaviour and thinking which cannot be understood fully, save by recognition of their anchoring in the past.'[29] Sapphire and Steel's enquiries parallel this methodology. They investigate each environment, using experience to guide them in drawing out the echoes of the past informing the present. Confined to the Jardines' house, Assignment One explores a property possessed by history, represented here by the time-break's antagonistic manifestations and Mr Jardine's (John Golightly) affection for antique clocks. There is little evidence in the *mise-en-scène* or the behaviour and costume of the characters that the narrative is set in 1979. Few contemporary objects are in evidence and tradition governs the household. Mrs Jardine (Felicity Harrison) recites nursery rhymes to her daughter; multiplication tables are learned by rote and there is a general sense of antiquity about the house. There are, as Steel observes, 'lots of old, old echoes'.[30] Knowing that a 'trigger', a 'pressure point',[31] must exist after their encounter with Time aboard the *Marie Celeste*, Sapphire and Steel 'study the present to bring out *all* of what lies in the present'. Once they discover that their enemy is using nursery rhymes as triggers, they can destroy it.

With its emphasis on reading before bedtime and other historically resonant customs, Assignment One reflects the conservative belief that history is expressed not simply in a linear fashion 'but in the persistence of structures, communities, habits, and prejudices generation after generation'.[32] Like Conan Doyle, Hammond uses his characters to defend these structures, practices and values, especially in Assignment One where the nuclear family and its property are central. Sapphire and Steel preserve the family unit and the traditions it follows. Although the return of Rob's and Helen's (Tamasin Bridge) parents can be read as a by-product of restoring the temporal order, Assignment One establishes the investigators as defenders of the family and its traditions. Throughout, Sapphire and Steel assure the children that their parents will be returned. Since the preservation of temporal harmony is inextricable from the preservation of the nuclear family, Assignment One shows Sapphire and Steel representing the customary conservative faith in the family as the mainstay of the social order.

Traditionally, 'much of the conservative veneration for the family lies in the historic affinity between family and property.'[33] In Assignment One, property plays a significant role in the temporal disorder. Time breaks through because the aggregation of antiques and old nursery rhymes wears thin the 'fabric' of temporality. In their battle with Time, Sapphire and Steel burn all the nursery rhymes they can find. Accordingly, one might assume the programme adopts an anti-materialist stance contrary to conservative thinking. However, at the conclusion, the family's books are restored with simulations. What the programme seems to be arguing at this point is that a large aggregation of traditions from the past is dangerous (the antiques and the nursery rhymes are too much for the fragile structure of time), whereas a lesser assortment (the antiques and faux children's books) are not a danger. Speaking metaphorically, *Sapphire and Steel* argues that time (and history) will tolerate the preservation of certain traditions providing others are replaced or substituted with new forms (which may resemble but are not identical to the original concepts). Whilst such a perspective follows the 'selective traditionalism' of conventional conservative thinking outlined by Nisbet,[34] it can also be linked more to the attitude of the Thatcher government. In signalling the tolerable and intolerable forms of the past, Assignment One echoes how Thatcher's Conservative Party during the same period advocated traditional values alongside an occasionally paradoxical 'break with the past' and a 'programme of reform'.[35]

This simultaneous preservation and overturning of established ideas is dramatised through Assignment One's narrative events. Gothic forces assault Sapphire and Steel as they defend the family and its house. These forces act generically, manifesting a power that threatens not merely property and social structure but the order – the bourgeois family – upon which that structure is founded.[36] Although the true menace remains unseen, its agents – manifestations of plague victims and Parliamentary soldiers from Cromwell's New Model Army – are potent symbols, especially at the end of the 1970s. As representatives of Cromwell's revolution, the parliamentarians function as images of social and political upheaval, civil war and strife. In the context of the late 1970s, they can be read as substitutes for what were then perceived to be contemporary agents of unrest, namely the unions. Although the analogy may be imprecise, the associations are clear: both parliamentarians and trade unions were seen as threatening to the fabric of their respective societies. After the Winter of Discontent, the historically confrontational trade unions were characterised as disruptive forces that needed reining in. In the run up to the 1979 general election, the Conservatives worked to convince the electorate that they could 'solve their central dilemma of dealing with the unions without a disastrous repetition of the 1974 confrontation' that toppled the Heath administration.[37] Like Sapphire and Steel, the Conservatives and, one assumes, the country were haunted by spectres of the past. The unions were one area where the Conservatives enforced their reforms; they were one of the ghosts the Thatcher government sought to exorcise.

The ethereal plague victims – summoned by the recitation of 'Ring-a-ring-a-roses' – are equally significant. The Winter of Discontent raised public awareness of the threats to health caused by uncollected refuse, disruption to water and sewage treatment, and the storing of unburied bodies in disused premises in Liverpool. Rats were more common in Britain's streets; whilst plague was not a concern, the historic reputation of the disease-ridden rat aroused fears of widespread illness. In Conservative opinion, the responsibility for this endangerment of public health was laid at the feet of the service-sector unions, which were now perceived to be resented by the population.[38] Hence the appearance of plague-ridden characters in *Sapphire and Steel* would have struck a resonant chord with contemporary audiences. The association of civil war soldiery with plague carriers is also noteworthy since as Stephen Porter observes, plague 'outbreaks … were greatly exacerbated by the civil wars in the 1640s…. Bristol was in the throes of a severe outbreak in September 1645 when it was captured by the New Model Army.'[39] The series seems to be drawing an analogy between the social and political situation of the 1640s and that of the late 1970s. If the Cromwellian Roundheads are equivalent to unruly unions, then the plague victims can be read as surrogates for a population fallen to their militancy.

Consequently, the banishment of these ghostly apparitions becomes synonymous with the Conservative desire to curb union power. In an interview with Brian Walden on 14 January 1979, Thatcher argued for the need 'to re-establish the authority of the government under the law' and insisted on an all-party accord to implement legislation revising the process of picketing, striking and negotiation. Underpinning this was her commitment to restricting the power of the unions.[40] She was advocating a reformation of the union movement to remove its socially disruptive influence. Since ghost stories deal with the insurrection rather than the resurrection of the dead, it is appropriate that the 'insurrectionary' activities of the public-sector unions should be represented by 'ghosts', whether they are described by *Sapphire and Steel* as 'visual refractions' or not.[41]

Like the ghost stories from which it borrows, *Sapphire and Steel* exploits its audience's fear of the irruption of disorder into an orderly world. However, where the ghost story displays 'a nostalgia for an older, more supernatural system of beliefs, and this nostalgia can be seen as inherently romantic',[42] *Sapphire and Steel* remains anti-nostalgic. Indeed its implicit critique of Mr Jardine's antiquarianism warns of the dangers of nostalgia, of adhering to too many things past. It is equally anti-romantic. By framing temporal disturbances as the result of sentimentality, it warns its audience against preserving too much from history. Although Julia Briggs argues that 'ghosts were a traditional medium of communication between the past and the present, the dead and the living, and thus the ghost story might be used to assert continuity at a time when it seemed threatened on many fronts',[43] the continuity suggested by the ghosts manifesting in Assignment One is unacceptable. They personify a time of discord and disease reappearing in the late 1970s that required a final relegation into history.

Confronting forces intent on temporal and social disintegration – indicated by the break-up of the Jardines' nuclear family – Assignment One emphasises the need to oppose negative influences from the past. By banishing these forces, *Sapphire and Steel* affirms what it perceives as good – the family, property, order and authority – over the negative influences of chaos. It confirms the need for strong governance while following Gothic conventions, where 'transgressions … allowed proper limits and values to be asserted at the closure of narratives'.[44] The 'proper limits and values' asserted at the conclusion of Assignment One can be seen to have a clear affinity with those of the incoming Conservative government.

Each of the following four assignments also dramatises themes echoing Thatcher's conservatism. Assignment Two achieves this directly in its treatment of the personae of dead servicemen and civilians returning in search of justice. As producer of the series, Shaun O'Riordan explains: Hammond 'was consumed with this idea of revenge after you'd been wrongly killed'.[45] Throughout the story, Tom Kelly gives a sympathetic performance as Pearce, a World War I soldier killed after the Armistice. The anger and injustice felt by Pearce, by a World War II pilot (David Cann), and by three civilians killed while testing a submarine, feed the parasitic Darkness which is manipulating them with promises of new life. When Sapphire and Steel buy the Darkness off with the life of Tully (Gerald James), a naive, middle-aged ghost-hunter, there is little evidence of Hammond's outrage for those 'mal-killed', as O'Riordan terms it.[46] Rather, Hammond validates the need for sacrifice. Tully, like Pearce and the rest, dies before his time, killed by an authority greater than he. With his death, the Darkness withdraws in a parallel of the German defeats of 1918 and 1945. Hence Assignment Two is not solely about injustice but also concerns itself with the need for sacrifice. By surrendering Tully to the Darkness, Steel affirms the value and importance of sacrifice for the 'greater good' of social and temporal stability.

Although the extent of the sacrifices expected of the British people under Thatcher did not become clear until 1980–81, the theme of sacrifice underlying her pre-election rhetoric may have provoked a comparable emphasis in Assignment Two. After she came to power it was obvious that, to arrest years of economic decline, her policies demanded a tightening of belts. As Kenneth Harris remarks: 'Thatcherism is … about *will*, and, in particular, the willing of the means as well as of the ends.'[47] Thatcher's means of opposing further deterioration in 1979 was Geoffrey Howe's radical 12 June budget, which saw public expenditure cut by £4 billion and VAT doubled to 15 per cent, with a reduction of income tax by 3p in the pound.[48] Thatcher's hard-nosed attitude towards economic reform through public spending control and the concomitant sacrifices required, which would lead to mass unemployment and social instability in the 1980s, is echoed in Steel's decision to feed Tully to the Darkness. Since the audience is not in a position to be harmed by Steel, it is likely to continue to accept him as a heroic figure. Though the conclusion to Assignment Two is chilling, the audience cannot help acknowledging the success of the programme's protagonists, in much the same way as 'those who remained unaffected applauded' the sacrifices required by Thatcher.[49]

Steel's willingness to sacrifice humans reappears in Assignment Three when he considers destroying an apartment building to restore a time break. 'What about the people downstairs?' Sapphire asks:

STEEL   That's their bad luck.

SAPPHIRE   You're talking about the lives of sixty-three people and fifteen animals.

STEEL   They'll be saving the whole of humanity. Human beings love a good sacrifice. Don't worry. When the building falls down, they'll blame the architect.[50]

Here, a characteristic deepening of cynicism informs Steel's Holmesian detachment and professional conviction. Such cynicism is not presented critically, however, since it is mitigated by wry humour (architects being blamed for defective buildings). From Christianity through ideas of patriotism to the remembrance of war dead, sacrifice is accepted as indicative of faith, honour, necessity and love. Just as the audience accepts that Tully's death is for the greater good, so it is likely to read the sacrifice of the apartment's inhabitants as an unavoidable consequence of preserving temporality. There is no irony in, or critique of, Steel's character; no sense that he is a satirical figure. Rather, the series suggests that strong leadership and social stability will require suitable sacrifices.

The relationship between Steel and Tully is also politically charged. Where Steel is a 'doer', Tully is an ineffectual 'talker'. Steel's dynamism further identifies him with Thatcher, who had grown tired of the empty rhetoric of earlier Conservative governments, which advocated change but failed to enforce it.[51] The division between Tory 'drys' – the doers – and 'wets' – the talkers – is reconfigured in Assignment Two to become a dialogue between Steel's coldly precise conviction and Tully's rather wet (in the usual sense) adherence to vague, conventional practices of ghost hunting. Tully's fussiness and middle-aged gallantry towards Sapphire mark him as a punctilious but ultimately inadequate individual. He has no imagination (suggested by his ownership of a one-eyed cat called Nelson), no understanding of what needs to be done and nothing to offer beyond the endless prattle of an enthusiastic amateur faced by consummate professionals.

A similar separation of doers from talkers is made in Assignment Three between the protagonists and Eldred (David Gant) and Rothwyn (Catherine Hall), time travellers on a research mission from the future. Isolated by a communications breakdown and powerless when their vivisected 'time unit' rebels, it is Sapphire, Silver and Steel who return them to the future. However, Assignment Three is less concerned with developing this wet/dry distinction than it is with dramatising another key contemporary Conservative concern: immigration. On first viewing there seems little indication of such a preoccupation, but *Sapphire and Steel* speaks in metaphors – both narrative and visual – and understanding what Rothwyn and Eldred represent exposes the subtext.

Again, Sapphire and Steel reunite a family: Eldred and Rothwyn regain their son after the time unit has transformed the boy. However, rather than being protected, the family is sent back to its future with their raging, malevolent time unit intact. As Steel remarks: it is 'their problem. They caused it. Let them suffer.... It doesn't belong here.'[52] The contrast between the treatment of the nuclear family in Assignment One and that in Assignment Three is partly a result of the attitudes held by the future society towards animals. Fifteen hundred years in the future, animals have been exterminated for being 'unclean'. 'Pieces' are 'kept alive' and 'propagated as pieces' for use by an obsessively sanitary human culture. Following this revelation, Sapphire, Silver and Steel literally turn their backs on Eldred and Rothwyn in a high angled shot that emphasises the difference in perspective between time traveller and time detective.

Sapphire's and Steel's outrage, which dramatises Joanna Lumley's well-publicised opposition to vivisection,[53] contrasts with Eldred's clinical stance. It also draws out the Assignment's ironic depiction of Eldred and Rothwyn who believe that the late twentieth century 'is a terrible part of time in which to be trapped.... It's brutal. It's cruel', where people like them 'would never survive'.[54] Neither Rothwyn nor Eldred perceives a society based upon vivisection as cruel. It remains for Sapphire and Steel to offer a more humane perspective. There is irony – or hypocrisy – here too, given Steel's previous willingness to sacrifice the population of the tower block, animals included, to mend the time break. However, the paradox is resolved by accepting the series' conviction that sacrifices are unavoidable and acceptable if there is no other alternative.

Vivisection, especially vivisection to facilitate the breaking of historical coherence, is shown to be unacceptable. Accordingly, Assignment Three establishes a cultural clash between the 'civilised' Sapphire and Steel and the 'barbaric' Eldred and Rothwyn. Where Silver's playful foppishness extends the cultured background of the time detectives already established by their middle-class personae, the effete Eldred emblematises the callous sterility of his time. Such a conflict reflects the concerns of more recent Gothic works, which deploy a 'fear of the barbaric not only from the past but also in the present and even the future'.[55] In Assignment Three, which adopts a conservative inversion of the liberal–radical perspective of progress, the barbaric descends on the present from the future. Individuals with alien and disruptive practices enter a British society they scarcely understand, where their lack of comprehension is signalled by their choice of anachronistic names. As temporal aliens, as immigrants from the future, they must be 'sent back'.

In suggesting that 'illegal immigrants' like Rothwyn and Eldred should be returned, *Sapphire and Steel* seems to subscribe to the contemporary Tory attitude towards immigrants and, possibly, to the late 1970s' Zeitgeist. On 30 January 1978, Thatcher warned of a Britain 'swamped' by black immigrants;[56] in an official policy statement on 7 April 1978, William Whitelaw 'promised a quota system to reduce immigration and a compulsory register of dependants'; and in July, extreme right-wing Conservative MP Enoch Powell criticised Thatcher for softening her earlier stance and promising merely to 'control the rate of immigration'.[57] The idea of defending Britain against foreign threats – real or imagined – informed the Conservative's defence policy, the pursuit of British interests in Europe and, post-*Sapphire and Steel*, the Falklands War. This 'new authoritarian ideology ... stressed the need for a state which would stand up to Britain's enemies abroad ... and at home'.[58] In Assignment Three, the authoritarian Sapphire and Steel act in this way, seeking out the foreign threat and exorcising a disruptive influence within.

It is important to note, however, that Rothwyn and Eldred are not sent home simply because their alien attitudes are anathema to Sapphire and Steel. They must be returned because their presence threatens the fabric of history. Their journey into the past and Sapphire and Steel's response stage a clash between the progressive rationalist view of the present 'as the beginning of the future' and the conservative stance, which 'is to see it as the latest point reached by the past in a continuous seamless growth'.[59] Hence Rothwyn and Eldred are rendered doubly repugnant through their relationship with vivisectionist technology and their ahistorical progressive rationalist attitude to the present. Their inappropriate names are not only a sign of their ignorance but also reveal a disregard for historical awareness that is the very antithesis of conservative views of the present. Again, *Sapphire and Steel* unites contemporary political attitudes with older conservative views.

Assignment Four's political subtext depends equally on metaphors. As several commentators have observed, the faceless Shape, haunting the pawnshop and bringing photographs to a semblance of life, alludes to the art of René Magritte.[60] Appearing in a variety of forms in a range of paintings, including *The Landscape of Baucis*, *The Road to Damascus*, *The Pilgrim* and *The King's Museum*, Magritte's faceless man is attired in bowler hat and modest suit. Although the Shape lacks the bowler hat, the business suit remains. Clearly, it is tempting to impose one or more of the various interpretations of Magritte's bowler-hatted man on to the Shape in search of an explanation for what it might signify. To do so, however, would be to overlook the political reading available. Well dressed but faceless, the Shape seems to symbolise the bureaucrat, the civil servant whose omnipresence is denoted by the Shape's occurrence in every photograph. It is an ideological image that reappeared in February 2004 when Conservative leader Michael Howard and shadow chancellor Oliver Letwin, surrounded by serried ranks of faceless, cardboard bureaucrats, promised to cut an unlikely £80 billion from Britain's civil service expenditure.[61]

Historically, the civil service has been a source of annoyance to the Conservatives. In its 1979 manifesto, the party stated its intention to cut public expenditure, including bureaucracy.[62] Indeed Thatcher demonised civil servants as social parasites, 'inefficient and overpaid'.[63] Her anti-bureaucratic ideology was based on her conviction that, corporately, the civil service was 'complacent, inert, pedantic and incapable of appreciating the need to devise or implement radical solutions to Britain's dire problems'.[64] Consequently, the civil service underwent radical cuts between 1979 and 1982, despite a lengthy dispute in 1981.[65]

Seemingly conscious of Thatcher's reservations regarding the civil service, *Sapphire and Steel* constructs the character of the Shape to reflect and emphasise public-sector shortcomings. Having trapped the landlord of a pawnshop in a photograph, the Shape continues to let out rooms above his shop. According to Liz, its surviving tenant, the Shape does not open the shop, work on the building, or bother Liz for rent, which she leaves on the stairs. Consequently, the assignment indicts the faceless bureaucrats of the civil service with indolence through the inaction of its featureless antagonist. This is a stance in keeping with Thatcher's attribution of Britain's economic decline to an inefficient public sector. [66]

Metaphorically, the Shape's ability to imprison people in old photographs signifies how the Conservative Party perceived the civil service as following practices that trapped society in traditional modes of bureaucratic administration like a fly in amber. Accordingly, Assignment Four echoes Thatcher's belief that 'the Establishment ... is absolutely at the heart of the British disease', specifically its economic decline.[67] The pawnshop emphasises this decline: 'It's a depressing place', Steel observes. 'There's nothing here but the belongings of the poor, the hopeless and the dead.'[68] The shop is a symbol for the condition of England in the months following the Winter of Discontent and prior to Thatcher's radical social reforms; a gloomy place caught between the consequences of economic atrophy, paralysing political traditions and social stagnation. It, like Britain, is a place where old things survive to trigger the return of unwelcome pasts on the present. Assignment Four's recurring rhyme, 'This is the way to London town', becomes a lament for how the capital and what it represented have deteriorated.

Caught in the conflict between the Shape and Sapphire and Steel, Liz is, as Andrew Martin suggests, 'one of those lost souls frequently found inhabiting '70s drama'.[69] The protagonists are less protective towards her than they are towards the Jardines, though they are not as callous in their treatment of her as they are in their dealings with Tully. It seems probable that their dismissal of her is predicated on the fact that she is indigent; a prostitute working in a club when she's 'allowed to'. Her valedictory speech, which emphasises her hopelessness, also alludes to the stagnant bureaucratic system represented by the photographs, the Shape and the ghostly 'children' it evokes: 'I feel like this lot [the people in photographs] sometimes. Looking like they've been somewhere, going somewhere, but when you think about it they're staying where they are. Going nowhere, right?'[70] The idea of 'going nowhere' is the key to Assignment Four. It defines the pawnshop, connotes a moribund bureaucracy and a weak economy, and summarises Liz's plight. Sapphire and Steel's indifference to her derives from the traditional conservative stance towards the poor and the disenfranchised. As Nisbet explains, the conservative 'argument may be stated easily: There are groups beginning with the family and including the neighbourhood and church, which are duly constituted to render assistance and in the form of *mutual-aid*, not high-flown charity from a bureaucracy.'[71] As representatives of an ambiguous but powerful authority, Sapphire and Steel do not 'render assistance' to Liz; they leave her to find assistance where she can.

However, contrary to their treatment of Liz, who must fend for herself, Sapphire and Steel defend the middle-class capitalists of Assignment Five. Lacking the subtle metaphors of Hammond's stories, Houghton and Read's screenplay exposes the series' right-wing stance directly. Modelled on the English country house murder mystery of the 1920s and 1930s, Assignment Five shows how an anachronistic party, hosted by Lord Arthur Mullrine (Davy Kaye) to celebrate the golden anniversary of the founding of Mullrine International, causes a bifurcation in time. This bifurcation is politically telling. In one continuum, scientist George McDee's (Stephen MacDonald) socialist desire to cure the world's diseases free of charge leads to disaster; in the other, competition between McDee's wife, Felicity (Nan Munro) and his lover, Arthur's sister, Emma (Patience Collier), brings about McDee's death and the rise of Mullrine International. In short, where socialism causes the extinction of the human race, competition and capitalist enterprise sustain it.

In their restoration of the correct timeline, Sapphire and Steel rescue the capitalist system and its representatives – Lord Mullrine; Tony Purnell (Christopher Bramwell), a merchant banker; Mullrine's deputy chairman, Felix Harborough (Jeffry Wickham); and Howard McDee (Jeremy Child), a partner in the company. None of these characters is depicted favourably, however. Mullrine is more concerned with the cost of his authentic suit than with the murders that occur. As well as sleeping with her boss, Lord Mullrine, Anne Shaw (Patricia Shakesby) is involved with Tony Purnell, who is being unfaithful to his girlfriend Veronica; George McDee is having sex with Emma and Felicity; and Felix is married to Annabel (Jennie Stoller), who is involved with Howard. Collectively, they are self-absorbed, decadent and vacuous. All are guilty of lying, hypocrisy and manipulation, yet their behaviour is treated ironically rather than satirically, as if the audience were witnessing the behaviour of spoiled children rather than pernicious adults. For example, when confronted with the mysteries of Time, Felix replies: 'I prefer to know where the next Range Rover is coming from.' Later, as Sapphire enlists Felix in her battle with Time, she ironically codenames him 'Brass', in acknowledgement of his preoccupation with money. When the cynical Howard makes his critical toast 'To Mullrine and McDee, to the millions they will make out of other peoples' pain and misery. To our hosts: charlatans and purveyors of blood',[72] his moral critique is undermined by the fact that he is blackmailing Purnell. Refusing to take a moral stance against these capitalists, Assignment Five shows the traditional conservative lack of interest in individual morality whilst recommending the benefits of capitalism to humanity.

Although private enterprise 'rated barely a mention in the Conservative Party's 1979 manifesto and played little part during Thatcher's first term',[73] Assignment Five acknowledges Thatcher's emphasis on individual endeavour. Indeed it is important to note how the story suggests that economic salvation lies in the hands of individuals rather than collectives. Mullrine and McDee are described as the 'whizzkids of the Depression', having founded an international company at a time of economic difficulty. The suggestion that intelligent and dedicated individuals can succeed in adversity is not only a key aspect of the American Dream but also an underlying principle of Thatcherism. Like Mullrine, Thatcher portrayed herself as a self-made individual, 'who by hard work, application and determination had made it to the top'.[74] Following the writings of the American economist Milton Friedman, she believed the free market to be the primary means of securing political freedom.[75] Sapphire and Steel support that principle by foiling an attempt to shift history away from Mullrine's stable capitalist venture to McDee's catastrophic socialist intention. Mullrine's capitalist exploitation of McDee's science is advocated as laudable because, as Assignment Five suggests, the enterprise of one dedicated, visionary individual, no matter how fussy or pompous he might be, is the cornerstone of a sustained and sustainable society.

The choice between political ideologies argued out in Assignment Five is elevated to direct struggle in Assignment Six, which opens in a deserted service station in 1981. Here Sapphire and Steel encounter an eloping couple (Edward de Souza and Johanna Kirby) from 25 July 1948; a ghostly figure of an old man (John Boswall) from 1925, and Johnny Jack (Chris Fairbank), a travelling player from 15 July 1957. Once the three men are revealed as Transient Beings, entities that once tried to recruit Sapphire and Steel but who now resent them for their achievements and independence, the protagonists realise that they are the victims of an elaborate trap. Using the Transients' time-travel device, they banish the old man and Johnny Jack into time; Silver disappears and a lacuna occurs. When Sapphire and Steel re-enter the café, seemingly in 1948, the woman explains chillingly: 'This is the trap. This place … is nowhere … and it's forever.'[76] She and her partner fade out of existence, leaving Sapphire and Steel trapped outside of time, staring through a window in space.

Despite its ambiguity, the adventure appears to dramatise a struggle between Thatcherite and centrist politics through setting and characterisation. Location is particularly significant as a site of conflict. The action occurs around a service station forecourt under a dominating fuel price sign. In the late 1970s and early 1980s, images of fuel and fuel prices were culturally charged, especially for Conservatives. The former Conservative government, led by Edward Heath, had lost a crisis election in February 1974. Although beset by difficulties, including a miners' strike, poor industrial relations and rising unemployment, Heath's government was toppled largely by the Arab–Israeli Yom Kippur War of 6–22 October 1973, when OPEC quadrupled oil prices, and by the miners' imposition of an overtime ban in November 1973.[77] The increase in international energy prices weakened Heath and strengthened the miners.[78] Memories of Heath's defeat were refreshed during the first Thatcher administration in 1979–80, when a second oil price explosion followed the deposition of the Shah of Iran. 'Stagflation', a term indicating a combination of slow growth and high inflation, threatened the world economy so that ghosts of the past returned to haunt the Conservative government. Hence the service station with its towering fuel price sign alludes to the cause of Heath's 1974 election defeat and the danger of further defeats arising from oil price instability. For modern Conservatives, it signifies a place of danger and political downfall. As such, it forms a suitable location for the battle between Sapphire, Silver and Steel and the Transient Beings.

Produced in autumn 1981, Assignment Six arguably alludes to the principal contemporary challenge facing the Tories: the founding of the Social Democratic Party (SDP) following the 'Limehouse Declaration' in February 1981. The SDP attempted to '"break the mould"of British politics'.[79] Its founding 'gang of four' – former cabinet ministers Roy Jenkins, David Owen, Shirley Williams and William Rogers – intended the SDP as a centrist party. Established by MPs previously active in the Gaitskellite Campaign for Democratic Socialism, which sought to reform Labour politics and electoral strategies, the SDP drew in 'apolitical idealists alienated by both the extremism of the far left and the abrasiveness of the Thatcherites'.[80] For most of 1981 and early 1982, it appeared that the SDP represented the only viable threat to Thatcher's Conservatives.[81] Although the SDP eventually failed to capitalise on its initial success, it appeared vigorous and promising in 1981. It is perhaps unsurprising, then, that Assignment Six sets its own 'gang of four' against its Conservative representatives.

Whilst they may echo in number Jenkins, Owen, Williams and Rogers, the Transient Beings are ciphers. Collectively, the four antagonists represent the kind of interclass and cross-generation appeal the SDP were hoping to achieve. Where the couple are of the professional middle classes and represent those members of the electorate in their twenties and thirties, the old man is an ageing independent businessman, whilst Johnny Jack is a member of the working class. The eloping lovers signify non-traditional freethinkers. From a conservative perspective, they stand for infidelity and, in their 14-year age difference, impropriety. They are the antithesis of Thatcher's advocated Victorian morality. The old man, juxtaposed with the young woman, suggests a new unity between the generations. Sharing his rustic, unpolished character and doll-festooned costume from the mumming plays (comedic remnants of pre-Christian rituals dramatising variously a conflict of character types or persons derived from history), Johnny Jack is the epitome of 'the common man'. [82] If this were not enough to identify him as a representative of the working class, his speech and declaration that 'The future could be a lot of fun – providing the price of a pint hasn't changed'[83] confirms his emblematic function through stereotyping.

Alluding to the political subtext underlying the challenge to Sapphire and Steel, the Transient Beings originate from three key years in British politics. Each date represents a significant moment for consensus politics. In 1925, Conservative prime minister Stanley Baldwin was establishing his 'New Conservatism' – seen to be 'principled, distinctive, accessible, moderate and unprovocative' – following his defeat of Labour's first prime minister, Ramsay MacDonald, in 1924.[84] The comparatively right-wing MacDonald later formed a

National Government of Coalition with Baldwin and the Conservatives in the early 1930s. As a consequence, the Labour Left vilified
him as a traitor to his party and his class. Importantly, though, both
MacDonald and Baldwin pursued one-nation policies; indeed, Baldwin
himself has been credited as one of the key architects of 'one-nation
conservatism', seeking a consensus with the unions and the working
class (albeit with the exception of the 1926 General Strike).[85] In 1925,
for example, he settled a coal crisis by granting miners more pay in
contravention of the wishes of the mine owners.

To substantiate the antagonism between consensus politics and
Thatcherite policies further, the eloping couple arrive with a copy
of the *Sunday Dispatch* for 25 July 1948 on the back seat of their
car. The newspaper draws attention to the fact that they originate
from a period of post-war consensus under Clement Attlee's Labour
Party. As Attlee's minister of health, Aneurin Bevan presided over
the passing of the National Health Service Act in 1946, which led to
the implementation of a state health service from 5 July 1948. After
the war, all political parties supported the founding of the welfare
state in response to the Beveridge Report.[86]

Although it could be argued that the couple simply signify a challenge to Conservatism from Labour policies, Attlee occupied a position
on the right of the Labour Party. Hugh Gaitskell, his successor as
Labour Leader, adopted a similar stance, and it was to this centrist
position that the SDP owed its origin. Hence the couple represent, in
part, both the contemporary challenge to the Conservative government
(the SDP) and an acknowledgement of the source of that challenge
(Attlee's and Gaitskell's position on the liberal left).

Emerging from this context, the couple critique the Conservative present of 1981: 'You've done nothing but throw your weight
around ever since you came here', the woman says to Steel. 'If this
is the future, the future you represent – well, you can keep it.'[87]
The woman's rejection of Steel's authoritarianism is, by association,
a rejection of Thatcher's authoritarian ideology. Hers is the voice of
both the post-war middle classes who rejected Churchill's government
in favour of the policies of Attlee and a contemporary audience
dissatisfied with Thatcherite policies. Importantly, Attlee's government
'led to a general acceptance of many of the main tenets of social
democracy: that capitalism could and should be made acceptable

to "ordinary people" by being regulated, humanised, and made to support a comprehensive system of social security'.[88] Thatcher's rejection of the consensus politics that emerged to support this view;[89] her anti-bureaucratic stance, her rejection of nationalisation and de-emphasising of the interventionist powers of the state, would place her in clear opposition to Attlee. It is no surprise that Sapphire and Steel, as Thatcher's representatives, are placed in direct conflict with the couple from 1948. Read in this way, the couple serve to remind the audience of the dangers arising from an earlier – and now re-emergent – political ideology.

Johnny Jack's origin does not appear coincidental either. He is transported from July 1957, the month in which Harold Macmillan claimed that, in Britain, 'most of our people had never had it so good'. It was a time when the 'embourgeoisement' of the working class was fully under way as consumerism and materialism began to take hold of the country.[90] Emerging from this context, Johnny Jack represents the 'common man' that both Macmillan and Gaitskell were eager to engage and to whom the SDP wished to appeal with its consensus approach. As a character from a mummers' play, Johnny Jack is also part of a form of entertainment intended to define a community, delineating those who are identified as members of that community and those who are classed as outsiders.[91] In this role, he represents a commonality that defines Sapphire and Steel as outsiders opposed to the consensus 'community' represented by the Transient Beings.

Hence the conflict between Sapphire and Steel and the Transient Beings can be read as a clash of Thatcherite politics with consensus politics, here represented by surrogates or avatars of the SDP's founders. In this context, Sapphire's statement that 'nothing of great historical importance' occurred in 1925, 1948 or 1957 marks her dismissal of any efforts towards political consensus.[92] The final triumph of the Transient Beings' collective over Sapphire and Steel may indicate, then, anxiety concerning the possibility of the SDP's success over Thatcher's conservatism; the victory of British political compromise and the consensus of centrist policies over radical agendas. Their designation as 'transient', on the other hand, may suggest an optimistic expectation of their brief attractiveness. Either way, Assignment Six finished production when the Tories were facing strong criticism and falling popularity, which would only be arrested in the wake of the Falklands War.

The presence of Johnny Jack perhaps provides an indication of how *Sapphire and Steel* as a whole might be read. Commonly, mumming plays are 'symbolic discourses on key issues prevalent in the communities [*sic*] mind which can be allied to existing story lines.'[93] In *Sapphire and Steel*, this 'symbolic discourse' is arguably a political one in which representatives of Thatcherite Conservative ideology overcome threats to that ideology. It is communicated using the 'existing story lines' of the detective genre, the ghost story and the Gothic. In hindsight, with the legacy of Thatcherism still inscribed on the British landscape and in the British psyche, perhaps the final expulsion of Sapphire and Steel at the conclusion of the series, by the ghosts of 1948, may not be such a cause for lament after all.

NOTES

1. For a detailed account of the origins of *Sapphire and Steel*, see www.the-mausoleum-club.org.uk/timescreen/Trial%204/sastart.htm; and producer Shaun O'Riordan's 1996 interview with Rob Stanley at www.dismal-light-net/sapphireandsteel/rs-oriordan.html (accessed 26 June 2003).
2. See P.J. Hammond, 'Introduction' in *Sapphire and Steel* (London: Virgin Books, 1992), p. 3.
3. http://home.iprimus.com.au/panopticon1/deadzones/ss2.html (accessed 20 June 2003).
4. Assignment Six was broadcast originally between 19 and 31 August 1982. As Andrew Martin points out, 'It was held over for almost a year after production after ATV, who originally produced the series, lost the Midlands region ITV franchise to Central Television.' See Andrew Martin, 'Fantasy Flashback: *Sapphire and Steel*', *TV Zone* 4 (March 1990), p. 30.
5. Peter J. Hammond in a letter to the author dated 8 November 2004.
6. David Butler and Dennis Kavanagh, *The British General Election of 1979* (London: Macmillan, 1980), p. 12; see also pp. 14–25.
7. Ibid., p. 41.
8. Thatcher received the sobriquet from Reginald Maudling during a speech at Kensington Town Hall in January 1976. See Kenneth Harris, *Thatcher* (London: Fontana, 1989), p. 111.
9. All characteristics attributed to Thatcher. See Butler and Kavanagh, *The British General Election of 1979*, p. 67.
10. Harris, *Thatcher*, p. 126.

11. Thatcher's authoritarianism in Cabinet is reported by Harris in *Thatcher*, pp. 120–22 and p. 132.

12. Stephen Knight, *Form and Ideology in Crime Fiction* (London: Macmillan, 1980) p. 67.

13. Butler and Kavanagh, *The British General Election of 1979*, p. 195.

14. Burke cited in Robert Nisbet, *Conservatism: Dream and Reality* (Milton Keynes: Open University Press, 1986), p. 35.

15. See Nisbet, *Conservatism*, p. 35.

16. Ibid., pp. 35–6.

17. Butler and Kavanagh, *The British General Election of 1979*, p. 155.

18. Knight, *Form and Ideology in Crime Fiction*, p. 128.

19. Ivor Crewe, '1979–1986', in Anthony Seldon (ed.), *How Tory Governments Fall: The Tory Party in Power since 1783* (London: Fontana, 1996), p. 404.

20. See Butler and Kavanagh, *The British General Election of 1979*, p. 139.

21. John Dearlove and Peter Saunders, *Introduction to British Politics* (London: Polity Press, 1985 [1984]), p. 291.

22. See ibid., p. 287.

23. See, for example, Nigel Andrews, 'Against the Elements', at www.the-mausoleum-club.org.uk/timescreen/Trial%204/sastart.htm; and David Sheldrick's 'Tales of Mystery and Imagination', at http://offthetelly.users.btopenworld.com/drama/sapphireandsteel.htm (accessed 4 February 2003).

24. See http://offthetelly.users.btopenworld.com/drama/sapphireandsteel.htm.

25. Nisbet, *Conservatism*, p. 23.

26. Ibid.

27. Knight, *Form and Ideology in Crime Fiction*, p. 86.

28. Steel (played by David McCallum) in Assignment One, Episode Three (1st tx. ITV, 17 July 1979).

29. Nisbet, *Conservatism*, p. 23.

30. Steel in Assignment One, Episode One (1st tx. ITV, 10 July 1979).

31. Sapphire (Joanna Lumley) in Assignment One, Episode One.

32. Nisbet, *Conservatism*, p. 24.

33. Ibid., p. 52.

34. See ibid., p. 26.

35. Crewe, '1979–1986', p. 395.

36. See Fred Botting, *Gothic* (London: Routledge, 1996), p. 7.

37. See Butler and Kavanagh, *The British General Election of 1979*, p. 60.

38. See ibid., p. 85; and Harris, *Thatcher*, pp. 101–5.

39. Stephen Porter, *The Great Plague* (Stroud: Sutton, 2003 [1999]), p. 21. Porter goes on to document the effect of the Civil War on the outbreak of plague (see pp. 21–3).

40. See Harris, *Thatcher*, p. 103.

41. See Assignment One, Episode Two (1st tx. ITV, 12 July 1979).

42. Julia Briggs, *Night Visitors: The Rise and Fall of the English Ghost Story* (London: Faber, 1977) p. 19.

43. Ibid., p. 110.
44. Botting, *Gothic*, p. 8.
45. Riordan, cited in Rob Stanley, 'Shaun O'Riordan – An Interview' at www.dismal-light.net/ sapphireandsteel/rs-oriordan.html.
46. Riordan, cited in ibid.
47. Harris, *Thatcher*, p. 127.
48. See Crewe, '1979–1986', p. 438.
49. Dearlove and Saunders, *Introduction to British Politics*, p. 291.
50. See Assignment Three, Episode One (1st tx. ITV, 6 January 1981).
51. Harris, *Thatcher*, p. 128.
52. Steel in Assignment Three, Episode Six (1st tx. ITV, 22 January 1981).
53. See, for example, www.all-creatures.org/ca/ark-192–church.html; www.uncaged.co.uk/iard.htm;www.sam.covington.btinternet.co.uk/sam_animals_ciwf.htm (all accessed 4 October 2004).
54. Rothwyn (played by Catherine Hall) in Assignment Three, Episode One.
55. David Punter, *The Literature of Terror*, Vol. 2: *A History of Gothic – The Modern Gothic* (London: Longman, 1996), p. 183.
56. Butler and Kavanagh, *The British General Election of 1979*, p. 20.
57. See ibid., p. 81.
58. Dearlove and Saunders, *Introduction to British Politics*, p. 287.
59. Nisbet, *Conservatism*, p. 25.
60. See, for example, Andrew Martin's comments at www.sflare.com/page2.html. (accessed 25 February, 2003).
61. See http://politics.guardian.co.uk/conservatives/story/0,9061,1144944,00.html (accessed 7 April 2004).
62. Butler and Kavanagh, *The British General Election of 1979*, p. 161.
63. Dearlove and Saunders, *Introduction to British Politics*, p. 291.
64. Harris, *Thatcher*, p. 129. For further discussion of why Thatcher opposed the civil service, see ibid., p. 129–31.
65. See Butler and Kavanagh, *The General Election of 1983* (London: Macmillan, 1984), p. 23.
66. See Dearlove and Saunders, *Introduction to British Politics*, pp. 291–2.
67. Sir John Hoskyns cited in Harris, *Thatcher*, p. 130.
68. Steel in Assignment Four, Episode One (1st tx. ITV, 27 January 1981).
69. Andrew Martin at www.sflare.com/page2.html.
70. Liz (Alyson Spiro) in Assignment Four, Episode Four (1st tx. ITV, 5 February 1981).
71. Nisbet, *Conservatism*, p. 61.
72. Howard McDee (played by Jeremy Child) in Assignment Five, Episode One (1st tv. ITV, 11 August 1981).
73. Crewe in Seldon, pp. 408–9.
74. Harris, *Thatcher*, p. 68.
75. See Dearlove and Saunders, *Introduction to British Politics*, p. 287.

76. Woman (played by Johanna Kirby) in Assignment Six, Episode Four (1st tx. ITV 31 August 1982).

77. See David Dutton, *British Politics since 1945: The Rise and Fall of Consensus* (Oxford: Basil Blackwell, 1991), pp. 68–9.

78. See Dennis Kavanagh and Anthony Seldon, *The Thatcher Effect* (New York: Oxford University Press, 1989), p. 9.

79. Kenneth O. Morgan, *Britain since 1945: The People's Peace* (Oxford: Oxford University Press, 1998 [1990]), p. 464.

80. Ibid.

81. See Arthur Marwick, *British Society since 1945* (London: Penguin, 2003 [1982]), pp. 231–2.

82. Keith Ford, www.wadard.co.uk/wadard/mummers.htm (accessed 25 August 2003).

83. Johnny Jack (played by Chris Fairbank) in Assignment Six, Episode Three (1st tx. ITV, 26 August 1982).

84. See Stuart Ball, '1919–29', in Seldon (ed.), *How Tory Governments Fall*, p. 260.

85. See http://core2.trg.org.uk/reformer/2000spring/historymen.html (accessed 24 September 2004)

86. See Marwick, *British Society since 1945*, pp. 27–39.

87. Woman in Assignment Six, Episode Two (1st tx. ITV 24 August 1982).

88. Colin Leys, *Politics in Britain* (London: Heinemann, 1983), p. 56.

89. See Dutton, *British Politics since 1945*, pp. 89–90.

90. It was this transformation of the working class that led to Labour being perceived as old-fashioned and associated with the past and post-war austerity. Such a perception provoked Hugh Gaitskell to attempt to modernise the party to make it more electable in the new consumer age.

91. See www.mystical-www.co.uk (accessed 25 August 2003).

92. Sapphire (played by Joanna Lumley), Assignment Six, Episode Three.

93. www.mystical-www.co.uk.

11

Counterpointing the surrealism
of the underlying metaphor
in *The Hitchhiker's Guide to the Galaxy*

M.J. SIMPSON

There is a popular perception that the television version of *The Hitchhiker's Guide to the Galaxy* is, frankly, not very good. Other than the subjective assessment of any given individual, there seems little to support this. When first broadcast in 1981, the programme was a resounding success with both audiences and critics. It won no fewer than three BAFTA (British Academy) awards, sold well overseas and has been repeated numerous times on both British terrestrial and satellite channels. It was released twice on video in the UK; on both VHS and laserdisc in the USA; and the 2002 British DVD release was lavished with critical praise and sold strongly (as did subsequent releases in the United States, Germany and Sweden). Yet received opinion still holds that the TV version of *Hitchhiker's Guide*, apart from the innovative graphical sequences, did not work.[1]

Part of the problem undoubtedly lies, or at least lay, with Douglas Adams, who frequently and publicly expressed dissatisfaction with the series, increasingly so as the years passed. His ire was largely aimed at producer/director Alan J.W. Bell (*Ripping Yarns* [BBC TV, 1979]; *Last of the Summer Wine* [BBC TV, 1973–]), whom he felt to be too conservative. On the other hand, some of Adams's own production suggestions – which were, thankfully, overruled – demonstrated his own capacity for completely missing the point.

The origins of *The Hitchhiker's Guide*, as has been well documented,[2] lie on Radio 4 in a six-part series first broadcast in 1978. By the time the television version premiered on BBC 2 in January 1981, there had been a further six radio episodes; two novels based loosely on the radio series, although not in the broadcast order; two long-playing records, which diverged from the radio series plot in quite significant ways, and three professional stage productions, all loosely adapted from the radio scripts but each of which treated the material in a new and innovative manner.

Unusually for a six-part serial, the first TV episode was filmed as a stand-alone pilot, although it was only ever broadcast as part of the series. It was shown three times before transmission: a special screening at the National Film Theatre (NFT) in front of an audience of sf fans to record a laughter track; to an audience of critics at the 1980 Edinburgh Television Festival; and at the Hitchercon 1 fan convention in Glasgow. The only significant differences between this version and the transmitted one were a slightly different title sequence (included as as 'easter egg' on the DVD release), a few very minor changes to some of the graphics, and John Lloyd's demotion from executive producer to associate producer. The NFT laughter track was never considered for broadcast but was merely for use when showing the programme to BBC executives to prove that it actually was funny!

The story opens with Arthur Dent (played by Simon Jones) waking up and spotting a bulldozer outside his house, which the council want demolished to make way for a bypass, an idea which appals Arthur but which will shortly recede into insignificance when a Vogon Constructor Fleet arrives to do the same thing to the Planet Earth. The dialogue between Arthur and council workman Mr Prosser (Joe Melia) is an example of Douglas Adams at his sparkling best:

PROSSER   But Mr. Dent, the plans were on display.
ARTHUR   On display? I eventually had to go down to the cellar to find them.
PROSSER   That's the Display Department.
ARTHUR   With a torch.
PROSSER   The lights had probably gone.
ARTHUR   So had the stairs.[3]

One of the joys of researching Adams's life and career as his biographer is the number of occasions when the perennial question

THE BYPASS AS A BAD THING   Arthur Dent (Simon Jones) and Ford
Prefect (David Dixon) refuse to take progress lying down in *The Hitchhiker's
Guide to the Galaxy* (BBC TV, 1981).

'where do you get your ideas from?' can be answered on his behalf. The concept of the bypass as a 'Bad Thing' dates back to 1965 when the Brentwood Junior School Debating Society, of which young Adams was an active member, argued the motion 'This House believes that the Brentwood by-pass will not benefit the people of Brentwood'. Another possible inspiration was a 1973 controversy, during Adams's time at Cambridge, over the university's proposed new radio telescope being threatened by construction of the Cambridge bypass. Around this time, Adams and his undergraduate writing partners Will Adams (no relation) and Martin Smith wrote and performed a sketch called 'How to Plan Countries'[4] about a man whose idyllic cottage is knocked down to make way for a motorway. Given Adams's propensity for reusing material, it is likely that much of the Arthur/Prosser dialogue originates from this sketch.

Perhaps the thing for which *The Hitchhiker's Guide* TV serial is best known is its use of 'computer graphics' to illustrate the narration. Certain poorly researched reference works persist in promoting the myth that these were done on a computer, and at least one unscrupulous computer artist has tried to take credit for them,[5] but it is well documented that no computers were used at any point during the making of the show. All the graphics were backlit cell animation designed to look not like computer graphics *circa* 1980 but to give the impression of futuristic computer graphics. Producing the graphics on a computer would have been phenomenally expensive at this time and would have looked like teletext.

That many modern-day explanatory graphics sequences in television documentaries bear a close resemblance to those created by Pearce Studios for *The Hitchhiker's Guide* TV serial more than twenty years ago may be an indication of how prescient the animators were, or it may be merely a remarkable coincidence. However, given the popularity of the serial, especially among those who work in computers, it seems very likely that many of the common stylistic motifs of modern television graphics can in fact be traced to the BAFTA-winning images in *The Hitchhiker's Guide*. In a sort of self-fulfilling prophecy – a recursive nostalgia if you like – computer graphics look like they do today because they are based on early pre-computer images of what computer graphics might look like in the future, and *The Hitchhiker's Guide* was both timely and pre-eminent in that respect. One can see something similar in the fact that early NASA spacesuits were silver for no other reason than that they were traditionally depicted as silver in comic strips and on sci-fi magazine covers.

It is notable in the first episode that although there is much narration, there is comparatively little animation. The first sequence, discussing Arthur Dent's alien friend, Ford Prefect (David Dixon), is half taken up with solarised footage of the forthcoming shots and also includes a specially shot dinner party scene. A later narration about the Vogon spaceships approaching Earth has one brief model shot and is otherwise composed entirely of stock footage from BBC science programmes. It shows the power of these graphic sequences that people remember them as accompanying all the narration. Interestingly, in these sequences, the actual words being spoken by the narrator of *The Hitchhiker's Guide* ('The Book', played by Peter Jones) do not appear on screen and instead we see only diagrams, tables and occasional paraphrasing from it as in 'This life form not ape descended'. This seems to be because the *Guide* itself, Adams's fictional idea of an electronic book from which these images are supposedly displayed, has not yet been introduced to us in the plot: a theory which is supported by similar sequences in later episodes when 'The Book' (i.e. Jones's character) is narrating but 'the book' (i.e. the fictional electronic guide) is not being accessed.

Though often derided for looking cheap, *The Hitchhiker's Guide to the Galaxy* was actually an extremely expensive programme to make for the time, to the extent that it sapped the entire special effects budget of the BBC Light Entertainment Department for 1980. A large part of this was due to the frequent use of unrelated cutaway scenes such as the aforementioned dinner party, which made *The Hitchhiker's Guide* something of a cross between a sitcom and a sketch show, with the narrative drive of the former but the set-up expense of the latter.

The dinner party, for example, has five non-speaking extras, for which the 1980 Equity rate was £22.50 a day, plus a chimpanzee, which cost more than his five fellow diners put together. Though the scene is shot silent against a black background, with no set or sound costs, there is a table with full dinner service, food and lit candles, plus costumes and make-up for the five human actors, and of course the actual camera crew to pay. And all this for a scene which lasts exactly eleven seconds! Likewise in the same episode, as the Vogon ships pass over London prior to destroying Earth to make way for a new hyperspace bypass, there are more extras in the pub (though one is Douglas Adams himself, presumably not being paid the Equity rate) and 26 people look up at the Vogon ships. Also there is a scene of two aliens drinking Pan Galactic Gargle Blasters, wearing £900-worth of futuristic costumes (though these were reused in the Milliways sequence in Episode Five, as were many other specially commissioned items).

The barman of the pub to which Ford Prefect takes Arthur for a final drink prior to Earth's destruction by the Vogons, with his limited knowledge of emergency procedures ('I thought we were meant to lie down or put a paper bag over our head'), is another 'where do you get your ideas from?' moment. Adams revealed in an early interview that the character was inspired by instructions on nuclear attack posters spotted in a former barracks that was used for rehearsals of a 1977 *Doctor on the Go* episode which he co-wrote.[6] (The fact that Adams attended the rehearsals for his sole episode of LWT's long-running *Doctor...* series [ITV 1969–77; BBC TV 1991] says a lot about his interest in the process of making programmes and possibly his determination to control, as far as possible, the fate of his own scripts.[7])

Of particular interest in terms of production detail are the closing scenes in Episode One of Ford and Arthur in the Vogon hold, which are not quite as good as they could be. David Dixon fluffs a line at one point and a half-second shot of 'Arthur' running across the hold is, notoriously, B-roll footage (i.e. footage from when the camera is left running between consecutive takes of the same shot) of actor Simon Jones going to his mark. This was due to a BBC technicians' work-to-rule at the time of production, which required a closedown at 10 p.m. prompt and prevented this scene being more carefully completed. Douglas Adams's inability to buckle down and write scripts or novels, resulting in a terrible rush before (or, increasingly, after) the deadline for delivery has been well documented. It is ironic that the first episode of *The Hitchhiker's Guide* TV serial displays a similar rushed ending.

Episode Two of the TV *Hitchhiker's Guide* – indeed, every episode – opens with narration, in this instance over famous shots of Douglas

Adams as an extra withdrawing money from a bank and then walking naked into the sea, leaving his clothes on the beach. A similar scene was used in the title sequence of the BBC comedy series *The Fall and Rise of Reginald Perrin* (BBC TV, 1976–80) and if this was not a direct reference to Perrin (and/or the 1974 fake suicide of disgraced MP John Stonehouse, who did the same thing in real life), it was certainly made with an awareness of the iconic image of clothes abandoned on a beach. The use of Adams himself was not planned but due to the contracted actor not turning up. This sequence, coupled with postings on naturism Internet forums by a gentleman named Douglas J. Adams, has led to a mistaken belief among certain parts of the British naturist community that Douglas Adams was one of their own!

The episode proper begins three and a half minutes in with Prostetnic Vogon Jeltz (Martin Benson) reading poetry to Arthur and Ford after his Vogon Constructor fleet has destroyed Earth. The Book's narration at this point cites the 'worst poet in the universe' as Paula Nancy Millstone Jennings of Greenbridge, Surrey, whereas in the radio series it was Paul Neil Milne Johnstone of Redbridge, a change made for legal reasons.[8] Also of note in this sequence are Arthur and Ford's pretentious critique of Jeltz's poem, reflecting Adams's wide reading of literary criticism for his English Literature degree at Cambridge. A reference to the 'Mid-Galactic Arts Nobbling Council', a slyly cynical dig at the Arts Council of England, became retrospectively ironic when Adams's close friend since Cambridge Mary Allen became secretary-general of the always controversial funding body in the 1990s.

The scenes with the Vogon Guard in this episode include two notable lines: 'I really wish I'd listened to what my mother told me when I was young...' was an old Cambridge Footlights joke, whose exact provenance was debated, though one informed source credits it to Adams's Footlights contemporary, lawyer-turned-presenter Clive Anderson.[9] The second, 'Da-da-da-dum!' – Ford's attempt to teach the Vogon Guard the opening of Beethoven's Fifth – was inspired by Adams' schoolmate David Wakeling, who would hum this single phrase repeatedly when checking 'lights out' at Brentwood School in his capacity as, appropriately, a prefect.[10]

Also in Episode Two, Arthur and Ford floating in space – facing, as Adams often put it, 'certain death' – is accompanied by one of the best known pieces of narration by 'The Book'. The odds against being picked up by a spaceship are said to be the same as the telephone number of a flat where Arthur once went to a nice party. Though it is never stated explicitly in the scripts, it is generally agreed that the girl whom Arthur met at the party in question was Trillian (played by Sandra Dickinson), who also met Zaphod Beeblebrox (Mark Wing-Davey) there, both principal characters who will later feature strongly in *The Hitchhiker's Guide*. In a short sequence, Trillian (whom we have not yet met) is seen from behind, being led away – as Arthur turns to pick up some drinks – by a hand on her shoulder, which retrospectively can be seen to be Zaphod's. There is even a quiet, overdubbed line, 'Is this guy boring you?', which is quoted by Arthur later on.

Douglas Adams was a lifelong party-thrower, and there are a great number of parties throughout *The Hitchhiker's Guide* saga: the scene with the chimpanzee in Episode One; the parties thrown by disreputable physicists, one of which led to the invention of the Infinite Improbability Drive; the flying party featured prominently in the third *Hitchhiker's* novel, *Life, the Universe and Everything* (1982), and so on. The telephone number of the party flat referred to above is, as has been explained assiduously by many sources, the actual number of a flat where Douglas did enjoy numerous parties. The flat was in Arlington Road and was owned by Jonathan Brock, a Footlights contemporary who went into law.[11] Adams maintained a lifelong interest in the comic potential of numbers, of which telephone numbers seemed a particularly rich source; indeed Eddie the computer observes later in this episode that 'most people's lives are governed by telephone numbers'.

When, subsequently in Episode Two, Arthur and Ford Prefect find their way on to the starship *Heart of Gold*, we finally encounter the other principal characters of *The Hitchhiker's Guide*: Zaphod, Trillian, Eddie the computer (the postdubbed voice of David Tate; Adams himself read the lines during filming) and Marvin the Paranoid Android (voiced by Stephen Moore). Used to working in the purely aural medium of radio, Douglas Adams had no real idea what any of his characters or machines in *The Hitchhiker's Guide* looked like, only what they did not look like, and this became a major stumbling block in the design of the robot Marvin. The late Jim Francis, a veteran of

Doctor Who and *Blake's 7*, was assigned the task of building the TV version's robotic character and found his sketches repeatedly turned down by Adams, though the author was able to offer no practical suggestions for improvements. Initially, Adams favoured using an actor wearing a silver leotard and silver body paint, something which had already been used on stage. When this idea was sensibly rejected, he took an entirely opposite view, which was that the costume should very definitely not look like an actor in a suit. Since there was no other way in 1980 of depicting a walking, humanoid robot, this was problematic to say the least.

Francis's final design, approved not so much because everyone involved liked it but because immovable location filming dates were fast approaching, incorporated one clever touch which actually suggested that there was no actor inside, or would have done had it not been quite so subtle. If one examines the circular elbow joints closely in the TV version of the robot, the metal on the inside of the joint would clearly cut off an actor's arm when the elbow is bent. The trick is that what appears to be stiff, curved metal is actually very thin, flexible metal which slides up inside the arm when the elbow bends. Like many technical aspects of the serial, this was an ingenious solution to a thorny problem, which went largely unnoticed by audiences and certainly entirely unappreciated by critics. Actor Stephen Moore was one of those unhappy with the final design of Marvin and declined to wear the costume, so he limited himself to voice duties while the actor who had been painted silver on stage, David Learner, portrayed the robot's body.

Equally, in the TV serial the *Heart of Gold* starship was a design which Adams had never thought through properly, describing it only as looking something like a running shoe – an idea taken literally by artist Chris Foss in a painting used on the covers of the 1988 British paperback editions of the *Hitchhiker's* novels. Ford's and Arthur's surreal surroundings when first picked up by the *Heart of Gold* elicit an important line, the meaning of which has changed completely over the years, and which, when fully understood, helps to emphasise how long ago the story was actually written. When Arthur's left arm disappears, he bemoans: 'How am I going to operate my digital watch now?' When that line was written in 1977 for the radio series of *Hitchhiker's Guide*, it was only five years after the launch of the Pulsar, the first digital watch. Adams had a lifelong fascination for gadgets and took particular amusement in those which used technology to do something that could already be done in a simple, and sometimes much better, manner. Most digital watches of the 1970s used LED (light emitting diode) displays and so could only be read by pushing a button – a thoroughly retrograde step from the traditional watch dial. This is what Arthur means by 'operate my digital watch', though the introduction of LCD (liquid crystal display) watches has changed the meaning to a question about how he will set the alarm or use the stopwatch. (LCD watches actually went on sale in 1973 but took a while to catch on.) And why does Arthur operate his watch with his left hand? Presumably because Adams envisaged him, like his creator, as left-handed. (Another line to change meaning over the years is in Episode One: the barman thanking Ford for letting him keep the change from a fiver went from gratitude to sarcasm to anachronism as beer prices rose. Six pints for under five pounds...)

The crew of the *Heart of Gold* were all based to some extent on people whom Adams knew personally, a technique which the author frequently used as he was notoriously bad at creating rounded characters, preferring them ready-made. Zaphod was based on Johnny Simpson,[12] a Cambridge roommate who put a great deal of effort into appearing relaxed. The character was also to some extent written to the strengths as an actor of Wing-Davey (a Footlights near-contemporary of Adams), just as Arthur and Ford were originally written to the strengths of Jones and Geoffrey McGivern (who played Ford on radio). A classic Zaphod line in this episode is: 'Which is the most nonchalant chair to be discovered in?' This is also a fine example of Adams using the Wodehousean technique of the displaced adjective – it is of course the occupant, rather than the chair, which is nonchalant.

Marvin the Paranoid Android was famously based on comedy writer Andrew Marshall (*Whoops Apocalypse!* [ITV, 1982], *2 Point 4 Children* [BBC TV, 1991–99], *Strange* [BBC TV, 2002]), and Adams took great delight in telling interviewers about the character's origins. Marshall, though somewhat flattered, feels that the situation has been somewhat exaggerated.[13] Trillian was ostensibly based on an ex-girlfriend of Adams, never specified.[14] Like many British male humorists, Adams had great problems in writing female characters, or feminine ones at least. Though Trillian featured strongly in the *Hitchhiker* novels *Life, the Universe and Everything* (1982) and *Mostly Harmless* (1992), she was absent from the fourth novel, *So Long, and Thanks for All the Fish* (1984), replaced by the equally two-dimensional character of Fenchurch – the young woman in a café in Rickmansworth seen briefly in the opening of Episode Two of the TV serial. Trillian was also absent from the second radio serial (BBC Radio 4, 1980), though that was partly because of the unavailability of the original actress, Susan Sheridan.

The opening narration of Episode Three, summing up the history of the Galactic Empire featured in *The Hitchhiker's Guide*, contains the one and only specific reference to another sf TV series (*Star Trek* [NBC, 1966–69]), in the rather obvious gag about 'to boldly split infinitives that no man had split before'. Though often described as a 'sci-fi spoof', *The Hitchhiker's Guide* plainly does not parody or lampoon any other iconic concepts from pop culture sci-fi, instead satirising the broader tropes of the genre in general, especially through the use of outrageous plot devices to allow faster-than-light travel (the Infinite Improbability Drive) or inter-species communication (the Babel Fish, a naturally occurring psychic translation device carried in the ear).

The most famous part of Episode Three is the sperm whale which materialises above the planet Magrathea when Arthur uses the unshielded Infinite Improbability Drive to transform the two nuclear missiles threatening the *Heart of Gold*. Douglas Adams claimed that the inspiration for this was the 1970s' American detective series *Cannon* (CBS, 1971–76), in which extras were frequently killed and nobody seemed to care, so he determined to create and then kill off an entirely irrelevant character, the whale, but damn well make the audience care about it. One reason why this sequence works so well is that it is a self-contained, stand-alone comedy monologue, something much more suited to Adams's Footlights-honed writing style than long-form narrative plotting.

The other missile becomes a bowl of petunias which thinks only 'Oh no, not again', and this stood as a good gag in its own right until the publication of *Life, the Universe and Everything* in 1982, which introduced the character of Agrajag. It transpired that this charac-ter had been reincarnated innumerable times and every single life

– including a brief spell as a petunia plant – had been terminated, often accidentally, by Arthur Dent. Though a fun concept which retrospectively explained the 'Oh no, not again' line in *The Hitchhiker's Guide*, this was literary 'back engineering' by Adams, who, when writing this Magrathean attack sequence for radio, TV and the first novel, intended the petunias gag to be nothing more than a non sequitur.

BBC TV productions such as *Doctor Who* (1963–89) and *Blake's 7* (1978–81) were stereotypically known for filming 'alien planet' sequences in Cornish quarries, and indeed the TV *Hitchhiker's* only major location work, apart from the scenes at Arthur's house, was in a Cornish quarry. It was not, as sometimes believed, the one which now houses the Eden Project biodomes, although it is only a few miles away. In summer 2002, an expedition by *The Hitchhiker's Guide* Appreciation Society located the specific quarry, which was extensively dug after the series was filmed but retains its distinctive conical waste-heap.[15]

Several other exterior scenes were filmed on a nearby beach, including the Sirius Cybernetics Corporation advert ('Your plastic pal who's fun to be with'), a bearded Arthur and Ford making landfall in Episode Six on a raft constructed from part of the Golgafrinchan 'B'-Ark and the previously mentioned footage of Douglas Adams walking into the sea. The location filming is commemorated by a definition in Adams's spoof dictionary, *The Deeper Meaning of Liff*: 'offleyhoo: (adj) ridiculously overexcited about going to Cornwall'.[16]

The scene in Episode Three in which Zaphod, Trillian and Ford explore the tunnel leading down under the surface of the planet Magrathea contains another brilliantly conceived but under-appreciated effect. Zaphod wears two pairs of 'Joo Janta 200 Super-Chromatic Peril-Sensitive Sunglasses', which we see turn totally black (to prevent the wearer from seeing something which might alarm him). The four lenses were polarising filters and a fifth filter was fitted on the camera; as long as all the filters were parallel, the sunglasses appeared clear, but turning the camera filter through 90 degrees rendered them opaque – to the camera.

The Joo Janta sunglasses had not featured in the original radio serial, but Adams loved the idea so much that he reused the same gag word-for-word several times: in Chapter 5 of the novel *The Restaurant at the End of the Universe* (1980), in an introduction to an American omnibus edition of *The Hitchhiker's Guide*, and in a 1984 computer game based on the serial, which included a pair of cardboard Joo Janta sunglasses among its packaged 'extras'. The concept's final appearance was the 2004 radio adaptation of the third novel, *Life, the Universe and Everything* (1st tx. BBC Radio 4, 21 September–26 October 2004).

When Adams was unable to find someone from his personal peer group on whom to base a character, he often resorted to basing it on a well-known actor. Slartibartfast (the venerable planet designer who specialises in fjords) was based on John Le Mesurier, but was played in the TV serial by Richard Vernon. The character's explanation of how the Magratheans had built Earth for the mice includes the TV serial's first use of the phrase which, more than any other, was bequeathed to the English language by Douglas Adams: 'life, the universe and everything'.

In Episode Four, there are two lengthy flashbacks, shown by Slartibartfast to Arthur, which feature computer operators named Lunkwill and Fook and their descendants (played by the same actors, Antony Carrick and Timothy Davies), Loonquawl and Phouchg. Adams clearly enjoyed the way in which names can evolve over time: another example is the character of Judiciary Pag LIVR in the *Life, the Universe and Everything* novel whose real name, Zipo Bibrok 5×10^8, is meant to suggest that he is in some distant way a descendant of Zaphod Beeblebrox. Ironically, these characters – Loonquawl, Fook and their descendants – are never explicitly named in the dialogue of the TV serial and so this is something which only those who have also read the novel would understand. It was typical of Adams to include such jokes in parts of the production script which would never actually be heard by audiences. An even more extreme case is the two cops at the end of Episode Four (played by Matt Zimmerman and Marc Smith), whose names in the script, Shooty and Bang Bang, are never even mentioned in the novel of *The Hitchhiker's Guide*.

There is a lovely gag in this brief Arthur–Slartibartfast scene between the two lengthy flashback scenes. When the Magrathean planet designer presses the eject button on the projection device he has been using to explain things for Arthur's benefit, a bright yellow item – presciently about the size of a 3.5 inch diskette, only introduced in 1980 – shoots out. The added (unscripted) sound of a small smash is an example of the care that was taken in post-production on the TV serial. Curiously, the planet Magrathea seems to have only one inhabitant in the TV version. The holo-recording from Magrathea which greets the *Heart of Gold* starship in Episode Three is also played by the actor Richard Vernon; although that character is called 'Magrathean' in the script, so far as audiences are concerned, it's Slartibartfast. Only the tannoy voice (played, as usual, by David Tate) betrays that anyone else has actually 'awoken' and is around on the planet. In a half-hearted attempt by the production team in Episode Four to alleviate this apparent cheapness, there is a matted-in shot of a robot on a lower level as an overhead gantry shot shows Arthur and Slartibartfast leaving the latter's workshop. However, it is not enough to convince the audience that Magrathea is populated and in fact serves only to confuse viewers as it looks a bit like Marvin.

The Vl'Hurgs versus G'Gugvunts sequence in the same episode (an entirely irrelevant aside about two warring planets) has been the source of much misinformation over the years. Looking for a way to represent the terrible war between the two races, the animators of the TV serial hit on the idea of depicting the conflict like a Space Invaders-style computer game (state of the art at the time but now charmingly archaic). Certain badly researched works, generally those which talk about the series' 'computer graphics', have spread the myth that an actual videogame was used here, when it is clearly more backlit cell animation.[17] Trillian's pet mice, Frankie and Benjy, are also revealed in this episode to be the extensions into our dimension of 'hyper-intelligent, pan-dimensional beings'. They are played, unsurprisingly, by two real white mice, although Adams, incredibly, had wanted them to be actors in mouse costumes (possibly inspired by the 1969 Monty Python sketch in which grown men admit to dressing like mice as some sort of perversion). Footage of the mice in *The Hitchhiker's Guide* is slowed down slightly and the random movements of their heads and mouths mean that at least some of the dialogue (voiced by Tate and Moore) matches up. (Live mice have also been used in some stage productions of *The Hitchhiker's Guide*, where once again their dialogue was sufficiently lengthy that some of it seemed to 'match up' – entirely randomly – with their movement).

Escaping from the mice, Arthur, Ford, Zaphod and Trillian are trapped behind a computer bank by the two galactic cops, Shooty and Bang Bang. Allegedly inspired by *Starsky and Hutch* (ABC, 1975–79), they, as with the previously mentioned *Cannon* inspiration, suggest that Douglas Adams had a real penchant for 1970s' American cop shows. The two characters at one point share an emphatic, single, face-to-face nod which is pure Laurel and Hardy, then their guns blast the computer bank behind which Arthur and his companions shelter, until eventually it blows up (this supposedly 'interior' sequence was in fact shot outside to allow for a really big explosion).

It is at this point that the TV serial, while remaining faithful to the radio version, diverges utterly from the 1979 *Hitchhiker's Guide* novel. Despite what Adams claimed (see below), the book was deliberately planned as an adaptation of only the first four episodes of the original radio serial in order to avoid using any material co-written with John Lloyd, with whom Adams had fallen out. In the novel, the computer does not explode; instead the guns fall silent and it transpires that the cops, who are described as wearing spacesuits, have died because their life-support systems failed. This in turn is traced to Marvin, still on the surface of Magrathea, who has struck up a conversation with the computer on the cops' spaceship and so depressed the device that it has committed suicide.

Many critics have cited the literary version of events as a sudden, arbitrary halt – generally believing Adams's much-repeated but utterly untrue assertion that he stopped the novel there because he was past his deadline and his editor had asked him to 'finish the page you're on'.[18] In fact, the book's story line is in many ways preferable to that of the radio and TV scripts because in the serial Arthur, Ford, Zaphod and Trillian find themselves unharmed, flung forward millions of years into the future to Milliways, 'the restaurant at the end of the universe'. Such is the pleasure that people find in the serial – and the episode in which the Milliways sequence occurs, Episode Five, is a particularly strong episode – that it has gone generally unremarked what an utterly arbitrary script link this is. The Shooty and Bang Bang scene is a smart bit of dialogue and unusually action-packed for *The Hitchhiker's Guide*; the entire Milliways sequence is a marvellous piece of not just Pythonesque comedy but also grand-scale science fiction. But the means of getting from one to the other – a huge explosion which sends the characters through time but does not even singe their clothing – makes no sense whatsoever.

Episode Five does have a unity, however, because it takes place entirely within one location, starting with the quartet's arrival at the restaurant and finishing as they depart its car park in a stolen space-ship. This strength of story line is backed up by sparkling dialogue; the largest, most complex set ever built for a BBC light entertainment show; as well as memorable incidental characters, who are given life in bravura performances by relatively well-known guest artists. Jack May, from long-running radio soap *The Archers* (BBC Radio, 1951–), plays salubrious restaurant head waiter Garkbit; David Prowse – Darth Vader himself – appears in a sharp suit as the bodyguard of dead-for-tax-reasons rock star Hotblack Desiato; and Peter Davison, then married to Sandra Dickinson, and who had just been cast as the new Doctor Who but was best known on TV as a vet in the series *All Creatures Great and Small* (BBC TV, 1978–90), is ironically cast as a talking cow. This 'dish of the day' sequence (in which the characters converse with a cow-like animal specifically bred to want to be eaten) remains one of the show's most memorable ideas. It was not, however, in the original radio serial but had been specially written for the re-recorded LP version and the disastrous 1980 West End stage production. A sadly lost scene in the Milliways sequence is a version of the bodyguard's monologue, shot full-length to show that former champion bodybuilder Prowse was genuinely holding David Dixon as Ford Prefect unsupported, at arm's length throughout. For some bizarre reason, a close-up (with Dixon standing on a box) was used instead. The original footage has been lost and even the photographs of it that existed are gone, lost with a collection of slides stolen from Prowse in the 1990s.

Douglas Adams was well known (or rather, became well known in later years) as a fan of 1960s/1970s rock music, and the whole concept of Milliways was inspired by a 1973 Procol Harum song, 'Grand Hotel'. Hotblack Desiato (his name taken by Adams from a firm of Islington estate agents) and his band Disaster Area allow Adams to have enormous fun spoofing rock star ideas and lifestyles. Specifically, the concept of a stage show which ends with a black 'stuntship' crashing into the sun is an allusion to the over-the-top performances of Pink Floyd and especially their 1968 song 'Set the

Controls for the Heart of the Sun'. Adams, despite being an impoverished graduate, had certainly seen the Floyd play at Knebworth in the 1970s when he was there helping Graham Chapman perform comedy sketches. He later used his fame to become friends with both Pink Floyd and Procol Harum and appeared on stage with both bands, the ultimate fan's dream.

The dialogue surrounding the telephone call from Marvin which ends this sequence is Adams at his finest:

ZAPHOD   They want to arrest me over the phone? Could be – I'm a pretty dangerous dude when I'm cornered.

FORD   Yes, you go to pieces so fast, people get hit by the shrapnel.

ZAPHOD   Hey, what is this? Judgment day?

ARTHUR   Oh – do we get to see that as well?[19]

All of this rather disguises the fact that the script link to the scenes in the Milliways car park is once again utterly arbitrary. There is absolutely no reason for the team – especially Zaphod – to leave early, missing both the end of the universe and dessert, in order to rush downstairs and see Marvin, for whom they show no concern or affection at any other time. In the radio serial, the black spaceship which they then steal is a Hagunnenon war-vessel and this version has occasionally been performed on stage with the alien pilot depicted using a specially commissioned inflatable monster. But the TV serial has the better known version, in which the spaceship is a huge prop from the Disaster Area stage show bound for the sun and our heroes are once again facing (as Douglas Adams liked frequently to point out with subtle irony) 'certain death'.

This sets the scene for Episode Six, in which our heroes escape 'certain death' via a randomly set teleport and Arthur and Ford materialise on board the Golgafrinchan 'B'-Ark vessel. Not only is this another arbitrary leap, albeit with slightly more technological justification than a time travel journey caused by an exploding computer, but it also means that Zaphod and Trillian depart the series suddenly and we never find out what happened to them. The 'B'-Ark sequence was, like the scenes with council man Mr Prosser at the start of the serial, an old script dusted down and reused. An earlier version can be found in the unproduced 1975 script *Our Show for Ringo Starr*,[20] which

Adams co-wrote with Graham Chapman, and before that the idea had been used in a rejected Adams *Doctor Who* script. In the *Ringo Starr* version, the 'useless third of the planet's population' – including management consultants, marketing executives and all sorts of bureaucrats and middle managers, who are packed into a giant 'ark in space' and sent to colonise another planet – originate not on an alien planet as in the planet Golgafrincham in *The Hitchhiker's Guide*, but on Earth (the list of those aboard included David Frost!).

In *The Hitchhiker's* version, the Golgafrinchan captain of the 'B'-Ark transporting his cargo (Aubrey Morris) spends his entire time in the bath. This is suspected as a self-reference by Douglas Adams, whose propensity for bathing was legendary. It is one borne out by the earlier 1975 version where the Captain's idiosyncrasy was that he was dressed as a turkey. Adams is known to have dressed as a turkey several times during his undergraduate period (photos exist!); possibly it was the only costume in his local fancy dress shop which fitted his 6' 5" frame. Thus we can see from this that Adams considered comedy writers such as himself to be prime candidates for the 'B'-Ark.

In this way, the TV version concludes where the first radio serial and the original pair of novels also finish – though each reached it by a different route, self-contradiction being one of the delights of *The Hitchhiker's Guide*. Arthur uses the Ark to get home, back to a pre-destruction Earth, where he has wanted to be all along. He has had an awfully big adventure but now things are back to normal, or as normal as they will ever be. The Earth is a beautiful, unspoilt planet and he has all the time in the world now to enjoy it. Although Adams later became an outspoken and respected pundit on ecological matters, when this ending was originally written for radio in 1977 – complete with accompanying soundtrack of Louis Armstrong's 'What a Wonderful World' – he had no real interest in science or nature, making this in retrospect a surprisingly sentimental ending to the sometimes cynical story of *The Hitchhiker's Guide* which had preceded it.

CONCLUSION

For all that purists prefer the books or the radio serial, the simple fact is that far more people (at least in the UK) have seen the TV version of *The Hitchhiker's Guide* than have ever read or heard it. The images of the characters and the illustrations of the ideas are those that are in the public consciousness, not least Arthur Dent in his dressing gown, an item of clothing never mentioned in the radio version or first two novels. An unfilmed scene for Episode Two of the TV version had Arthur changing into a silver spacesuit for the remainder of the serial, but even Douglas Adams had to admit that the dressing gown fitted the character better, symbolising his search for comfort, normality and tea.[21]

When the TV serial debuted in January 1981, most critics loved it, although in tabloids and broadsheets alike it was common practice to trot out 'jokes' about things being 'out of this world' or 'lost in space'. Herbert Kretzmer in the *Daily Mail* called *The Hitchhiker's Guide* 'great stuff',[22] while the *Daily Telegraph*'s Sylvia Clayton described it as 'a very English science fantasy' and said the production was 'full of life and invention'.[23] Christopher Reid, however, in a typically po-faced *Listener* review, found the first episode 'thin on jokes, overweight on whimsy',[24] and Richard Ingrams observed in the *Spectator* that 'I didn't laugh once.'[25]

The *Guardian*'s reviewer called the show a 'brilliantly witty blend of deft writing and acting with the latest jollities video technology can devise'[26] – which is an important point. The serial may look dated and quaint now but at the time it was considered, quite rightly, to be at the cutting edge of broadcast video techniques. Miles Kington in *The Times* very astutely pointed out that 'the special effects and noises boys could not possibly hope to win against the budget of something like *Star Wars*, but they earn an honourable draw'.[27] The *Daily Star* devoted almost a page to the show, with photos of extras on the Milliways set, while in the *Daily Express*, *The Hitchhiker's Guide* received the accolade of being referred to in a Giles cartoon.

More than 20 years on, the television *Hitchhiker's Guide to the Galaxy* stands up to inspection, helped certainly by the superb work done on the 2002 DVD release version with its plethora of extras and detailed, witty on-screen commentary notes. People's perceptions of the show may have changed over the years, just as the lines about digital watches and six pints of bitter have mutated in meaning, but the TV serial itself – scripts, performances, design, production, editing, music – remains as popular and relevant as ever. If it seems to have dated more than the radio version, that could be for several reasons, not least that 'futuristic' costumes and hairstyles always reflect their date of true creation. More to the point, although the TV *Hitchhiker's Guide* was at the cutting edge when it was made in 1980, that edge has moved on considerably since then as science fiction has proliferated on the big and small screens. Post-1978 advances in radio techniques, such as they are, are much less obvious. The 2004 radio revival of *The Hitchhiker's Guide* was recorded and mixed using state-of-the-art digital technology and was only the second British radio programme broadcast in Dolby 5.1 surround sound, yet it was still essentially a combination of music, sound effects (many produced physically in the studio) and voices. By comparison, the long-awaited feature film version released in 2005 (USA/UK; dir. Garth Jennings) is a million miles from the TV serial, not only because of the vastly increased budget but also because special effects technology – digital, prosthetic and animatronic – have developed beyond all recognition in the intervening quarter-century. But if longevity and an ability to appeal to subsequent generations are the marks of a classic, then it is an appellation which the TV version of *The Hitchhiker's Guide to the Galaxy* truly deserves. And remember: it did win *three* BAFTAs.

NOTES

1. For example: 'Considering the awesome aural visions suggested by the radio, the TV equivalents were always bound to be second best.... For this and other reasons, the TV version of *The Hitchhiker's Guide to the Galaxy* is considered ... a poor cousin to the radio original.' Mark Lewisohn, *The Radio Times Guide to TV Comedy* (London: BBC Books, 1998), p. 321.
2. See, for example, Neil Gaiman, *Don't Panic! The Official Hitchhiker's Guide to the Galaxy Companion* (London: Titan Books, 1988) and Roger Fulton, *The Encyclopaedia of TV Science Fiction* (London: Boxtree/Independent Television Books, 1990), pp. 186–8. Yet the origins are evidently not sufficiently documented for the many sources over the years who have cited the radio series as 'based on the book', including, on one notorious occasion, the *Radio Times* itself.
3. Episode One, *The Hitchhiker's Guide to the Galaxy*, wr. Douglas Adams, prod./dir. Alan J.W. Bell (1st tx. BBC 2, 5 January 1981).
4. First performed in the Footlights smoking concert, *Duplicator's Revenge*, on 25 October 1973.
5. 'Sophisticated computer animation converted the viewer's screen into the Guide when necessary.' Jon E. Lewis and Penny Stempel, *Cult TV: The Essential Critical Guide* (London: Pavilion Books, 1993), p. 20.

6. Douglas Adams, interview with David Howe and Owen Tudor, published in the *Doctor Who* fanzines *Beka* and *Oracle* in 1978.

7. The episode in question is 'For Your Own Good', co-written with Graham Chapman, first broadcast on ITV, 20 February 1977.

8. For a detailed explanation of the situation, the views of the real Paul Neil Milne Johnstone, and a photograph of Adams and Johnstone together at school, readers are directed to my book *Hitchhiker: A Biography of Douglas Adams* (London: Hodder & Stoughton, 2003; rev. edn Coronet, 2004).

9. The source in question being, in fact, Adams's Footlights contemporary, Clive Anderson.

10. Though the actual word used at Brentwood School was 'praepostor'.

11. See, for example, the footnote to 'Fit the Second' in Geoffrey Perkins (ed.), *The Hitchhiker's Guide to the Galaxy: The Original Radio Scripts* (London: Pan Books, 1985; rev. edn 2003), p. 51.

12. No relation to the present author.

13. Simpson, *Hitchhiker*, p. 107.

14. Ibid., p. 106.

15. ZZ9 Plural Z Alpha, 4 The Sycamores, Hadfield, Glossop, Derbyshire SK13 2BS.

16. Douglas Adams and John Lloyd, *The Deeper Meaning of Liff* (London: Pan/Faber & Faber, 1990).

17. See once more, Lewis and Stempel, *Cult TV*, p. 20.

18. See, for example, Neil Gaiman, *Don't Panic! Douglas Adams and The Hitchhiker's Guide to the Galaxy*, 3rd edn (London: Titan, 2002), p. 55.

19. Episode Five, *The Hitchhiker's Guide to the Galaxy*, wr. Douglas Adams, prod./dir. Alan J.W. Bell, 1st tx. BBC 2, 2 February 1981.

20. Published in Graham Chapman, *OJRIL: The Completely Incomplete Graham Chapman* ed. Jim Yoakum (London: Batsford, 1999).

21. From the third novel on – *Life, The Universe and Everything* (1982) – Arthur's dressing gown is referred to in print.

22. Herbert Kretzmer, TV review, *Daily Mail*, 6 January 1981.

23. Sylvia Clayton, TV review, *Daily Telegraph*, 6 January 1981.

24. Christopher Reid, TV review, *The Listener*, 8 January 1981.

25. Richard Ingrams, TV review, *The Spectator*, 8 January 1981.

26. Peter Fiddick, writing about the serial in the *Guardian* later that week, managed not only to mishear and hence misquote a line of dialogue but also confused John Lloyd with his *Not the Nine O'Clock News* (BBC TV, 1979–82) co-creator Sean Hardie.

27. Miles Kington, TV review, *The Times*, 8 January 1981.

12

'OK, homeboys, let's posse!' Masculine anxiety, gender, race and class in *Red Dwarf*

ELYCE RAE HELFORD

Set in a futuristic and potentially post-patriarchal environment and shunning embodied female characters until its sixth series, the popular sf TV sitcom *Red Dwarf* (BBC TV, 1988–99) offers a compelling take on gender identity. The programme follows a small group of twenty-something male humans and humanoids living on *Red Dwarf*, a deep space mining ship, three million years in the future. Dave Lister (played by Craig Charles), a sloppy working-class Liverpudlian, is the former lowest ranking crew member and apparently last surviving human. He is accompanied by a hologram of his dead bunkmate, Arnold Rimmer (Chris Barrie), a neurotic middle-class white man and former second lowest ranking crew member. Holly (Norman Lovett), the image of a white, working-class male head that personifies the ship's computer, has restored Rimmer to keep Lister sane. With them is the Cat (Danny John-Jules), a young black feline-man with an American accent who evolved from the offspring of Lister's cat (over the millions of years Lister was in the ship's 'stasis chamber'). Beginning in Series Three, the crew is joined by Kryten (Robert Llewellyn), a white, male-modelled cyborg, who acts as technical adviser, domestic servant and companion. The only regular female cast member in the first six series is a second version of Holly (Hattie Hayridge), a young blonde female image that replaces the original male computer image during Series Three through Five. By Series Six, the crew has lost contact with *Red Dwarf* and lives on the shuttle *Starbug* without Holly.

Only in Series Seven does a primary embodied female character, officer Kristine Kochanski, join the cast. Kochanski dated then dumped Lister when the crew was alive. She is the object of Lister's dreams of a life back on Earth; however, the woman who accidentally joins him in Series Seven comes from an alternate universe. The original Kochanski (C.P. Grogan), whom we see through flashbacks and temporal anomalies during the first six series, is a working-class-gal-made-good: tomboyish, intelligent and friendly. Both Kochanskis are knowledgeable and capable; yet the second Kochanski (Chloe Annett) is selfish, spoiled and an upper-class snob.

Red Dwarf's futuristic scenario in Series One through Six offers a speculative representation of what might have been a potentially post-patriarchal space: a world where patriarchal standards of male attitude and behaviour could have been irrelevant, even replaced by something new. When the sitcom introduces a woman, we can thus trace her impact upon this potentially 'beyond gender' scenario.[1] By examining what *Red Dwarf* says about gender construction and masculine anxiety, we find some of the messages available in television texts for cultural consumption and contestation. Accordingly, we can gain valuable insights into some of the ways in which Western masculinities are constructed through media representation. And we can see how difficult it is to envision new understandings of gender, even within speculative contexts. Ultimately, through *Red Dwarf*, we grasp the degree to which 'changing the definitions of manhood will require a serious confrontation with [mediated] images' as well as 'structural realities'[2] and that just projecting ourselves into an imagined future will not solve the problems men experience living up to today's standards.

Like Antony Easthope's perspective in *What a Man's Gotta Do: The Masculine Myth in Popular Culture* (1990), the following chapter proceeds from the contention that 'to be male in modern society is to benefit from being installed, willy nilly, in a position of power. No liberal moralising or glib attitudinising can change that reality. Social change is necessary and a precondition of such change is an attempt to *understand* masculinity, to make it visible'.[3] To 'understand' means to reject 'attempts to treat masculinity ... as the normative referent against which standards are assessed' and to analyse it instead 'as a problematic gender construct',[4] not unlike feminist studies of femininity. Study of representations of masculinity, like those in popular television, can make such norms and imperatives visible, comprehensible and available for dispute and revision. And science fiction visions of man's future help us to see how tenacious our norms and imperatives are.

Though following a pro-feminist approach to men's studies is essential to cultural transformation, attention to sets of social expectations for men must not blind us to the oppressiveness of gender-typing within patriarchy for women. Even as we acknowledge that 'men who find it difficult or objectionable to fit into the patterns of traditional masculinity often find themselves castigated and alienated',[5] express low self-esteem or exhibit antisocial behaviour, we must simultaneously retain focus on the oppression of women. If not, we emphasise the burden of masculine roles for men while ignoring the simultaneous privileges they may receive, often whether they 'fit' masculine stereotypes or not. Such a misguided perspective may 'tacitly assume and promote a liberal notion of the formal equality of men and women', when, in reality, women are still far from achieving political and economic justice.[6] Therefore, even as this study focuses on *Red Dwarf*'s representations of the difficulties inherent in patriarchal demands on men, it also refers to the ways in which the male characters maintain Western patriarchal perspectives, often reducing women to objects.

For the first six series, *Red Dwarf* emphasises the behaviour of and relationships between the members of its all-male crew. Significantly, with humanity virtually extinct, there is nothing left to prove to superior men (the ship's captain, other officers, fathers and so on) and no competition for women. Thus the men in theory could be free to challenge the gender norms that may have oppressed them. Rimmer could admit his sexual inexperience openly, cease his admiration for military generals and warlords, and drop his ineffectual bravado. Lister could abandon his impossible dream of playing provider for a family on a farm on Earth. Yet they do not.

Kryten, likewise, could question his feminised role as domestic servant and, consequently, his tendency to bolster the stereotypical masculinity of his companions. Lister does encourage Kryten to break his programming but gives this up relatively quickly, showing respect for his 'mechanoid' companion while simultaneously enjoying the privilege of having someone else do the laundry and cook. Perhaps this relationship, in part, encourages Northern (English) working-class Lister to develop through the series from rumpled slob to leather-wearing tough (if in appearance more than behaviour) and occasional hero. Although Lister's encouragement of Kryten's feminisation is passive, Rimmer's is not. Rimmer constantly props up his weak masculine ego by giving Kryten orders, ridiculing his programming for domestic duties, calling him demeaning names and attempting (ineffectually) to catch him making errors. The fragility of Rimmer's ego is a constant source of conflict, humour and even plot development throughout the series. Moreover, Rimmer ridicules Lister, Holly and the Cat, as well as Kryten. The Cat laughs it off most easily: he is a Southern dandy obsessed with his own superficial attractiveness and the pursuit of (non-existent) mates, yet he loves to taunt the others with how undesirable they are. Generally, then, in this potentially post-patriarchal space, there is still an obsolete and detrimental anxiety over gender roles.

Gender-typed behaviour and conflict escalate when the crew encounter occasional female or female-like beings. For example, they meet female types as 'opposites' in an alternate universe ('Parallel Universe'); as Genetically Engineered Life Forms or GELFs ('Polymorph', 'Camille', 'Psirens' and 'Emohawk'); 'wax droids' ('Meltdown'); videogame characters ('Better Than Life') and holograms ('Holoship' and 'Quarantine').[7] Both primary character interaction and plots that bring the characters into contact with female beings highlight an ongoing conflict between the post-patriarchal possibilities of this imagined future and the continued maintenance of oppressive, archaic gender norms. This conflict leads to the repeated playing out of the male characters' struggles to live up to Western norms of manhood – however diverse such norms are relative to class, race and region (Northern or Southern English) – within the specific context of a future that exaggerates, through humour, the meaninglessness of such struggles.

At first glance, then, *Red Dwarf* offers viewers a humorous, anachronistic bastion of stereotypically masculine behaviour. Lister, for example, exemplifies a working-class, Northern English perspective. Thus he ineffectually defends his enjoyment of watching videotapes of topless female boxing ('The Last Day', Series Three, 1st tx. BBC 2,

19 December 1989) and scorns his female opposite for crude, 'masculine' behaviour that parallels his own but sleeps with her anyway ('Parallel Universe'). Yet, enacting a more middle-class, white male stereotype, he sometimes hides his objectification of women behind superficially liberated platitudes. In a lecture to Rimmer, he opines: '[Y]ou see [women] as some alien species that needs to be conquered with trickery. They're not; they're people' ('Parallel Universe'). [8] The more blatantly sexist, though higher-class, Southern prep-school boy Rimmer reveals that he relies on books such as *1001 Chat-Up Lines* and the use of hypnotism to get dates ('Parallel Universe') and repeatedly brags about his sexual exploits aboard *Red Dwarf*. When the crew attempts to rescue a group of women aboard a crashed ship (where they first meet Kryten), Rimmer pretends to be the heroic captain of *Red Dwarf*, including rolled-up socks in his trousers and what Lister calls a 'Clive of India' look ('Kryten', Series Two, 1st tx. BBC 2, 6 September 1988).

Most of these examples, however, are complicated by context to reveal the characters' inability to uphold ultramasculine norms. For example, Lister is horrified to learn that he may be pregnant after sleeping with his opposite in her female-dominated universe. The overconfidence that leads him to dub his partner 'Miss Yo-Yo Knickers' becomes a feminised insecurity as he rails against exploitative sexual predators (women) who have sex without first ensuring that their partners (men) have taken proper precautions against pregnancy ('Parallel Universe'). Even more significantly, over the course of several episodes, we learn that Rimmer's big sexual encounter was his *only* sexual encounter; that it lasted twelve minutes and that his partner had concussion at the time ('Thanks for the Memory', Series Two 1st tx. BBC 2, 20 September 1988).

By comparison, the Cat's gender identity is far less developed. Much of the viewers' attention is focused on the Cat's vanity, style, heterosexual desire and powerful sense of smell. These traits, along with his pronounced canines and dark skin, are all identifiable as part of a feline heritage. However, he is humanoid and thus his masculinity (as human) is significant for discussions of gender representation in the programme. Like Lister and Rimmer, the Cat often fits Western stereotypes of masculinity in behaviour and attitudes; yet he, too, is a failure. He talks constantly about finding a mate but never does. He is a virgin whose pre-adolescent sexuality is coupled with a cultural innocence arising from his lack of experience in the human world. Only in videogames does he meet his hypermasculine goals, being so popular that he can reject even Marilyn Monroe (a repeated symbol of female perfection for the crew; see 'Better Than Life', 'The Last Day' and 'Meltdown').

More common are representations of the Cat as possessing an immature, narcissistic sexuality, exemplified well when he meets a 'pleasure GELF' (a metamorph that imitates the ideal love object of the observer) and sees himself ('Camille'). He is even feminised in his characterisation as a stereotypical Southern dandy: he has an enormous and flamboyant wardrobe, an obsession with his reflection and a penchant for preening. Actor Danny John-Jules, who portrays the Cat, has emphasised this feminisation in interviews: 'He's probably like a little girl the first time she puts on makeup and says "Hey, this stuff looks good...".'[9]

In addition to the masculine stereotype of obsession with sexual potency and the feminine stereotype of obsession with appearance, the Cat's identity is also very much about race. It is significant that John-Jules reads the pink suit he wore in the first episode as feeling 'like an old Cab Calloway suit'.[10] Furthermore, the Cat's link to African-American maleness is made plain through his portrayal by a black actor and his character's pointedly American accent and 'black' speech cadences. One powerful stereotype invoked by the Cat, particularly for US audiences, is the 'Sambo'. The myth of the lazy black man has been central to white America's need to deny that black men's labour built the nation, to 'erase the significance of Black male labor from public consciousness'.[11] Popular media thus actively remade enslaved black men into 'lazy and shiftless' Sambos, 'cartoon-like creatures only interested in ... having a good time'.[12] We see this mythic figure survive beyond the present into *Red Dwarf*'s fictional future. For example, in one early episode, Lister becomes ill and passes out. The Cat refuses to carry him to the sick bay, despite there being no one else to do it. When the helpless holographic Rimmer demands that he stop eating lunch and help, the Cat selfishly finds the request absurd. Later, when Lister is lying in bed, the Cat decides to be generous. He brings Lister a 'gift': an orange peel and empty grape stems. This effort so exhausts the Cat that he steals the blanket off Lister's feverish body and lies down for a nap ('Confidence and Paranoia', Series One 1st tx. BBC 2, 14 March 1988). Even more plainly, when forced to work to earn his meals, the Cat states: 'I do not do the "w" word' ('Queeg', Series Two 1st tx. BBC 2, 4 October 1988). Of course some, especially British, audiences, may read such behaviour not through race but through English class and region. A refusal to work or dirty oneself is also a classic representation of the English dandy; it helps heighten English North–South antagonism in the series in terms of the Cat being seen here to put on Southern aristocratic airs. Laziness-with-style is a key dandy trope.

Though the Cat is the only clearly marked 'black' character in the programme, race is also occasionally foregrounded through Lister. Though his racial heritage is never mentioned, Craig Charles has skin colour, facial features and a dreadlocked hairpiece that signify him as African rather than Anglo. Hints of racial/cultural identification can also be found within interactions between Lister and the Cat. For example, in 'Backwards' (Series Three, 1st tx. BBC 2, 14 November 1989), they must rescue Rimmer and Kryten. While the white duo find a way to survive on this reverse-running Earth (largely due to Kryten's efforts), Lister and the Cat play the fool, exemplifying US myths of black male ignorance and failure as they misread signs and decide they are in Bulgaria. More specifically, we see stereotypical urban American blackness encoded when they rap together, the Cat providing a backbeat while Lister chants: 'We didn't come here lookin' for trouble; we just came to do the Red Dwarf shuffle.' For British audiences, this may echo as a critique of British boys' emulation of African-American youth culture.

Such representation continues when the crew must band together to save their lives in Series Five's 'Demons and Angels' (1st tx. BBC 2, 19 March 1992). When Rimmer thinks he alone is safe from harm, he is unmoved by Lister's description of the foursome as 'Boys from the Dwarf' or the Cat's reference to the group as 'the Posse' and his assertion that 'if one of us is in a fix, the homeboys band together' (followed by a hip-hop wrist-shake performed by Lister and the Cat – joined, with less effectiveness, by Kryten). Yet when Rimmer's own life is in danger, he jumps in with a forced 'OK, homeboys, let's posse', revealing his lack of knowledge of the patterns of this

THE BOYS FROM THE DWARF with Holly the computer.

kind of black slang and thus verifying his (white) cultural isolation from the others.

As with all interpretations, however, there are others. The racist limitations discussed above can also be interpreted as parody. In such a reading, overkill in the Cat's characterisation arguably reveals the ridiculousness of African-American male or dandy stereotypes. What we can call the Cat's 'hyperracialised' or 'dandified' persona can also be read as active performance. It is not a tool to hide and cover a 'real' male experience or group identity but rather, as Mary Ann Doane argues in an examination of filmic femininity and the concept of the masquerade, a 'decorative layer which conceals a non-identity'.[13] From this perspective, the Cat character 'effects a defamiliarisation of ... iconography'.[14]

Similarly, Lister and the Cat's rapping, which can be interpreted as articulation of the stereotype that all young black men rap when alone together, can also be read otherwise. The lines we hear are based on the 1985 Chicago Bears' 'Superbowl Shuffle', not a true hip-hop perspective. This moment can, through parody/masquerade, be understood as the failure of Lister and the Cat to uphold stereotypes.

Through such a perspective, we laugh not at Lister and the Cat or at British youth emulating US black youth style but at the idea that all young African American men (can) rap. And we find a link in the programme between critiques of hyperracialisation and hypermasculinisation as unrealistic and unproductive norms.

Ultimately, whether subversive masquerade or racist/classist cartoon, the Cat is figured largely through stereotype. By contrast, Kryten, though limited by his programming, is a more complex and emotionally healthy 'male' than his crewmates (at least until Series Seven). His feminised status as servant is balanced by impressive technical knowledge and physical strength (echoed in a costume that mimics a well-muscled male body). This cyborg figure thus emerges as the most effectively gender-balanced (though not gender-transgressive) character in the programme. For example, when he does have the opportunity for a love affair (with a blob-like GELF in 'Camille') he is nurturing, non-objectifying and unselfish. Thus where the Cat may be read as lampooning an always-adolescent (black) male sexuality, Kryten enacts the voice of mature and emotionally healthy (white) male adulthood, ironically within a non-human body. Yet 'ironically' is perhaps imprecise here, for as Donna Haraway has argued: 'Cyborg imagery can suggest a way out of the maze of dualisms in which we have explained our bodies and our tools to ourselves.'[15]

Kryten is a cybernetic fusion of organic tissue and mechanical body. He looks and sounds white and male but his simulation of white maleness makes plain Western patriarchy's desire to replicate its white male standard endlessly through its technology and creation of mechanical slaves. Furthermore, his white maleness is flawed: his head is angular, hairless and the subject of ridicule by the other crew members and he does not wear clothes but rather a permanent black metallic suit. His physicality invites a more complex reading of Kryten via race. Just as he exhibits feminine behaviour within a hypermasculine body, he arguably blends white master and Black servant/slave images through appearance and manner. His face mimics Caucasian appearance while his body is entirely (coded through its darkness as) B/black. Behaviourally, Kryten enacts this complexity through his technical authority coupled with his menial role. Thus we can see in Kryten a masquerade that, even more obviously than the Cat's, highlights the limitations of that which it replicates. Kryten's human creators purposefully made him less than but similar to white men, yet his very imperfection and knowledge of his own subservience create a figure that sees and enacts the limitations in both master and servant/slave, masculine and feminine and white and minoritised identities. He emerges, thereby, as more than the sum of his parts.

A particularly compelling example of the use of his gender-balanced and racially doubled persona occurs when alien technology accidentally renders Kryten entirely human ('DNA', Series Four, 1st tx. BBC 2, 21 February 1991). He is unsurprised to find that he takes the form of a white male. He immediately scorns the company of his spare mechanical heads, makes fun of mechanoids as stupid and inept, becomes obsessed with his large genitals and finds himself lusting after vacuum cleaners in an objectifying manner. We see that once he loses his cyborg form, he loses his ability and desire to see the world from a disempowered position. As he gains true white male status, his behaviour becomes rigidly gendered and racially typed.

Interestingly, Lister enjoys Kryten's company far less when he becomes human and suggests that he return to his mechanoid status. Although Lister claims Kryten is never fully human, it seems that he is intolerable to Lister precisely because he has become too 'human' (meaning white and male). Lister as well as Rimmer feel safer knowing that, though they were formerly the lowest ranking crew members aboard Red Dwarf, they would always rank higher than the servant Kryten. A human Kryten, with all his competencies still intact, is unacceptable to them. Ultimately, Kryten's cyborg state is what helps him to see and productively critique (by embodying) the dualisms that trap human consciousness. At the end of the episode, Kryten decides to go back to being a cyborg, an identity with which he is happiest. Generally, then, we can see in Kryten an effective response to – though not transcendence of – gendered and racialised binarisms, symbolising an 'infidel heteroglossia'[16] against which the other characters' more rigid identities may be read.

Holly, in his first form, echoes some of Kryten's complexities. He appears white and male and his face is more fully human than Kryten's, yet he is only a talking head on a screen. Similarly, he is in control of the ship, apparently representing more master than servant; however, he often makes mistakes in his calculations while

Kryten does not. That he lacks the mature sexuality of Kryten and speaks informally, with a heavy Northern working-class accent (while Kryten always speaks more formally, even calling the others 'sir', with a Canadian accent), are perhaps the most significant reasons the crew interacts more casually with Holly than with Kryten. To be sure, where Rimmer makes fun of both Holly and Kryten, Lister treats both with respect. Yet Holly is more clown than threat to Rimmer and more servant than ship's master to Lister.[17]

When Norman Lovett left the show after Series Two, the writers used his exit to break up their all-male scenario and add an interesting momentary gender complexity to Holly. In Series Two's 'Parallel Universe', Holly shares a brief flirtation with 'Hilly' (Hattie Hayridge), his feminised computer 'opposite'. In the first episode of Series Three ('Backwards'), we learn that Holly has decided to swap personalities and now appears identical to Hilly (though 'he' still goes by the already feminine name of Holly). Though by necessity divorced from biology, this computerised sex change still gives viewers a new perspective on the formerly stereotypical 'male' character. In the identity swap, we can read a critique of male fears of loss of masculine ego. Because Holly sees nothing wrong with becoming feminised, neither may the viewer.

Nevertheless, the changes that occur when the ship's computer goes from white male to white female are significant. The new Holly is generally desexualised and seems to have little effect on the masculinities of the male characters. This offers a positive message about female versus male technical competence in the eyes of the crew. However, the new Holly also manifests traits identifiable as stereotypically white-feminine, particularly an accentuated naive stupidity. The 'male' Holly was occasionally inadequate but the new 'female' Holly is far more so. Holly's portrayer, Hattie Hayridge, seemed well aware of this writing limitation. During an interview given between Series Four and Five (entitled 'Don't Call This Computer a Dumb Blonde') she expressed her hope that in the upcoming series, 'they might make [Holly] more intelligently sarcastic rather than stupid'.[18] Apart from one episode in which she is momentarily made brilliant ('White Hole', Series Four, 1st tx. BBC 2, 7 March 1991), Holly remains a static figure. In addition, Holly's role shrinks considerably once feminised. This may signify sexism in the writing of the programme but it can also be read as a symptom of the tension in maintaining the 'female' Holly within the generally masculinised play of *Red Dwarf*. Such a reading is supported when we note the significant increase in tensions between the sexes and manifestations of strongly gender-typed behaviour during Series Seven, with its inclusion of Kristine Kochanski.

However variously gendered and racialised they are, the Cat, Kryten and the two Hollys retain fairly static identities. Lister and Rimmer, by comparison, are more dynamic characters (at least within individual episodes: more often than not, as in most sitcoms, changes in personality are not maintained over time). Along with this relative dynamism comes complexity of behaviour. Certain of Lister's and Rimmer's actions and attitudes are difficult to qualify as either masculine or feminine and exemplify the possibilities for gender play that placement of the characters in a potentially post-patriarchal space can allow. For example, in 'Queeg' Lister takes a sex quiz from a woman's magazine with obvious delight. He checks off the box that says he wears a 'sexy black negligee' to bed, squeezes his chest and decides that his 'boobs' are 'definitely too large' and is thrilled to learn that his rating makes him 'one foxy lady: sensuous, sexual and you don't mind showing it'.

More significantly, gender roles are thrown fully into question when Lister decides to give Rimmer a piece of his memory as a gift to commemorate Rimmer's 'deathday' ('Thanks for the Memory'). Lister chooses the time of his relationship with Lise Yates, a woman he seems primarily to remember as a great sex partner and booster of his self-confidence because of her attraction to him. Through a machine capable of such a transfer, Lister loads the Lise Yates era into Rimmer's hologrammatic brain. When Rimmer wakes, he is transformed from a self-pitying failure into a secure, self-confident individual who 'remembers' the power of the love he shared with Lise. Through Rimmer's description of this wonderful, caring woman, Lister becomes aware of his folly in having ended his brief relationship with her, just to 'play the field'. Lister recognises his own masculine immaturity through Rimmer's uncharacteristically adult understanding of the relationship with Lise. Thus this scene also shows Rimmer's ability to grow as a character. We learn that he, too, has the potential to reach beyond relationships with women that are purely objectifying.

Yet Rimmer refuses this growth: upon learning that he never really knew Lise, he immediately demands to have the memory removed and recollection of the days since the transfer stripped from the minds of Lister, the Cat and even Holly.

Perhaps the most striking aspect of gender relations in *Red Dwarf* prior to Series Seven, however, is the programme's engagement with homoeroticism, especially with Rimmer as the desiring/repressing subject. Rimmer frequently attacks Lister's sexuality, attempting to exhibit a sexual self-confidence he does not possess. He thereby only illustrates excessive insecurity over issues of sexuality and desire. Typical are scenes such as the moment in 'Polymorph' when Lister's boxer shorts turn out to be a genetically engineered mutant and begin shrinking on his body. Lister falls to the floor in agony and begs Kryten to take off his pants. Kryten, coincidentally sporting a vacuum hose attached to his 'groinal socket', stops his cleaning duties and comes immediately to Lister's aid. He bends before the writhing Lister and pulls off his shorts. With utter predictability for anyone familiar with this type of formulaic sitcom moment, Rimmer arrives and announces: 'You'll bonk anything, won't you, Lister? Not even an android's safe from your vile appetites.'

Yet this kind of homophobic disparagement becomes a more complex expression of gender anxiety and homoerotic desire in Series Four's 'Dimension Jump' (1st tx. BBC 2, 14 March 1991). Here Rimmer reacts with obvious jealousy to a handsome and heroic alternate-universe version of himself called 'Ace'. First, Rimmer attacks Ace by identifying him as inadequately masculine and therefore gay. He tells his companions: 'I bet you anything he wears women's underwear. They're all the same, his type. Rough and tumble, hurly-burly macho marines in public and behind closed doors he'll be parading up and down in his taffeta ballgown, drinking mint juleps and whipping the houseboy.' Then, as Ace develops a friendship with Lister that is closer than Rimmer's, he begins to make homophobic allusions to their relationship. Ace defends Lister's heterosexuality, telling him to ignore Rimmer's jibes and get back to fixing *Starbug* (the crew's shuttle was accidentally disabled by Ace's ship). In response, Rimmer snipes: 'Yes, the sooner we get back, the sooner you can climb into a nice soapy bath together and play "Spot the Submarine".' Finally, after Ace has saved *Starbug*, successfully operated on the Cat's leg (injured in the accident) and taught Kryten to play the piano, Rimmer responds to Lister's admiration with: 'So, is it going to be a simple Registry Office or a full church do for you two?'

The homophobic attacks here are obviously clichéd and offensive, not unlike the scene in 'Polymorph'; however, the number of these predictable attempts at ridicule and disparagement make them something more. Rimmer is revealing deep anxiety at losing his only human friend to Ace, a more capable and desirable version of himself. Through such interactions, we come to see that the homophobic masculine norm that Rimmer embraces with gusto is overcompensation for insecurity and arguably an ineffectual masking of taboo homosexual desire. Furthermore, Rimmer may be accusing Lister of deferring to a social better since Rimmer's insecurities regarding his sexuality come second only to his frustrated attempts to achieve higher social rank.

Fear of being unmasked leads to Rimmer's attempts to feminise Lister, to cast suspicion elsewhere. This is a repeated interaction throughout *Red Dwarf* and determines much of the tension between the characters. Lister is the frequent butt of jokes, insults and competitive discussions about women and sex. Though his relationships with women are apparently little more successful than Rimmer's, Lister is far more experienced. Despite this, Rimmer is determined to seem the more successful of the two. To prove the success of his techniques for picking up women, for example, Rimmer asks Lister to 'be a woman ... sort of on your own, in a bar, short leather mini-skirt, peep-hole bra' ('Parallel Universe'). He then attempts to seduce Lister. The joke that ensues, as Rimmer tries unsuccessfully to get Lister to respond correctly to his weak pick-up line, masks the sexual implications of the scenario. Rimmer grows increasingly frustrated as Lister fails to give the right replies and quickly moves to a discussion of his alleged sexual conquest of a woman with this line and through use of the hypnotic 'mesmer stare'.

At times, Rimmer's feminising of Lister is even more blatant. After calling him a 'sad, middle-aged woman' in 'Bodyswap' (Series Three, 1st tx. BBC 2, 5 December 1989) , Rimmer learns that it is possible to have his consciousness placed inside Lister's body. Though he ostensibly desires this transaction to be temporarily alive and embodied again, in the context of the programme's homoerotic moments,

Rimmer's occupation of Lister's body is an expression of masked sexual desire. That Rimmer then uses Lister's body to gorge himself on food, cigars and sex with 'Rachel' (a blow-up doll) signifies both the unleashing of repressed desire (in patently Freudian terms) and the desire to be (with/inside) Lister. The sharing of Rachel reveals a triad which, like the Lister–Ace–Rimmer threesome, suggests that the third figure (Rachel; Ace) is merely a device for allowing a man to maintain a homophobic stance while simultaneously revealing an undeclared and undeclarable homosexual desire.

Rimmer's non-traditional gender identity and (homo)sexualisation exhibit another facet when the character is overtly feminised. Particularly common, for example, are scenarios that offer alternative feminine or female versions of Rimmer. Aside from Ace, most of the alternative Rimmers are female, as in Rimmer's female opposite ('Parallel Universe') and female Rimmer 'clones' ('Rimmerworld', Series Six, 1st tx. BBC 2, 4 November 1993); or feminine, as, when suffering from a hologrammatic virus, Rimmer dons a gingham dress and blonde braids ('Quarantine'). In 'Demons and Angels', we meet the best and worst of Rimmer (and the rest of the crew), divided into two beings: the 'low' and the 'high'. While the 'high' Rimmer and all of his shipmates are feminised through their flowing robes, gentle voices and penchant for dance, of the 'lows' only Rimmer appears in drag, complete with garter-belt and fishnets, resembling Frank N. Furter from *The Rocky Horror Picture Show* (dir. Jim Sharman, UK, 1975). As a 'low', Rimmer enacts the homosexual slang connotations of his name. By comparison, rather than being feminised, the 'low' version of Lister is both hypermasculinised and racialised, resembling a Mexican bandit from a Hollywood 'B' Western.

Perhaps the most disturbing feminised image of Rimmer, however, occurs in Series One's 'Balance of Power' (1st tx. BBC 2, 29 February 1988), when Rimmer takes over the body of (the original) Kochanski and illustrates that non-traditional masculinities, gender anxiety and homoeroticism do not prevent the sexist objectification of women. The episode focuses on Lister's attempt to pass the chef's examination so that he can become Rimmer's superior, demand the return of Kochanski's personality disk (which Rimmer has hidden) and bring her back as a hologram. Rimmer resorts to desperate measures to thwart Lister's efforts. In Kochanski's body, he sashays into the classroom where Lister is taking his exam. His portrayal of a woman is predictably clichéd and offensive, as well as homoerotically suggestive when Rimmer tells Lister to have sex with 'her' (while his mind is inside). It becomes quickly obvious to Lister that this is not Kochanski. When his plan fails, Rimmer asks Holly to give him his own body back. The swap works, almost, and Rimmer finds himself back to normal, with the exception of his possession of Kochanski's right breast. At first he complains but then he decides to tell Holly to take his time and leaves the room, squeezing 'his' new-found body part. Rimmer's self-groping is worthy of commentary not for the gender-bending implications – which we see numerous times throughout the programme, as we have seen – but for the objectification of a woman's body and Rimmer's obvious enjoyment of this form of exploitative pleasure.

Though Rimmer is feminised in various ways and tries to feminise Lister intermittently during Series One through Six, the homoerotic desire functions in one direction only. In general terms, Lister's attitude towards Rimmer ranges from respectful tolerance to outright exasperation. Even Lister's adoration of Ace never includes reference to homosexual desire apart from Rimmer's jibes. It is not until the seventh series that the possibility of Lister's possession of repressed homosexual desire emerges. In Series Seven's 'Blue' (1st tx. BBC 2, 14 February 1997), Lister deals with feelings of loss after Rimmer, in an earlier episode, leaves the crew. Despite the new presences of the glamorous alternative Kochanski on board, Lister no longer has his foil and actually begins to miss Rimmer, calling him a 'unique' and 'special' friend. The Cat and Kryten think Lister has gone mad. But we as viewers see the appropriateness of his nostalgia when Rimmer rematerialises in Lister's sleeping quarters and the two have a talk that quickly becomes ripe with deep affection and sexual innuendo. Rimmer asks Lister to confirm that he cares less for his new crewmate (Kochanski) than he cared for him. As Lister answers Rimmer's queries, he comes to fill the feminised role of the passive lover who has been waiting, faithfully, for a wandering man's return:

RIMMER   Is she [Kochanski] as good as me?

LISTER   Well, she's been here a few weeks and she hasn't quoted one Space Corps directive.

[*Both gently laugh.*]

RIMMER   She's pretty attractive, though, isn't she?

LISTER   Is she? I haven't really noticed....

RIMMER   So she's not as attractive as me, then?

LISTER   Don't be daft. She couldn't hold a candle to you, man.

RIMMER   Oh, you're just saying that.

LISTER   I'm not. I've... um... I've missed you, man.

RIMMER   And I've missed you, too, Listy.

LISTER   Oh, Rimmer.

[*They embrace.*]

RIMMER   Dave...

LISTER   Don't ever leave us again.

RIMMER   I won't. I won't.

LISTER   Do you promise?

RIMMER   Oh, Listy.

LISTER   Rimsy...

[*They kiss.*]

In the midst of the lovers' clinch, we cut to Lister, waking from a dream. He rolls out of bed, furiously wiping his tongue, horrified at himself and his apparent desires. We see here an unleashing of repressed male desire.

The excessiveness of this dream arguably moves the undertones of Lister/Rimmer desire into overt parody. Moreover, and predictably for a sitcom that matches hypermasculinity with powerful anxieties over gender roles, parodic critique quickly returns to a more traditional portrayal of repression later in the episode. Lister is 'cured' of his Rimmer adoration on a ride through a frightening artificial reality 'museum' called 'The Rimmer Experience', designed by Kryten and based upon Rimmer's logs. Nostalgic emotional closeness gives way to more typical competitive distance as scenes displaying Rimmer's selfishness, pomposity and lies remind Lister how arrogant and ignorant his ex-bunkmate was. This also allows Lister effectively to re-repress his temporarily unveiled desire and for the programme to retreat from the boldness of its exceptional dream scene.

That Kryten created this ride may seem a simple act of kindness between friends or a way for this servant/companion to fill his role properly; however, the situation is more complex, particularly in terms of gender. The new Kochanski has offered her own feminised, therapeutic counsel to Lister regarding his friendship with Rimmer. Kryten calls her advice 'psychobabble' and offers his 'Rimmer Experience' instead, reflecting scorn for feminine and middle-class models of friendship. This tension between Kryten and Kochanski, moreover, illustrates the significant changes in the programme when Kochanski is added to the crew. Generally, the relative complexity of gender representation in the male characters of *Red Dwarf* during its first six series becomes more simplistic and extreme during Series Seven. The arrival of Kochanski (and the loss of Rob Grant as one of the programme's key writers) shifts focus, tensions and representational patterns significantly for all the primary characters.

Even by Series Four, Grant and Naylor knew that the programme was 'very male-oriented' and that if they were going to add a new character (after Kryten in Series Three), it should be a woman.[19] However, says Grant, they were also 'worried about that altering the air; there was an important air of sexual frustration about the ship.'[20] A first solution was to introduce the female version of Holly. Yet one of the writers' continuing 'deep regrets' was that they had not 'been able to pursue Lister's unrequited love for Christine [*sic*] Kochanski.'[21] When they could not get the original actress for the part, they held off – until Grant left the programme and Chloe Annett was hired to replace C.P. Grogan as Kochanski in Series Seven.

Once Kochanski comes on board, much of the programme's focus shifts to her acclimatisation and relationships with other characters. Lister, for example, spends most of his time trying to make this alternative version of his ex-beloved happy and attracted to him. However, it is Kryten who is most affected by Kochanski's presence and who arguably becomes the centre of the series' commentary on gender roles. In contrast to the Cat and Lister, Kryten is not at all attracted to Kochanski, though he is obsessed with her. Considered logically, the two should like each other, for they have much in common. Kochanski knows a great deal about technical matters, is excellent at problem solving and has as much concern for cleanliness and etiquette as Kryten. Instead, they compete. Kryten is jealous of Lister's attraction to Kochanski, insecure about his future with the two if they become a couple, and frustrated with her ability to replace him as both technical consultant and friend. Furthermore, the even posher Kochanski threatens Kryten's status as classier than Lister or Rimmer. Because he is not adept at direct expression of his feelings (significant in terms of gender and class status), he instead picks on feminised trivialities, tangling with Kochanski over where to put the salad cream and which drawer her underclothing belongs in. Kochanski, of course, does not want to usurp Kryten's role as maid; in fact, she treats him as more of a servant than he is accustomed to. And we soon see that the conflict between them is about far more than food handling or laundry.

Kochanski's presence signals a crisis for the formerly gender-balanced mechanoid. Kryten knew that Rimmer's obnoxiousness and the Cat's self-centredness left him Lister's closest friend. Typical for representations of male–male friendships and working-class masculine stereotypes, the two never speak about this directly. Kochanski, however, is a direct threat. Hence Kryten's attitude and behaviour – which have heretofore vacillated between his originally programmed proper servant-class decorum and the working-class masculinity he has developed with Lister's encouragement and assistance – shift significantly in Kochanski's presence. He expresses his emotions directly and effusively. When he confronts Lister, his dread bursts out of him: 'She can't stay here, sir. She just can't!' ('Ouroboros', Series Seven, 1st tx. BBC 2, 31 January 1997). There are both over-protective mother and jealous lover-types in his attitude and tone here and throughout Series Seven. When Lister asks why Kochanski must leave, Kryten's voice rises to a 'hysterical' squeak (that we come to hear whenever he expresses fear and anxiety in this series) and cries: 'She's going to take you away from me.' Lister tries to pacify him but Kryten is not dissuaded from his bleak fantasy. Even Lister's firm reassurance, 'There's no one I care about more than you', is met only with Kryten's desperate feminised (and homoerotic) bid for affection in his reminder: 'I'd never dump you like she did, never.'

Jealous affection for Lister is not the only trait that keeps Kryten from closeness with Kochanski. Her higher class status distances her from all the other characters. When it becomes clear to her that she will be staying with the men, she spends much of her time heaping insults on the lifestyle of the crew. This alternates with moping and sobbing over her lost life aboard a cleaner, better-equipped, alternative ship with a smarter, more sensitive, and more heroic version of Lister. Despite great differences in attitude and lifestyle, Lister and even the Cat do make attempts to relate to Kochanski's stereotypically gender- and class-defined perspectives. Kryten, however, does not. Thus the Cat and particularly Lister find themselves in the midst of a war between Kochanski and Kryten for control of life on *Starbug*: will it become a classier, feminised ship in which pub games involving drinking and flatulence are replaced by drawing room games involving hummed opera passages? The tension reaches its violent climax when, on the anniversary of Kryten's joining the crew, Kochanski sets up an artificial reality excursion to '*Pride and Prejudice* World' ('Beyond a Joke', Series Seven, 1st tx. BBC 2, 21 February 1997). Kryten, meanwhile, has prepared a special meal and celebration for himself. When the three others wander into the dining area to tell Kryten about the game, he ignores their idea and beckons them to partake in his culinary masterpiece. His role as feminised servant is obvious in the fact that he did the cooking for his own anniversary dinner, as well as in the others' casual dismissal of his efforts. Kochanski, by contrast, fulfils the upper-class white feminine role of 'mistress' (as she controls the men's actions) or 'woman on a pedestal' (as they look up to and/or desire her), when she giddily glorifies her youth spent in 'Jane Austen World' videogames. Despite an inability to relate to her love of historical romance, Lister and the Cat do want to please Kochanski by seeming classy. They eventually even render the game masculinely palatable by attempting to seduce the female members of the Bennett family within the '*Pride and Prejudice* World' scenario.

Meanwhile, having offered what he thought was an even more impressive upper-class pleasure (the extravagant meal) and been rejected, Kryten grows furious. The feminisation of Kryten through his adoration of Lister and mother/maid role also has a 'masculine' side, made evident when the mechanoid brings violence into his desire for revenge against Kochanski. Kryten enters the Austen game through a fused connection with a World War II combat game. When he appears, he does so in an army tank that pops out of a calm lake beside the gazebo in which Kochanski, Lister and the Cat sit, sipping tea with various Austen characters. Menacingly, Kryten declares: 'Perhaps I didn't make myself clear. I said, "Supper is ready".' He then blows them up. The others, too shocked to speak, simply stare at Kryten and the dead fictional characters all around. Clearly, servant-class masculinity wins this round.

However, this scene is atypical. Immediately after the explosion, Kryten returns to his role as overbearing mother/insecure wife figure. He fusses over the dinner, fishing for compliments; then, when they are not forthcoming, he whines about how unappreciated he is and that his 'fingers are practically worn down to the exoskeleton'. He continues clamouring until he literally blows his top. His exploding head perfectly exemplifies a sexist vengeance, a violent end deservedly enacted upon Kryten as a shrewish housewife stereotype whose hysteria rightly destroys 'her'. Further complicating this representation, we learn that the malfunction is a result of Kryten's 'negadrive', a file that holds all of his anger, jealousy and resentment and blows when it is full. This special repository was installed intentionally by Kryten's female creator, Professor Mamet, who modelled the Kryten-type series of mechanoids on a lover who jilted her, a 'pompous, ridiculous looking, mother hen clucking' man. This information offers the possibility of a new, anti-feminist reading to the programme. Kochanski is the 'bitch' who ruins male camaraderie; now Kryten becomes the innocent victim of an anti-male revenge plot for which a woman (Mamet) is ultimately responsible.

Ultimately, Series Seven brings a highly competent woman aboard the ship; a strong, intelligent, well-educated individual who could help to challenge sexist stereotypes and further the potentially post-patriarchal nature of the programme. However, placed as she is within an anachronistically masculine crew (written with far less subtlety than in series past), Kochanski emerges as a disruptive, hyperfeminised, classist stereotype who inspires even greater rigidity of gender roles in the male members of the crew. At the close of Kochanski's first series with the 'boys from the Dwarf', the space of the sitcom is arguably more patriarchal and less futuristic than ever.

Whether exemplifying the objectification of women by men who attempt to live up to rigid patriarchal standards of manhood, the emotional trauma suffered by these men as they inevitably fail in their attempts, or the potential for reconfigured masculinities (including the pleasure and pain of homoerotic desire), *Red Dwarf* offers sf scenarios and broad humour that address the problematics of gendered subjectivities in terms far richer than we might expect from a situation comedy. In addition, by projecting this struggle into a potentially post-patriarchal future, the programme illustrates the tenacity of patriarchal norms. Although there is no practical value in working to uphold rigid masculine or feminine ideals, the characters generally rely on this binarism to provide a conclusive way of knowing both self and world. For viewers, this seemingly trivial sitcom thus offers an important articulation of the complexities of patriarchal gendering. In addition, *Red Dwarf* illustrates how truly difficult it can be to rid ourselves of such standards.

NOTES

1. This chapter shares some of its structure and emphasis with an earlier essay of mine on *Red Dwarf*: 'Reading Masculinities in the 'Post-Patriarchal' Space of *Red Dwarf*', *Foundation* 64 (1995), pp. 20–31. I read *Red Dwarf* as an American; hence my interpretations of gender, race and class in the series necessarily emphasise my US media culture context. Of course, I also address the British context for production and reception of the series. For this, I am extremely grateful to Farah Mendlesohn's patient discussion with me of the British reception of *Red Dwarf* and her insights, particularly regarding race. Moreover, with Series Eight having already aired (in 1999) and the possibility of a future *Red Dwarf* film, my analysis and conclusions necessarily rest at an arbitrary but significant point in the development of the programme. I leave it to other critics to explore the eighth series and any feature film that eventually emerges, to conduct audience studies and to explore themes other than gender.

2. Michael S. Kimmel, 'Foreword' in Steve Craig (ed.), *Men, Masculinity, and the Media* (Newbury Park CA: Sage, 1992) p. xii.

3. Antony Easthope, *What a Man's Gotta Do: The Masculine Myth in Popular Culture* (Boston: Unwin Hyman, 1990), p. 7.

4. Kimmel, 'Considering Men and the Media', in Craig (ed.), *Men, Masculinity, and the Media*, p. 2.

5. Ibid., p. 3.

6. Tania Modleski, *Feminism without Women: Culture and Criticism in a 'Postfeminist' Age* (New York: Routledge, 1991), p. 6.

7. 'Parallel Universe', Series Two (1st tx. BBC 2, 11 October 1988); 'Poly-morph', Series Three (1st tx. BBC 2, 28 November 1989); 'Camille', Series Four (1st tx. BBC 2, 14 February 1991); 'Psirens', Series Six (1st tx. BBC 2, 7 October 1993); 'Emohawk', Series Six (1st tx. BBC 2, 28 October 1993); 'Meltdown', Series Four (1st tx. BBC 2, 21 March 1991); 'Better Than Life', Series Two (1st tx. BBC 2, 13 September 1988);

'Holoship', Series Five (1st tx. BBC 2, 20 February 1992); 'Quarantine', Series Five (1st tx. BBC 2, 12 March 1992).

8. All quotations are transcribed from videotapes of the televised episodes. I have used *Primordial Soup: Red Dwarf Scripts* and the novel(isation) *Red Dwarf: Infinity Welcomes Careful Drivers* when necessary and appropriate to clarify language or spelling. See Rob Grant and Doug Naylor, *Primordial Soup: Red Dwarf Scripts* (Harmondsworth: Penguin, 1993) and *Red Dwarf: Infinity Welcomes Careful Drivers* (Harmondsworth: Penguin, 1989).

9. Joe Nazzaro, 'This Cat is Cool: An Interview with Danny John-Jules', *Stasis Leak 2* (1993), p. 35.

10. Ibid., p. 34.

11. bell hooks, *Black Looks: Race and Representation* (Boston: South End Press, 1992), p. 90.

12. Ibid.

13. Mary Ann Doane, 'Film and the Masquerade: Theorizing the Female Spectator', in John Caughie, Annette Kuhn, Mandy Merck and Barbara Creed (eds), *The Sexual Subject: A Screen Reader in Sexuality* (London: Routledge, 1992) p. 234.

14. Ibid., p. 235.

15. Donna Haraway, 'A Cyborg Manifesto: Science, Technology, and Socialist-Feminism in the Late Twentieth Century', in *Simians, Cyborgs, and Women: The Reinvention of Nature* (New York: Routledge, 1991), p. 181.

16. Ibid.

17. Interestingly, in one episode, Holly briefly adopts an African-American male appearance ('Queeg'). He exhibits a personality directly taken from Morgan Freeman's drill sergeant character in the film *An Officer and a Gentleman* (dir. Taylor Hackford, USA, 1982) while his name, Queeg, is obviously an ironic allusion to *Mutiny on the Bounty* (dir. Frank Lloyd, USA, 1935; remade US 1962, dir. Lewis Milestone), as the easygoing Holly pretends to lose control of the ship to this aggressive and cruel alternate persona. The violent dangerousness of the black man in the racist white American imagination (see hooks, p. 89) is seen here, though tempered for the sitcom format. Queeg overworks and underfeeds the crew but the cruellest he gets is taking over the hologrammatic body of the unsympathetic Rimmer and making him jog around the ship after falling into unconsciousness.

18. Hattie Hayridge, cited in Nazzaro, 'Don't Call This Computer a Dumb Blonde: An Interview with Hattie Hayridge', *Stasis Leak 1* (1992), p. 26.

19. Joe Nazarro, 'Writing for *Red Dwarf*: An Interview with Rob Grant and Doug Naylor', *Stasis Leak 1* (1992), p. 7.

20. Rob Grant, cited in Nazzaro, 'Writing for *Red Dwarf*', p. 7.

21. Ibid.

13

British apocalypses now – or then? *The Uninvited, Invasion: Earth* and *The Last Train*

CATRIONA MILLER

Since the television film of *Doctor Who* in 1996 (USA/UK; dir. Geoffrey Sax; writer Matthew Jacobs), British-made science fiction on television had been sporadic at best but in the late 1990s a flurry of indigenous sf dramas appeared on British screens: *The Uninvited* (1st tx. ITV, 25 September–16 October 1997); *Invasion: Earth* (1st tx. BBC 1, 8 May–12 June 1998) and *The Last Train* (1st tx. ITV, 7 April–6 May 1999). It seems no coincidence that these serials appeared at the same time as fears about the approaching millennium were filling the media. A concern with the 'end of the world' is a common feature in science fiction and in British science fiction in particular, but, as this chapter will show, there were also antecedents in the apocalyptic literature of Jewish and Christian tradition.

Each of these three serials, in its own way, imagined possible catastrophic fates for humanity from a British perspective, as Britain's cosy island shores were assaulted time after time. Although the alien conspiracy in *The Uninvited* is global, England is where the critical action takes place. In *Invasion: Earth*, aliens are shot down over Scotland. Whilst the incursion is revealed to be global, the decisive moments happen in the Scottish town of Kirkhaven. In *The Last Train*, as in *Threads* (BBC, 1984), the apocalypse is viewed from Sheffield and beyond.

Science fiction is sometimes seen as a predominantly American genre, particularly with regard to film. As I.Q. Hunter has put it, the 'critical consensus remains ... that British sf [film] is a poor thing, responsive at periods to national discourses, but too often a shadow of its more ambitious, confident, expensive and expansive American counterpart.'[1] The same might very well be said about British science fiction on television, where *Star Trek* (NBC, 1966–69; 1987–2005), *Babylon 5* (Rattlesnake Productions for Warners, 1993–99) and *Stargate SG-1* (MGM 1997–) have all had bigger budgets and (arguably) bigger ideas than any potential British equivalents.[2]

In literary terms, however, British science fiction has respectable canonical progenitors, even in the apocalypse genre, such as Yeats's poem 'The Second Coming' (1919), or T.S. Eliot's *The Waste Land* (1922). In a more obvious sf mode, Mary Shelley's *The Last Man* (1826) and H.G. Wells's short story 'The Star' (1897) very obviously address the 'end of the world', and it can be argued that the three television dramas of the 1990s are, in fact, the extension of British science fiction's traditional obsession with catastrophe. In comparison to American science fiction, British narratives have tended to be 'characterised by gloom and doom'.[3] H.G. Wells may have been writing at the height of the British Empire but he also inhabited the *fin de siècle* of the nineteenth century with its morbid fears about degeneration, sexual excess and hygiene.

British science fiction's chief concern, it has been argued, has been with disasters arising from 'a threatened or an actual incursion into private space, represented by Island-nation, home territory or insular Self'.[4] This is the end of days as envisaged by British writers. Certainly *The Uninvited* is a straightforward invasion narrative, as is *Invasion: Earth*. *The Last Train* is less obviously about invasion, but at the same time the island-nation of Britain is catastrophically affected by a meteor strike in Zambia, causing, among other things, the establishment of non-indigenous plants on British soil (in an apparent nod to John Wyndham's 1951 *The Day of the Triffids*). 'The seeds were thrown up into the atmosphere', explains scientist Harriet in the drama (played by Nicola Walker).[5]

Critical responses to these dramas were mixed, with most considering them (to varying extents) enjoyable hokum. The *Guardian* referred to *The Uninvited* as 'corny and far-fetched ... it's like a rickety fifties body-snatcher movie tarted up with pre-millennial trappings like cynical Wapping journalists and cyber-caffs',[6] while the *Independent* referred to its 'almost touching devotion to the clichés of the science fiction conspiracy drama'.[7] *Invasion: Earth* was viewed as 'ambitious, ludicrous, good-looking stuff',[8] while *The Last Train* was 'a bizarre mix of the plausible and the deeply silly'[9] and 'a real, old-fashioned sci-fi thriller'.[10]

Overall, there was a sense in which the critics struggled to take television science fiction seriously. In more than one piece, the reviewer spent some time wondering if the small screen could possibly live up to its big screen counterparts.[11] However, according to Jed Mercurio, writer of *Invasion: Earth*, 'Sci-fi enables you to deal with themes on a grand scale, such as the fate of all mankind, which you don't get in a cop show'.[12] The ability of science fiction to deal with 'themes on a grand scale' is thus not simply dictated by budget, since big ideas can be explored not only on the cinema screen but in television's more intimate space.

Certainly all three dramas set out to deal with big themes. *The Uninvited*, allegedly springing from an idea by Leslie Grantham,[13] concerns the infiltration of humanity by a group of aliens drawn to Earth by its increasingly polluted atmosphere; the less oxygen, the better the planet suits them. In order to facilitate their plans for global domination, the aliens plan to stage a major nuclear detonation in the Antarctic, destroying the ozone layer and melting the ice caps. The destruction of human civilisation will in this fashion strengthen theirs. Into the midst of their plans stumbles ex-photo journalist Steve Blake (Douglas Hodge), who rapidly embarks on a one-man crusade to end the alien invasion.

As the Scottish *Daily Record* pointed out, a serial about aliens with world domination on their mind, masquerading as not-so-ordinary folk, seemed to be lifted straight from John Wyndham's *The Midwich Cuckoos* (1957) and *Invasion of the Body Snatchers* (dir. Don Siegel, USA, 1956), by way of *The X-Files* (Fox Television, 1993–2002).[14] Ultimately, however, as one reviewer put it, 'in any kind of plausibility face-off, *Teletubbies* (BBC TV, 1997–2001) would win hands down'.[15]

The Uninvited does seem to suffer from some plot difficulties: in the final showdown, Blake is fooled into entering an army base full of the aliens. Armed only with a fire axe and a plucky girlfriend, he makes his final stand. 'What are you going to do with that axe, Stephen?' taunts Gates (Leslie Grantham). 'Going to kill us all?' As it turns out, this is exactly what he does. Blake breaches a fortunately situated pipe full of pure oxygen and kills the aliens – that is *all* the aliens throughout the world, because, luckily, the aliens are somehow linked into a gestalt intelligence. As the head alien helpfully explains, the invaders 'seem to have a collective mentality, which may give them certain shared weaknesses'.[16] In other words: kill one, kill them all. This is a fortunate circumstance, to say the least, for Blake and the rest of humanity.

In this end-of-the-world scenario, the build-up of greenhouse gases makes Earth an increasingly attractive proposition to the non-oxygen-breathing aliens, which have, apparently, enjoyed a previous period of residence in the early days of Earth's atmospheric evolution (about 5 billion years ago), though whether they are another breed of 'terran' or genuine extraterrestrials is never made clear. Despite this, the message to be more ecologically aware is made explicit, however common this trope might be to science fiction.

In 1998, BBC Scotland (in a co-production with the American Sci-Fi Channel) made an expensive foray into science fiction. *Invasion: Earth* reputedly cost £750,000 an episode, making it one of the most expensive drama serials ever made, in the same league as *Brideshead Revisited* (Granada Television for ITV, 1981).[17] Rather like *The Uninvited*, the serial was apparently intended to be Britain's answer to *The X-Files*.[18] Indeed both dramas are likely to have been commissioned as a result of the American show's success.

Scripted by Jed Mercurio (the writer of hospital drama *Cardiac Arrest*, BBC TV, 1994–96) and intended to be a special effects extravaganza, *Invasion: Earth* concerns the fate of humanity as Earth is caught in the crossfire of a war between two alien species. The serial contains a variety of standard science fiction tropes: the invasion of Earth from outer space and other dimensions, revelations about the fate of alien abductees, as well as bio-colonisation and the heroics of a chosen few (in this case, civilian scientists and NATO personnel) who stand against overwhelming odds.

Initially, it appears that two forces are ranged against humanity. As the Scottish *Daily Record* explained: 'The bald-headed, doe-eyed Echos are the classic benign extra-terrestrials. The nDs – the non-dimensionals – are pure evil energy who devour whole planets.'[19] It becomes clear, however, that the Echos are victims of the nDs.

'ONLY THE DEAD SHALL SEE THE END OF WAR'   Humanity fights
for survival in *Invasion: Earth* (1998).

Having overcome the Echos, the nDs arrive on Earth to 'farm'
humanity for their biotechnology. They have no interest in humans
except insofar as they can be harvested.[20] Civilian scientist Amanda
Tucker (Maggie O'Neill) is colonised by alien biology just as surely as
the countryside itself is overrun. As Charles Terrell (Anton Lesser),
the alien abductee puts it, the nDs have a simple philosophy: 'They
come. They conquer.'[21] Negotiation is not an option, as hapless
computer buff Nick (Paul J. Medford) discovers when attempting
to communicate with them using his laptop. He is sucked into the
nD structure and suffers an untimely death.

At first it appears as if the Echos will be useful allies with superior
technology and advanced space travel. However, in Episode 3, 'Only
the Dead' (1st tx. BBC 1, 22 May 1998), we find that their response
to the nD incursions is to commit mass suicide. As Terrell explains to
the others: 'The Echos are a highly compassionate race. They would
rather lose their own lives than be put to some violent purpose.' He
quotes Plato: 'Only the dead shall see the end of war.'[22] Whilst this

is certainly one moral response to overwhelming odds, according to *Invasion: Earth* it is not the twentieth-century human way. Nevertheless, the series has an unusually pessimistic outlook.

In *The Uninvited*, Blake may have been able to save humanity with nothing more than a fire-axe, but things are less simple for those facing the nDs. At first it seems that the ingenuity of human scientists has saved the day, as RAF pilot Chris Drake (Vincent Regan) and Tucker deliver a payload of 'virus' into the bio-structure of the nD stronghold. Perhaps an American series might have stopped there; it was certainly good enough for the pilots in Hollywood blockbuster *Independence Day* (dir. Roland Emmerich, USA, 1996). But two years later, success in *Invasion: Earth* is more short-lived. Almost immediately, the alien bio-structure returns larger than ever. 'There must be others existing in parallel', suggests an increasingly distraught Tucker in the sixth and final episode, 'The Shatterer of Worlds': 'When one matrix is destroyed another folds down.... There could be layer upon layer, stacking up through the dimensions, an infinite number.'[23]

Ultimately, rather than be subsumed by the bio-farming nDs, a nuclear device is set off on mainland Britain destroying the alien's foothold, at least for now. In the process, heroine Amanda Tucker and a large tract of Scotland are also wiped out. 'They'll know', says General Reece (Fred Ward), 'if we're ready to destroy one place, we'll be ready to destroy every place and destroy everybody they use. A scorched earth until they stop.... We'll blast every blade of grass and they'll know we'll fight and never, never give in.'[24] These are bold words but also a stark ending for a piece of popular entertainment – a fiery apocalypse and a whiteout. It is rare for a mainstream drama to end with the total annihilation of humanity, as it tends not to sit well with audience expectation and limits commercial potential, although at least one newspaper report seemed to imply that a second series was not out of the question.[25]

By way of contrast, *post*-holocaust stories have much greater potential for commercial development and leave room for more positive outcomes. In 1999, ITV produced post-holocaust drama *The Last Train*. Scripted by ex-*This Life* writer Matthew Graham,[26] *The Last Train* is 'your basic post-apocalyptic nightmare, complete with contaminated water and packs of Rottweilers trying to pick off small children.'[27] It was Granada's most expensive drama of the year, costing around £5 million,[28] most of which went into images of a post-catastrophe Sheffield.

The story tells of an asteroid collision with Earth, although unlike the Hollywood blockbusters *Armageddon* (dir. Michael Bay, USA, 1998) and *Deep Impact* (dir. Mimi Leder, USA, 1998), the narrative is less concerned with the lead-up to the impact than it is with its aftermath. The drama follows the fate of a small group of passengers on a London-to-Sheffield train who, having been frozen by gas from a mysterious canister carried by MOD scientist Harriet Ambrose (Nicola Walker), emerge some years later to face the consequences of a global catastrophe. Perhaps because BBC TV dramas like Terry Nation's *Survivors* (1975–77), *Day of the Triffids* (1981) and *Threads* (1984) had already addressed the breakdown of society in some detail, *The Last Train* is more interested in transplanting ordinary people into an extraordinary situation and following their quest, than in charting the exact detail of civilisation's demise.

Harriet tries to persuade the rest of the disparate group of ex-passengers that they must find ARK, a government bunker in Scotland, where she is convinced her boyfriend is waiting for her, along with whatever is left of civilization. The group of train wreck survivors – among whom are thief Mick (Treva Etienne), policeman Ian (Christopher Fulford), unhappily pregnant Roe (Zoe Telford), Jandra (Amita Dhiri, also from *This Life*) and her two children – agree. On their journey, they encounter Hild (Caroline Carver), a pregnant young woman and survivor, who is being hunted by her own savage-looking people. Hild and the child she carries become increasingly important as the narrative unfolds.

The Last Train seems to keep asking the question, what is the price worth paying to ensure survival? And in this drama the characters face a constant stream of moral choices. In Episode One, Mick tries to leave the others to fend for themselves, taking an all-important van with him. In Episode Two, Harriet seems happy to give up hope and let Mick and Ian die with her in the booby trap set by her boyfriend. It is Ian who deciphers the clues that allow them to escape. Later in the episode, Harriet destroys a well to ensure that the others continue their journey to ARK. In Episode Three Jandra's son Leo (Sacha Dawan), in a teenager's fit of rage, is responsible for his mother's fatal accident, after he finds her making love with

Ian. In Episode Five, Colin (Steve Huison), another of the survivors, jealous of Mick and Roe's growing relationship, attempts to force himself on Roe. Colin is the most obviously disturbed character of them all, continuing to wear his business suit and carry his briefcase throughout. Still angry with Mick in Episode Six, he closes the door to ARK on Mick and another of the train's passengers, Austin (James Hazeldine), leaving them to be crucified by Hild's people.

Throughout, Harriet single-mindedly (even selfishly) drives the group forward to her goal – to find Jonathan Geddes (Ralph Brown) and ARK – but when at last they arrive in Scotland hoping to find 'civilization', or at least what remains of it, they discover Geddes is an old man, alone in the ruins.[29] The passengers of the last train between London and Sheffield discover they had been frozen for 50 years, not the few months they initially assumed, and Harriet finds that those who had been lucky enough to have a place in ARK were defrosted from suspended animation after only ten years and left the installation. Acceding to Geddes's wishes, Harriet smothers him.

The narrative depicts a catalogue of distrust, betrayal and murder. In the blank slate of the post-apocalypse, where a fresh start seems possible, people are shown to be just as corrupt and selfish as they were in the old order. Even the inhabitants of the village of Mareby, which is depicted almost as a model village – a potential paradise amid the destruction caused by the meteor – were unable to maintain their oasis and gradually abandoned the place, leaving only an old man, Mark (Kenneth Colley), and his barren daughter behind to dream of renewal. Mark covets Hild and her child as avariciously as her own people.

The Last Train ends with the birth of Hild's baby and the revelation that her people are the children of ARK, the descendants of those who left. This is the remnant of humanity that Harriet has worked so hard to find. This *is* civilisation. The survivors of the train wreck and the survivors of the apocalypse are left to try to find some kind of future together. As in *Invasion: Earth*, humanity is in the grip of a catastrophe not of its own making, but the response here is different. Survival in *Invasion: Earth* was unlikely. In *The Last Train* it seems possible, although the suspicion is that life after the end of the world is every bit as morally compromised as it was before.

Thus the late 1990s saw three television dramas depicting the end of civilisation and possibly life itself in the British Isles, common enough themes in science fiction in general and, as noted, in British science fiction in particular. The end of an old world order and the start of a fresh new one have been imagined many times but, given the particular context of this cluster of dramas, it is difficult to avoid the implication that these shows were a commissioning response to the approaching millennium. As Robert Hanks of the *Independent* observed at the time: 'With the new millennium just around the corner, I suppose it was only a matter of time before television started spouting end-of-the-world sagas.'[30]

Such *fin de siècle* concerns were not unique to the 1990s. Despite the logical and rational understanding that these centennial endings are entirely artificial (and entirely dependent upon the acceptance of the Christian calendar), 'the terminal decades of a century suggest to many minds the death throes of a diseased society and the winding down of an exhausted culture', as Elaine Showalter has argued.[31]

Yet, in addition to the ending of a mere century, the 1990s contained a much rarer frisson – the end of a millennium; a frisson that appeared to lead to a variety of extreme reactions, for it seemed as if signs of 'millennial angst' were not confined to fictional scenarios. In 1993, the FBI intervened in Waco, Texas, leading to the Branch Davidian suicides and the deaths of 85 people. In 1995, 16 members of the Solar Temple cult committed suicide in Switzerland and Canada. Also in 1995, the Aum Shinrikyo ('Supreme Truth') cult in Japan carried out sarin gas attacks on the Tokyo subway, leading to seven deaths and 500 people requiring medical attention. The cult's beliefs placed a firm emphasis on the writings of Nostradamus and were dominated by millennial visions and apocalyptic scenarios. In 1997, 39 members of the Heaven's Gate cult 'beamed themselves up to the stars from the mansion near San Diego they called their "ship"' to join, they believed, aliens on a spacecraft tracking the Hale–Bopp comet. Among their number was the brother of Nichelle Nichols, the actress who played Lieutenant Uhura in *Star Trek*.[32]

Most of the population, it is true, were not prone to such extremes as these; nonetheless there was widespread unease about the predicted computer meltdown caused by the 'millennium bug'. This widely anticipated computer problem was the result of hardware and software which used only the last two digits of the calendar year, rather than all four and it was thought that essential systems could be vulnerable when they ticked over from '99' to '00', making some of them interpret the year as 1900. Estimates of the damage that could be caused ranged from global meltdown to minor irritation. 'Some people', claimed the BBC website dedicated to the Y2K problem, 'have gone as far as to take measures to prepare themselves for the collapse of civilisation.'[33]

There were also fears that the millennium bug could jeopardise the safety of Britain's nuclear power stations, causing facilities dependent on the nuclear plants – like the national grid and local telecommunications networks – to fail.[34] In December 1999, a United Nations report indicated that the six major oil-producing states (responsible for more than half the world's oil reserves) might not be Y2K compliant in time.[35] It was also feared that some Russian nuclear reactors, including those discarded from submarines, would be vulnerable to Y2K problems, with potentially catastrophic consequences.[36]

In Britain, all leave for the National Crime Squad was cancelled at the turn of the millennium due to fears of crimes connected with the millennium bug (such as failing alarm systems or collapsing public utilities causing blackouts),[37] while the armed forces were put on high alert to deal with any protracted outbreaks of public disorder.[38] People were advised that there was no need to hoard food as city and county councils were laying in stocks of food, as well as medical equipment, heating and lighting,[39] and there was a live UK government website carrying millennium bug updates, where staff were monitoring television and Internet news feeds, as well as incoming bulletins from consular staff around the world.[40] There were also worries for financial institutions, which could potentially lose records for bank accounts, pensions, investments and mortgages. Websites sprang up advising people to stockpile cash and liquefy their assets before credit cards and cashpoint machines stopped working. Banks and building societies responded by printing millions of copies of a leaflet entitled 'Your Money and the Millennium' to allay concerns.[41]

On the BBC's *Talking Point* website, where the debate in July 1999 was the question 'Millennium Bug – Reality or Rumour', a variety of opinions were expressed: 'As a computer professional I am very alarmed at the level of preparedness in this country', said one correspondent. 'The only reason why the government is not shouting hard enough is because it does not want to panic people', said another. 'The reality is that if a few computers crash, it may be the computers that are controlling a nuclear plant.' This respondent went on to suggest that this could eventually lead to looting, with police powerless to prevent it. Another contributor pointed out that the vast majority of microprocessors likely to be affected were not in computers but embedded in systems that controlled aeroplanes, satellites, cars, elevators and so on: 'How can we be sure that all of these have been checked and replaced?' he asked.[42]

The end of the first millennium, the year 999, had also been a period of strange omens, comets and a time of chaos and instability – leading, many feared, to a heavenly battle between the Antichrist and the Messiah.[43] The 1990s, too, had its comet (Hale–Bopp) and its fears of destabilisation that would bring about the end of civilisation as we knew it, though perhaps without the war between angels and demons. In philosophy, too, the end of history was declared in 1992, when Francis Fukuyama argued that although normal life persisted, history had already come to an end.[44] This was the end of an old epoch: a time of transition, a moment for a new beginning. It is hardly surprising that science fiction television picked up on such themes. The end seemed to be nigh.

This 'sense of an ending',[45] as Frank Kermode termed it, leads to a consideration of the purpose that these dramas might serve. Naturally, one could just suggest that they are a rather cynical attempt to exploit commercially the millennial angst described above, but this question of 'apocalypse' can be considered in a wider context too. Despite their 'popular' origins, it is possible to regard *The Uninvited*, *Invasion: Earth* and *The Last Train* as something more than just 'corny and far fetched', albeit entertaining, drama.

According to Kermode, our interest in endings (even self-created endings) derives from 'a common desire to defeat chronicity, the intolerable idea that we live within an order of events between which there is no relation, pattern, mutuality or intelligible progression'.[46] How do we deal with infinity and aimlessness? We invest the final decades of a century with rich symbolic meanings of death and rebirth to mark a time of transition, a time of change. In *fin de siècle* times, we consume collective dramas about apocalypse and post-apocalypse survival and imbue them with the focus of our anxieties. Society itself therefore creates these 'endings' in the ongoing flow of time, for 'although the idea of a world without end or purpose is logically coherent, infinite duration is difficult to conceive and the notion of eternal aimlessness repugnant'.[47]

However, despite the fact that as it moved into the twenty-first century, Western culture was outwardly increasingly secular rather than religious, the symbolic language and metaphors of these dramas owe a great deal to Jewish and Christian apocalyptic writings. After all, science fiction is by its nature a symbolist genre and 'any symbolist movement in literature ... will tend to re-use a set corpus of symbols'.[48] The pessimistic concern with the end of the established order echoes a pessimistic strain in apocalyptic literature proper: a literature born of crisis and written for the consolation of the persecuted. Often these writers had no faith in progress and did not believe there would be an orderly evolution to a better world. Wars, famines, earthquakes, fire from the sky, or floods were commonly mentioned.[49]

These three British television dramas from the 1990s depict the 'end times' in different ways and offer different responses to the apocalypse event, but they do seem to draw upon common apocalyptic traditions to realise their visions. Although the term 'apocalypse' is frequently employed in writing about this kind of 'end time' imagination in science fiction, whether with regard to film, television or literature, it is rarely understood in its original context. The term does deserve closer inspection as it is a loaded word and potentially a problematic one.

'Apocalyptic'[50] is a term today 'popularly associated with fanatical millenarian expectation'[51] and yet the word 'apocalyptic' is derived from the Greek word *apokalypsis* (found in Revelation 1:1), which means 'uncovering' or 'revelation'. As Leon Morris states: 'Literature bearing this name may thus be expected to be largely taken up with revealing what has been hidden.'[52] Hence, although 'apocalyptic' is often used today to mean a sense of future expectation and of endings, in fact what it strictly implies is a revelation of that which has been hidden. In this stricter historical sense, 'apocalyptic' is usually taken to refer to a body of writing produced in Jewish circles between 250 BCE and 200 CE, before subsequently being taken up by Christianity.[53] It is a record of divine disclosures made known through the agency of angels, dreams and visions concerning transcendent reality and final redemption.

Taken in a more literary sense, 'apocalyptic' is a diverse genre, a hybrid from which it is possible to tease out certain common features. Often revelations are made through 'other world' journeys, and a rich (and in some cases impenetrable) symbolic language is employed. Most tracts are clearly the product of their political and economic times, designed to encourage the oppressed, while, as mentioned, a degree of pessimism, a concern with the 'end' of history and cosmic cataclysm, also appear as common themes. As the biblical Book of Daniel states: 'the coming end will be a time of anguish, such as has never occurred since nations first came into existence.'[54] Confusion around this term 'apocalypse' arises because 'on any showing, apocalyptic grades off into other styles of writing. Many ancient books are partly apocalyptic and partly something else.... The boundaries of apocalyptic are not well defined and those who know most about it are least apt to be dogmatic.'[55]

To employ the term 'apocalypse' therefore is to imply an ancient tradition and writings concerned with an eschatological crisis that leads to a cosmos restored. However, given its rather precise meaning, some caution may be necessary when applying the idea of 'apocalyptic' to the science fiction genre because, at least on the surface, *The Uninvited*, *Invasion: Earth* and *The Last Train* are part of the secular genre of science fiction and would seem to have little concern with any kind of religious viewpoint. However, 'modern media, particularly television and film, occupy a role in our society analogous to religious narratives, art and drama in the premodern period ... as a source of theatre for the collective imagination',[56] and these end-of-the world dramas seem, by their very nature, to utilise symbolism drawn from more ancient 'end of days' narratives.

For example, *The Uninvited* suggests that humanity has put itself at risk by polluting its own environment. As one character points out, because of our carelessness 'We invited them back, so to speak.' In this scenario, nuclear catastrophe would be followed by environmental restructuring to suit the aliens. There are parallels in the description from the apocryphal 'Apocalypse of Peter',[57] a well-known text in early Christianity: 'And the stars shall be melted by flames of fire, as if they had not been created, and the firmaments of the heaven shall pass away for lack of water and shall be as though they had not been.'[58] Humanity's environmental niche would thus be no more. Creation is undone.

Invasion: Earth, however, sees Earth helplessly caught between two 'heavenly armies': the angelic Echos (the symbol Terrell uses to summon the Echos looks like a pair of angel's wings[59]) and the demonic, ruthless nDs, with their nightmarish, parasitic forms. Written in around 100 CE, the Jewish apocryphal apocalyptic text 2 Esdras says: 'Calamities are sent forth and shall not return until they come over the earth. The fire is kindled and shall not be put out until it consumes the foundations of the earth.'[60] Likewise, General Reece can see no way forward but to use nuclear weapons to destroy the very thing that brings the nDs to Earth – life itself. Fiery apocalypse and the destruction of all things can be the only results. However, 'true' apocalyptic texts, in Jewish and Christian writings, never speak unambiguously about the 'final destruction of all human life'.[61] Rather, they tend to offer a vision of holocaust (the temporary triumph of the powers of evil) followed by rebirth and revival (the intervention of God).

Where *The Uninvited* manages to avert the threatened tragedy and *Invasion: Earth* succumbs to it, by way of contrast *The Last Train* tries to imagine what might come *after* the apocalypse, when only a remnant (albeit not a very righteous remnant) of humanity has survived the harrowing. As 2 Esdras puts it: 'The beginning of sorrows, when there shall be much lamentation; the beginning of famine, when many shall perish; the beginning of wars, when the powers shall be terrified; the beginning of calamities, when all shall tremble. What shall they do when the calamities come?'[62] Written shortly after the Roman destruction of the temple in Jerusalem, 2 Esdras sees the end of civilisation and asks the question, what shall be done? All that the remains of humanity in *The Last Train* seem capable of is an attempt at survival, although ultimately this drama epitomises these two key elements of the apocalyptic – the end of all things and their paradoxical renewal – and so it is perhaps appropriate that the last of these three dramas ends with the birth of a child and the possibility of reconciliation.

In applying the term 'apocalyptic' to these television dramas, it is implied that something is uncovered, or revealed, by these series.

Indeed, it can be argued that they show unconscious processes depicted in conscious symbolism. The unconscious unease generated by the ending of a century and a millennium is expressed through these dramas about the end of the world, since 'myths and culture live in a co-determining dialectic'.[63] These are secular and not religious narratives, and yet at the same time it is possible to see in them another layer of meaning, their metaphoric significance going beyond simple millenarianism. Historical context is important and useful in decoding the anxieties that may motivate these disaster scenarios, but in moving beyond the outward signs of millennial angst it is possible to uncover another meaning in this cluster of apocalyptic dramas: meaning related to the *fin de siècle*, yet at the same time working on a more personal level of the psyche.

Creation myths can be understood as myths of awakening towards consciousness, while myths of destruction and the end of times can be seen as their opposite – a move towards death. As one Jungian psychologist suggests: 'People who are emotionally gripped by a story or an idea repeat it endlessly and cannot stop talking about it or telling and retelling it.... It is a means of abreacting a strong emotional impact.'[64]

These three dramas explore different and extreme images of 'the end', of death on a grand scale. Some characters endure; others do not. Blake survives in *The Uninvited* as a standard hero who overcomes evil and saves the world. The world is left outwardly unchanged – the aliens are defeated and die all over the world; their deaths falsely attributed to an unknown virus, as a final journalistic voice-over in the drama implies. Amanda Tucker, the nD-infected scientist of *Invasion: Earth*, is unable to overcome the 'demonic' infestation of the aliens, but instead of becoming their creature, she chooses, rather like the equally afflicted Ripley (Sigourney Weaver) in *Alien3* (dir. David Fincher, USA/UK, 1992), self-immolation in the nuclear destruction of Kirkhaven. In *The Last Train*, all of the characters face the possibility of death. Some survive – Colin escapes the vicious dog attack that claims several of the other passengers in the hours immediately after they leave the train wreck, but as time goes on, others are less fortunate. Jandra dies because of her son's actions, while ultimately Mick and Austin are crucified by Hild's people.

The end of civilisation and personal death are closely linked, but ultimately what meaning might be drawn from this would appear to depend upon individual perspectives. Writers on the subject of apocalypse tend to suggest that there are two types of 'ending' – endings which explore a sense of ultimate purpose or destination, a *telos*, and endings which speak only of an end, a *terminus*. The teleological understanding perhaps implies a more religious viewpoint, while the *terminus* implies a more secular point of view. Science fiction seems to waver between the two. John J. Collins, a leading writer in the field of biblical apocalyptic literature, suggests that the genre is designed to challenge world-views in what he calls a 'revolution of the imagination'. To imagine apocalypse is to challenge common perceptions; he calls it a revolution because it can 'foster dissatisfaction with the present and generate visions of what might be. The legacy of the apocalypses includes a powerful rhetoric for denouncing the deficiencies of the world. It also includes the conviction that the world as now constituted is not the end.'[65] These late 1990s' TV dramas can function, too, as cautionary tales with purpose. We may not be able to avert tragedy and destruction as such (asteroids and aliens) but whereas religious apocalypses speak of restoration and the possibility of 'a new heaven and a new earth',[66] where the new city of Jerusalem is rebuilt ('its radiance like a most rare jewel, like a jasper, clear as crystal.'[67]), these secular narratives seem to indicate that humanity must change or it will doom itself – either through nuclear holocaust, or through civilised humanity's apparently innate inability to cooperate even in ecological matters essential to survival.

Others would argue that although science fiction has its strand of 'end times' narratives, concerning itself with images of nuclear holocaust, ecological catastrophe, sexual decadence and social collapse, these are not usually intended to effect personal spiritual transformation.[68] The dramas can equally be read as narratives that speak only of *terminus*, implying that there is little that can be done. If survival is possible, it is random. There is no meaning, and such choice as we have is only how we will face our ends.

In all three works, we are treated to the spectre of the end of the world, with all the 'sensual elaboration' of fantasy that Susan Sontag in *The Imagination of Disaster* argues is the source of their appeal.[69] It is possible to understand *The Uninvited*, *Invasion: Earth* and *The Last*

Train as dramas that respond fairly directly to anxiety surrounding the ending of the second millennium in which the culture of the Western world-view is programmed to look for these periodic termini. It is impossible to accept an ongoing flow of undifferentiated time and so our calendar produces convenient moments of completion, conclusion and ending. In Britain, towards the end of the 1990s, the internal psychic state of the nation was projected outwards on to these dramatised apocalypses of the imagination.

Science fiction may not be apocalyptic literature in the strict traditional sense, and these sf TV dramas, on one level, can simply be seen as the slightly 'corny and far-fetched', albeit entertaining, hokum mentioned earlier. Then again, like all useful myths, archetypes, stories and narratives, the apocalyptic paradigm can be 'modified again and again to serve a whole range of interpretive and speculative purposes'.[70] *The Uninvited, Invasion: Earth* and *The Last Train* reflected the times in which they were produced, perhaps offering a cautionary perspective, as traditional apocalyptic literature once did. At the same time, they inhabited more individual psychological territory, exploring the terrain of more personal endings. At the end of the 1990s, they drew upon tropes of apocalyptic writing and catastrophe traditions within British science fiction in order to explore the possibilities of three very British 'apocalypses now', or rather (in view of their transmission at the end of the last millennium) 'then'.

NOTES

1. I.Q. Hunter, 'The Strange World of the British Science Fiction Film', in I.Q. Hunter (ed.), *British Science Fiction Cinema* (London: Routledge, 1999), p. 6.
2. Note the concern to show that *Invasion: Earth* had a big budget to lavish on its special effects, as mentioned later in the chapter.
3. Nicholas Ruddick, *Ultimate Island: On the Nature of British Science Fiction* (Westport CT: Greenwood Press, 1993), p. 33.
4. Ibid., p. 109.
5. Harriet Ambrose in Episode One, *The Last Train* (1st tx. ITV, 7 April 1999).
6. Adam Sweeting, *Guardian*, 26 September 1997.
7. Thomas Sutcliffe, *Independent*, 3 October 1997.
8. Harriet Lane, *Observer*, 8 May 1998.
9. Robert Hanks, *Independent*, 16 May 1999.

10. Peter Paterson, *Daily Mail*, 8 April 1999.

11. *Invasion: Earth* was unfavourably compared to American blockbuster *Independence Day* (dir. Roland Emmerich, USA, 1996).

12. Peter Millar, *Sunday Times*, 12 May 1998.

13. Tony Purnell, *Daily Mirror*, 26 September 1997.

14. John Millar, *Daily Record*, 10 October 1997.

15. Thomas Sutcliffe, *Independent*, 3 October 1997.

16. Episode 4, *The Uninvited* (1st tx. ITV, 16 October 1997).

17. Aidan Smith, *Scotsman*, 14 April 1998.

18. Peter Millar, *Sunday Times*, 12 April 1998.

19. John Millar and Kathleen Morgan, *Daily Record*, 15 April 1998.

20. In this, the nDs seem to be a purely organic version of the Borg, a race of cyborgs which first appeared in the *Star Trek: The Next Generation* episode 'Q-Who' (1st tx. NBC, 5 August 1989).

21. Charles Terrell (played by Anton Lesser), 'Only the Dead', Episode 3 of *Invasion: Earth* (1st tx. BBC 1, 22 May 1998).

22. 'Only the Dead'.

23. 'The Shatterer of Worlds', Episode 6 of *Invasion: Earth* (1st tx. BBC 1, 12 June 1998).

24. 'The Shatterer of Worlds'.

25. Millar and Morgan, *Daily Record*, 15 April 1998. The apocalyptic nuclear climax of *Invasion: Earth* is comparable to the conclusion of the 1979 *The Quatermass Conclusion* (Euston Films for Thames) though the latter did not, however, 'end with the total annihilation of humanity'. See James Chapman's chapter, '*Quatermass* and the Origins of British Television sf', in this volume for further discussion.

26. *This Life* (BBC 2, 1996–7).

27. Eddie Gibb, *Sunday Herald*, 4 April 1999.

28. Gareth McLean, *Scotsman*, 10 April 1999.

29. Interestingly, Scotland is where Terry Nation's *Survivors* also seek to find renewal.

30. Robert Hanks, *Independent*, 16 April 1999.

31. Elaine Showalter, *Sexual Anarchy: Gender and Culture at the Fin de Siècle* (London: Virago, 1991), p. 1.

32. Arnold Kemp, *Observer*, 30 March 1997.

33. http://news.bbc.co.uk/hi/english/static/millennium_bug/countries /default.stm (accessed 31 August 2004).

34. Nick Paton Walsh, *Observer*, 21 August 1999.

35. Industrial Staff, *Guardian*, 20 December 1999.

36. Neil McIntosh, *Guardian*, 26 May 1999.

37. Duncan Campbell, *Guardian*, 18 January 1999.

38. David Gow, 'Y2K Special Report', *Guardian*, 28 October 1999.

39. http://news.bbc.co.uk/hi/english/static/millennium_bug/bugtown/ shops.stm (accessed 31.8.04).

40. The website address was www.millennium-centre.gov.uk. The site is no longer active.

41. Rupert Jones, *Guardian*, 20 February 1999.

42. http://news.bbc.co.uk/1/hi/talking_point/398248.stm (accessed 31 August 2004).

43. Michael Staunton, *Guardian*, 31 December 1998.

44. See Francis Fukuyama, *The End of History and the Last Man* (Harmondsworth: Penguin, 1992).

45. See Frank Kermode, *The Sense of Ending* (Oxford: Oxford University Press, 1967).

46. Frank Kermode, 'Waiting for the End', in Malcolm Bull (ed.), *Apocalypse Theory and the Ends of the World* (Oxford: Blackwell, 1995), p. 250.

47. Bull, *Apocalypse Theory and the Ends of the World*, p. 1.

48. Adam Roberts, *Science Fiction* (London: Routledge, 2000), pp. 16–17.

49. See Leon Morris, *Apocalyptic* (London: Inter-Varsity Press, 1972).

50. In academic writing on this subject, the term 'apocalyptic' is usually used both as a noun and as an adjective. I have chosen to follow this convention here.

51. John J. Collins, *The Apocalyptic Imagination* (New York: Crossroad Publishing Company, 1984), p. 1.

52. Morris, *Apocalyptic*, p. 20.

53. BCE means 'Before The Common Era' (also known as the Christian Era), and means essentially the same as the common usage, BC ('Before Christ'). CE is a designation for the period of time from AD 1 onwards. Any year AD is the same year CE, thus AD 500 = 500 CE. The terms permit the use of the Julian and Gregorian calendar without necessarily referring to the Christian god (as non-Christians interpret the term as 'Common Era' rather than 'Christian Era'). The usage of the designation is common in academic circles and non-Christian historical writings.

54. Daniel 12:1.

55. Morris, *Apocalyptic*, p. 24.

56. Stephen O'Leary, 'Apocalypticism in American Popular Culture', *The Encyclopedia of Apocalypticism*, ed. Stephen J. Stein (New York: Continuum, 2000), p. 392.

57. 'Apocryphal': meaning that although it is a Christian text, it is not included in the canonical scriptures of the Bible.

58. 'The Apocalypse of Peter', in Bart D. Ehrman, *Lost Scriptures* (Oxford: Oxford University Press, 2003), p. 283.

59. See Episode 3 of *Invasion: Earth*, 'Only the Dead' (1st tx. BBC 1, 22 May 1998).

60. 2 Esdras, 16: 14–15. This is an apocryphal text found in some bibles which include intercanonical and apocryphal writings, such as the Jerusalem Bible.

61. John J. Collins, 'Apocalyptic Eschatology as the Transcendence of Death', *Visionaries and Their Apocalypses*, ed. Paul D. Hanson (London: Fortress Press, 1983), p. 65.

62. 2 Esdras, 16:18.

63. Richard M. Gray, *Archetypal Explorations* (London: Routledge, 1996), p. 197.

64. Marie Louise von Franz, *Patterns of Creativity Mirrored in Creation Myths* (New York: Spring Publications, 1972), p. 132.

65. Collins, *The Apocalyptic Imagination*, p. 215.

66. Revelation 21:1

67. Revelation 21:11

68. Bull, *Apocalypse Theory and the Ends of the World*, p. 5.

69. See Susan Sontag, *Against Interpretation and Other Essays* (London: André Deutsch, 1987).

70. David Seed (ed.), *Imagining Apocalypse* (London: Macmillan, 2000), p. 12.

Further reading

Archer, S., and Nicholls, S. (1998). *Gerry Anderson: The Authorised Biography*. London: Legend.

Atwood, T. (1983). *Blake's 7: The Programme Guide*. London: Target.

Barr, C. (1986). 'Broadcasting and Cinema 2. Screens within Screens', in C. Barr (ed.), *All Our Yesterdays: 90 Years of British Cinema*. London: British Film Institute.

Bignell, J., and O'Day A. (2004). *Terry Nation*. Manchester: Manchester University Press.

Bradbury, K.C. (2004). *Portal to Infinity: An Independent and Unauthorised Guide to BBCTV Doctor Who*. Indiana: 1st Books Library.

Buxton, D. (1990). *From The Avengers to Miami Vice: Form and Ideology in Television Series*. Manchester: Manchester University Press.

Caughie, J. (2000). *Television Drama: Realism, Modernism and British Culture*. Oxford: Clarendon Press.

Carraze, A., and Oswald, H. (1990). *The Prisoner: A Televisionary Masterpiece*. London: Virgin Publishing.

Chapman, J. (2002). *Saints and Avengers: British Adventure Series of the 1960s*. London and New York: I.B. Tauris.

Clute, J., and Nicholls, P. (eds) (1993). *Encyclopedia of Science Fiction*. London: Orbit.

Cook, J.R. (2003). 'The Year of The Sex Olympics (1968)/Alice in Wonderland (1966)', *Film International* 4.

Cook, J.R., and Murphy, P. (2000). 'After the Bomb Dropped: The Cinema Half-Life of The War Game (1965)', *Journal of Popular British Cinema* 3.

Cooke, L. (2003). *British Television Drama: A History*. London: BFI.

Cornell, P., Day, M., and Topping, K. (1996). *The Guinness Book of Classic British TV*, 2nd edn (Enfield: Guinness Publishing).

Cull, N.J. (2001). 'Bigger on the Inside... *Dr. Who* as British Cultural History', in Graham Roberts and Philip M. Taylor (eds), *The Historian, Television and Television History*. Luton: University of Luton Press.

Davies, S.P. (2002). *The Prisoner Handbook*. London: Pan–Macmillan.

Dessau, B. (1992). *The Official Red Dwarf Companion*. London: Titan Books.

Dicks, T., and Hulke, M. (1972). *The Making of Doctor Who*. London: Pan.

Evans, C. (ed.) (1969). *Mind at Bay*. London: Panther.

Evans, C. (ed.) (1970). *Mind in Chains*. London: Panther.

Fairclough, R. (2002). *The Prisoner: The Official Companion to the Classic TV Series*. London: Carlton Books.

Fulton, R. (1997). *The Encyclopedia of TV Science Fiction*. London: Boxtree in association with Independent Television Books.

Gerani, G., and Schulman, P. (1987). *Fantastic Television: Pictorial History of Science Fiction, the Unusual and the Fantastic on TV*. London: Titan Books.

Gaiman, N., Simpson, M.J., and Dickson, D.K. (2002). *Don't Panic: Douglas Adams and The Hitchhikers Guide to the Galaxy*. London: Titan Books.

Grant, R., and Naylor, D. (1993). *Primordial Soup*. Harmondsworth: Penguin.

Grant, R., and Naylor, D. (1994). *The Making of Red Dwarf*. Harmondsworth: Penguin.

Grant, R., and Naylor, D. (1996). *Son of Soup*. Harmondsworth: Penguin.

Gregory, C. (1997). *Be Seeing You…: Decoding The Prisoner*. Luton: University of Luton Press.

Haining, P. (1999). *The Invasion: Earth Companion*. London: TV Books Incorporated.

Halliwell, L., with Purser, P. (1986). *Halliwell's Television Companion*, 3rd edn. London: Grafton Books.

Hammond, P.J. (1992). *Sapphire and Steel*. London: Virgin.

Hearn, M., and Archer, S. (2002). *What Made Thunderbirds Go! The Authorised Biography of Gerry Anderson*. London: BBC Books.

Helford, E.R. (1995). 'Reading Masculinities in the "Post-Patriarchal Space" of *Red Dwarf*', *Foundation* 64.

Hills, M. (2001). *Fan Cultures*. London: Routledge.

Howarth, C., and Lyons, S. (2000). *Red Dwarf Programme Guide*, 3rd. edn. London: Virgin.

Howe, D.J., Stammers, M., and Walker, S.J. (1992). *Doctor Who: The Handbook – The Fourth Doctor*. London: Virgin Publishing Ltd.

Howe, D.J., Stammers, M., and Walker, S.J. (1993). *Doctor Who: The Handbook – The Sixth Doctor*. London: Virgin.

Howe, D.J., Stammers, M., and Walker, S.J. (1994). *Doctor Who: The Handbook – The First Doctor*. London: Virgin.

Howe, D.J., Stammers, M., and Walker, S.J. (1997). *Doctor Who: The Handbook – The Second Doctor*. London: Virgin.

Howe, D.J., and Walker, S.J. (1995). *Doctor Who: The Handbook – The Fifth Doctor*. London: Virgin.

Howe, D.J., and Walker, S.J. (1996). *Doctor Who: The Handbook – The Third Doctor*. London: Virgin.

Howe, D.J., and Walker, S.J. (1998). *Doctor Who: The Handbook – The Seventh Doctor*. London: Virgin.

Howe, D.J., and Walker, S.J. (2003). *The Television Companion: The Unauthorised and Unofficial Guide to Doctor Who*. Tolworth: Telos.

Hoyle, F., and Elliot J. (1975). *A for Andromeda* [1962]. London: Corgi.

Hunter, I.Q. (ed.) (1999). *British Science Fiction Cinema*. London: Routledge.

Huxley, A. (1932). *Brave New World*. London: Chatto & Windus.

Jacobs, J. (2000). *The Intimate Screen: Early British Television Drama*. Oxford: Oxford University Press.

Jeffries, S. (2001). *Mrs. Slocombe's Pussy: Growing Up in Front of the Telly*. London: Flamingo.

Jenkins, H. (1992). *Textual Poachers: Television Fans and Participatory Culture*. London and New York: Routledge.

Johnson, C. (2002). 'Exploiting the Intimate Screen: *The Quatermass Experiment*, Fantasy and the Aesthetic Potential of Early Television Drama', in Janet Thumim (ed.), *Small Screens, Big Ideas: Television in the 1950s*. London and New York: I.B. Tauris.

Johnson, C. (2005). *Telefantasy*. London: British Film Institute.

Kneale, N. (1959). *The Quatermass Experiment*. London: Arrow Books.

Kneale, N. (1960). *Quatermass and the Pit*. London: Arrow Books.

Kneale, N. (1960). *Quatermass II*. London: Penguin Books.

Kneale, N. (1976). *3 TV Plays: The Road; The Year of the Sex Olympics; The Stone Tape*. London: Fantasy Ferret.

Kumar, K. (1987). *Utopia and Anti-Utopia in Modern Times*. Oxford: Blackwell.

Leman, J. (1991). 'Wise Scientists and Female Androids: Class and Gender in Science Fiction', in John Corner (ed.), *Popular Television in Britain: Studies in Cultural History*. London: BFI.

Lewis, J.E., and Stempel, P. (1993). *Cult TV: The Essential Critical Guide*. London: Pavilion Books.

Lewis, L. (ed.) (1992). *The Adoring Audience: Fan Culture and Popular Media*. London: Routledge.

Mangan, M. (ed.) (1990). *Threads and Other Sheffield Plays*. Sheffield: Sheffield Academic Press.

Miller, J.S. (2000). *Something Completely Different: British Television and American Culture*. Minneapolis: University of Minnesota Press.

Muir, J.K. (1997). *Exploring Space 1999: An Episode Guide and Complete History of the Mid 1970's Science Fiction Television Series*. North Carolina: McFarland.

Nation, T. (1976). *Survivors*. London: Weidenfeld & Nicholson.

Nelson, R. (1997). *TV Drama in Transition: Forms, Values and Cultural Change*. London: Palgrave–Macmillan.

Newman, K., and Petley, J. (1998). '*Quatermass* and The Pen: Interview with Nigel Kneale', *Video Watchdog* 47.

O'Brien, D. (2000). *SF:UK. How British Science Fiction Changed the World*. London: Reynolds & Hearn.

Orwell, G. (1949). *Nineteen Eighty-Four: A Novel*. London: Secker & Warburg.

Paget, D. (2000). 'Disclaimers, Denials and Direct Address: Captioning in Docudrama', in John Izod and Richard Kilborn (eds), *From Grierson to the Docusoap: Breaking the Boundaries*. Luton: University of Luton Press.

Palgut, T. (2003). *The Prisoner: The Village Files*. London: Titan Books.

Petley, J. (1989). 'The Manx-Man', *Monthly Film Bulletin* 662.

Pirani. A. (1989). *The Complete Gerry Anderson Episode Guide*. London: Titan Books.

Rakoff, I. (1999). *Inside The Prisoner: Radical Television and Film in the 1960s*. London: Batsford Press.

Richards, J. (2003). *Doctor Who – The Legend: 40 Years of Time Travel*. London: BBC Books.

Rogers, D. (1989). *The Prisoner and Danger Man Book*. London: Boxtree.

Rolinson, D., and Cooper, N. (2002). '"Bring Something Back": The Strange Career of Professor Bernard Quatermass', *Journal of Popular Film and Television* 30/3.

Segal, P., and Russell, G. (2000). *Doctor Who: Regeneration: The Story Behind the Revival of a Television Legend*. London: HarperCollins.

Simpson, M.J. (2001). *The Pocket Essential Hitchhiker's Guide*. London: Pocket Essentials.

Simpson, M.J. (2004). *Hitchhiker: A Biography of Douglas Adams*. London: Coronet.

Simpson, P., et al. (2002). *The Rough Guide to Cult TV*. London: Rough Guides.

Stevens, A., and Moore, F. (2003). *Liberation: The Unofficial and Unauthorised Guide to Blake's 7*. Tolworth: Telos Publishing.

Tracey, M. (1982). 'Censored: *The War Game* Story', in Aubrey Crispin (ed.), *Nukespeak: The Media and the Bomb*. London: Comedia.

Tulloch, J. (1990). *Television Drama: Agency, Audience and Myth*. London: Routledge.

Tulloch, J., and Alvarado, M. (1988). *Doctor Who: The Unfolding Text*. London: Macmillan.

Tulloch, J., and Jenkins, H. (eds) (1995). *Science Fiction Audiences: Watching Star Trek and Doctor Who*. London: Routledge.

Vihimagi, T. (1994). *British Television: An Illustrated Guide*. Oxford: Oxford University Press.

Ward, M., Perry, C., and Down, R. (2004). *Out of the Unknown: A Guide to the Legendary BBC Series*. Bristol: Kaleidoscope Publishing.

Webb, N. (2004). *Wish You Were Here: The Official Biography of Douglas Adams*. London: Headline.

Welsh. J. (1983). 'The Modern Apocalypse: *The War Game*', *Journal of Popular Film and Television* 11/1.

Notes on contributors

JAMES CHAPMAN is Senior Lecturer in Film and Television History at the Open University. He has wide-ranging research interests in the history of British popular culture. His books include *Licence to Thrill: A Cultural History of the James Bond Films* (1999), *Saints and Avengers: British Adventure Series of the 1960s* (2002), and *Past and Present: National Identity and the British Historical Film* (2005), all published by I.B. Tauris. He is general editor of the *Popular Television Genres* series and is currently writing a cultural history of the classic British sf TV series *Doctor Who*.

JOHN R. COOK is Senior Lecturer in Mass Media at Glasgow Caledonian University. He is the author of two successful editions of the first full-length academic study of the work of the late television playwright Dennis Potter: *Dennis Potter: A Life on Screen* (Manchester University Press, 1995, 1998), as well as co-editor (with Vernon W. Gras) of *The Passion of Dennis Potter: International Collected Essays* (St. Martin's Press, 2000). A specialist in TV history, in 2003 he was invited by the British Film Institute to research and provide detailed voice-over commentaries for the BFI DVD release of director Peter Watkins's famous BBC TV film *Culloden* (1964). He has been a fan of British science fiction TV since childhood.

NICHOLAS J. CULL is Professor of Communications at the Annenberg School for Communications, University of Southern California, Los

Angeles. British-born, he has published widely on propaganda and popular culture in Britain and the United States, including the essay 'Bigger on the Inside... *Doctor Who* as British Cultural History', in Graham Roberts and Philip M. Taylor (eds), *The Historian, Television and Television History* (University of Luton Press, 2001), which presented new material from the BBC archives.

ELYCE RAE HELFORD is Professor of English and director of women's studies at Middle Tennessee State University. Her research centres on representations of gender, race and feminism in science fiction and fantasy literature, television and film. She is editor of *Fantasy Girls: Gender in the New Universe of Science Fiction and Fantasy Television* (Rowman & Littlefield, 2000), co-editor of *Enterprise Zones: Critical Positions on Star Trek* (Westview Press, 1996) and author of articles and book chapters on such subjects as *Buffy the Vampire Slayer* and *Xena: Warrior Princess*. She is currently indulging herself in writing a book of erotic prose and poetry, tentatively entitled *The Secret Sex Lives of Inanimate Objects*.

UNA McCORMACK has conducted research into online fan communities and is the author of several articles in this area. She teaches organisational theory at the University of Cambridge and is a professional writer of fiction.

CATRIONA MILLER is a Lecturer in Media at Glasgow Caledonian University, where her research interests include the vampire myth in particular and the horror genre in general, Jungian film studies and the archetypal dimensions of science fiction and fantasy. She is currently preparing a new monograph on *Female Cult TV Heroines* for I.B. Tauris.

ANDY SAWYER is the librarian of the Science Fiction Foundation Collection at the University of Liverpool Library, and course director of the M.A. in Science Fiction Studies. He has published on children's/young adult sf, John Wyndham, telepathy, *Babylon 5*, 'reverse-time narratives' and Terry Pratchett. He co-edited the collection *Speaking Science Fiction* (Liverpool University Press, 2000). He is also reviews editor of *Foundation: The International Review of Science*

Fiction and associate editor of the forthcoming *Encyclopedia of Themes in Science Fiction and Fantasy* (Greenwood Press).

DAVID SEED studied at the universities of Cambridge, Leicester and Hull. He holds a chair in American Literature in the School of English, Liverpool University. He has published books on Thomas Pynchon, Joseph Heller and American science fiction and the Cold War, among others. He is the editor of the *Science Fiction Texts and Studies* series from Liverpool University Press and is a member of the editorial board of the *Journal of American Studies*. In 2001 he was elected fellow of the English Association.

SUE SHORT lectures in media and film studies at Birkbeck College and London Metropolitan University. She has published articles on science fiction in a variety of books and journals; her first book, *Cyborg Cinema and Contemporary Subjectivity*, was published by Palgrave Macmillan in 2004. She is currently completing a new book on female representation in contemporary horror, as well as planning to co-edit an encyclopedia of sf adaptations.

M.J. SIMPSON is regarded as the world's leading authority on the life and career of Douglas Adams. He is the author of *The Pocket Essential Hitchhiker's Guide* (Pocket Essentials, 2001) and *Hitchhiker: A Biography of Douglas Adams* (Hodder & Stoughton, 2003). His website, Planet Magrathea (www.planetmagrathea.com), carries daily updates on the legacy of Douglas Adams. He is research archivist for the Official *Hitchhiker's Guide* Society (www.zz9.org).

PETER WRIGHT is Senior Lecturer in Literature and Film Studies at Edge Hill College of Higher Education. He is author of *Attending Daedalus: Gene Wolfe, Artifice and the Reader* (Liverpool University Press, 2003). He has also written articles on British science fiction film, Edgar Rice Burroughs and *Doctor Who*.

Index